VBA Programming for Microsoft Project

'98 through 2010

with an Introduction to VSTO

Rod Gill
Microsoft Project MVP

VBA Programming for Microsoft Project
'98 through 2010 with an Introduction to VSTO

Copyright © 2011 Rod Gill

Publisher: Chefetz LLC
Author: Rod Gill
Tech Editor: Jack Dahlgren
Copy Editor: Rodney L. Walker
Cover Design: Emily Baker

ISBN: 978-1-934240-21-2

LCCN: 2011920851

Published and distributed by Chefetz LLC dba MSProjectExperts, 90 John Street, Suite 404, New York, NY 10038. (646) 736-1688 http://www.msprojectexperts.com

MSProjectExperts publishes a complete series of role-based training/reference manuals for Microsoft's Enterprise Project Management software including Microsoft Project and Microsoft Project Server. Use our books for self-study or for classroom learning delivered by professional trainers and corporate training programs. To learn more about our books and courseware series for Administrators, Implementers, Project Managers, Portfolio Managers, Resource Managers, Executives, Team Members, and Developers, or to obtain instructor companion products and materials, contact MSProjectExperts by phone (646) 736-1688 or by email info@msprojectexperts.com.

Contents

Contents

Contents

About the Author

Rod Gill is founder of New Zealand based ACE Project Systems Ltd. He has been involved with project management his entire career and with the advanced use of Microsoft Project since its release. Apart from doing project management training, consulting, and Project Server implementations, Rod has a regular sideline in VBA development, mostly for Microsoft Project.

After 8 years of software engineering to develop control systems and their operator interfaces, Rod was drawn to VBA development and integrating Microsoft Project with other systems. Rod is a long-time Microsoft Project Most Valuable Professional (MVP), first winning this prestigious technical award in 1998 for his contributions to the Microsoft communities. Rod's passion for Microsoft Project and Project VBA, together with his passion for helping others, has kept him in the forefront of using Microsoft Project. Contact Rod online in the TechNet forums, or e-mail him at:

rodg@project-systems.co.nz

Download the Sample Files

You can find sample code and other macros that accompany this book by pointing your browser to the following URL:

http://www.msprojectexperts.com/vba2010

Author's Introduction

Becoming a Project Guru

A Project Guru is not just a power user. Project Gurus are great at managing and reporting on project information. Data management and reporting is what makes VBA so useful and productive.

While it can certainly add to your productivity to add a feature to make something quicker and easier, managers are more commonly impressed when large amounts of information are quickly and accurately managed, updated and reported on. Therefore, VBA can be a very powerful tool whose effective use leads to you being seen as a Guru in the use of Microsoft Project.

Project VBA can help you:

- Understand and use your application better

- And your team become more productive

- Add value to your information

- Eliminate boring and repetitive work

- Make following processes easier and more reliable

- Become more useful and valuable at work

- Stand out as a Power User/Guru

But wait, there's more:

- If you know Project VBA, Excel VBA is easy to pick up

- VBA lets you integrate the power of Project and Excel almost seamlessly

- Good schedulers are likely to have the right aptitude to program in VBA

- VBA can be used with any active project

- Works with or without Project Server

- VBA written for Project 98 still works in Project 2010 – so great compatibility

To justify and expand on these points I am going to describe some real life examples from my past contracts though the organizations shall remain nameless!

Lessons from an outsourcing project

First, I was involved in implementing Project Server for a global organization going through the pains of outsourcing their IT operations. For various reasons, there was a shared Project Server implementation with a number of clients and a prohibition on all but the most basic of customizations.

With 30 plus projects to report each week and for management to review apples for apples across all projects and their programs required a new approach. Did I forget to mention that the servers were in America and the projects managed in New Zealand and that there was a 200+ millisecond latency (technical translation: very slow performance)? Well imagine managers spending two days a week opening Project Web App (PWA) views that took 2 minutes to fully display and did not hold the information they were interested in anyway because of the block on customization.

All project managers ended up manually preparing Excel reports weekly. Consequently, they often left schedules untouched for many weeks.

I pointed out that almost all the data required by management was either in Project Professional or in PWA's Risks and Issues. I proposed that if project managers updated their schedules in Project Professional, Issues and Risks in PWA, I could produce an automated report reading data directly from the remote SQL Server in Excel.

The following week management opened a spreadsheet in Excel, selected a project from a drop down list and within 3 seconds separate, formatted worksheets displayed lists of milestones, current tasks, and issues and risks.

Project managers spent less time creating better quality reports: a great win-win. Moreover, it encouraged following the process. To update a schedule, click a button for the report. The bonus was up-to-date schedules for resources and time management of remaining work.

One day, I was collaborating on a particular project over the coffee pot when I overheard a woman bemoaning her lot: she had 1,800 reports in Excel to convert to pdf format and then move to different folders (one folder per report) on a web server – manually every week! While this was a temporary role, it had been going on for a month with at least six more to go before the report numbers were due for heavy pruning. From her voice, it sounded like she was already trying to fit one of her arms into one of those special white jackets with no opening to their sleeves.

I asked the innocuous question: "So why don't you automate the job?" The threat-laden reply was "could you?" "Yes if you get my manager's permission." Five minutes later, I was writing VBA code in Excel to create 1,800 pdf files from 1,800 Excel files.

I asked for and received in Excel a list of every report, the full path and location of the source .xls file and the full path of the destination folder for the new pdf file.

For me it was then a simple job of looping through each file, opening it in Excel, printing to pdf, then moving the resultant pdf file to the correct folder. The only holdup was sourcing a pdf printer that was controllable from VBA. We settled on Adobe Acrobat, as there was already a spare license available for installation.

Three days manual labor was now 60-minutes having lunch watching Excel VBA do its work! Between you and me, it is embarrassing having someone kiss the ground you walk on.

As another side effect, they extended my 3-month contract (on short-term rates) to 15 months (on short-term rates) as they did not want me out of their sight after that little demonstration of productive work. So knowing VBA can make you wealthier as well. If you know VBA for Project, VBA for Excel is easy to learn and vice versa.

Lessons from a Refinery Upgrade

In a more recent project, I was one of several planners scheduling a refinery upgrade. Once again, numerous opportunities arose to write creative solutions that either manipulated large amounts of data usefully or eliminated boring work to save time and frustration and improve data accuracy.

Given the nature of refineries, there is a lot of inter-disciplinary work, so each scheduler might have to work in most schedules. As a result, each scheduler would leave each file in a state they preferred. We were all skilled schedulers; but we each had our own preferred layouts. In addition, scrolling to the current date was also tedious as each schedule spanned at least six months.

My solution was a VBA macro that ran when any project opened. Each scheduler had their own view and table in a common Global.mpt file so the *project_open* event read the name of the currently logged-in user, then applied the appropriate view and table. Finally, the code scrolled the Gantt timescale to the current date.

This was so seamless that the other schedulers complained when the same things did not happen on their home copies of Project! The win was avoiding the frustration and delays of always seeing other people's views and achieving productivity from the moment the file opened.

> **i**   This example's code is in Module 08: *Controlling Microsoft Project Using Events*

Another productive macro was one involving pipes. Refinery upgrades have pipes, more pipes and then yet more pipes. Fabrication and installation of all pipes need tracking. Instead of multiple tasks for each pipe (one drawing could have 20 sheets, each one a separate piece ready for transport by truck) a spreadsheet did the detailed tracking. Each pipe piece had a count of welds, bolt ups, flanges, supports, etc. Percentage progress was then a function of how many of each was actually complete. When a weld was completed, the actual weld count incremented and the total percent complete for that pipe piece automatically updated. With fixed price, hours were not relevant, but physical progress, including painting and delivery, was.

In the schedule, there was one task for each pipe for fabrication and one for installation. I wrote a Project VBA macro that read percentage progress from the tracking information in the active spreadsheet and updated the schedule accordingly.

A separate spreadsheet, for site personnel to fill in, covered progress for all steps required to install the pipes.

What was a tedious calculation (summing progress for many sheets into one pipe progress value) became a quick click of the mouse to update all pipe fabrication or installation tasks for the active project. The schedule now clearly stated progress and dates for each pipe without needing many hundreds of tasks for tracking the basic (but important) details. One task for a pipe replaced potentially 50 or more fabrication tasks.

This example is a good one to emphasize the value of Project and Excel working together managing a large volume of important data.

Lessons from a Project Conference

At the 2009 Microsoft Project Conference in Phoenix Arizona, I attended a session on writing PSI code for Project Server. One of the learning points was that you cannot update resource rates in Project Server 2007 using PSI (small bug fixed in 2010).

During the lunch break that followed, I spent 20 minutes writing a piece of code to read new rates from an Excel spreadsheet and update the corresponding resources in Project Professional. Another good example of how VBA can showcase you as the Project Guru that you are!

Anyone with good VBA skills can make their managers look good and in uncertain times enhance their job prospects.

When to use a Project Add-in

A Project add-in is a customized set of features that appears built into Microsoft Project. However, you must code the features using Visual Studio and distribute and deploy them separately from Project.

Use an add-in when:

- You need to incorporate features only available to .Net languages such as C# and VB.Net

- You need to interact with other applications that VBA cannot work with

- You need more code security so no one can edit or otherwise change your code (for example, shrink wrapped application extensions for sale)

- The bulk of your code processes information outside Project and you need more speed

There is a strong debate over whether C# or VB.Net is the better language. For the purposes of this book, I am assuming that most readers are more familiar with VBA. Therefore, I use the development approach for add-ins that starts by getting your code working in VBA then copy and pasting it into VB.Net for your add-in. VB.Net is, therefore, easier to learn (for people who learned VBA first) and is the tool I use in this book. C# developers are more likely to be proficient in its use and can easily translate to C#. They need no help from me!

When to use Project Server Interface (PSI) Code

PSI code is almost exclusively the domain of skilled C# developers with a good grasp of Web Services. As such, PSI coders are most likely to be developing applications to sell to the Project Server community or work for a large organization with a large Project Server environment to support.

PSI code is good for:

- Developing interfaces between Project Server and other business applications at the Server level (e.g., in-house accounting or timesheet software)

- Working with Server data not in the reporting database, but in Project Server

- Impersonating different users in Project for various workflow processes

PSI code is verbose (compared to VBA) to the extent that a 20 line VBA macro can often do what a 100 line PSI interface would do. However, VBA cannot update Server data without publishing projects from Project Professional and PSI code is constrained by Project Server's limited scheduling engine when it comes to scheduling, while VBA has Project Professional's full scheduling capabilities available. The right tool for the right job, therefore, depends on your skill sets and what you want to achieve. This book covers VBA and using VB.Net to develop add-ins for Project.

> **i** See the book *Programming Project Server* for all PSI-related development needs.

Developing appropriate quality levels

If you are developing a VBA macro for yourself and others to use, the initial quality required is whatever it takes to make the code work! As you are there, you are readily available to fix any bugs that crop up and make any changes or essential improvements.

When you write code for someone else to use at a different site, then you need to step the quality up a gear. Error handling is required to handle all likely errors (such as referencing blank rows or opening files that do not exist).

Developing add-ins for Project that are to be sold to other organizations requires the highest level of quality as bugs are not expected and the add-in needs to handle all sorts of user errors. However, there is a train of thought that says "the more idiot proof any software is, the bigger the idiot that will come along and use it!"

Final Note

If you have any problems getting any of the code in this book to work, please email me and I will do what I can to help you. I wish you well in your development endeavors. May all your code work first time, make you look like the Project Guru you really are and may developing in Project give you much satisfaction and improved job prospects.

Rod Gill
Matakana
New Zealand
rodg@project-systems.co.nz

SECTION 1

MICROSOFT PROJECT VBA ESSENTIALS

Learning Objectives

After completing this section, you will be able to:

- Use formulas to replace some of your VBA code
- Write Project VBA code to control Microsoft Project
- Write Excel VBA code to control Microsoft Project

Introducing Project VBA

Project VBA is Microsoft's implementation of VBA into Microsoft Project. All the common VBA code is available in Project VBA, as is the common Visual Basic Editor (VBE). This book assumes that you know the basics of VBA common to all Office applications. If you do not understand or are not sure about the basics of VBA, review the introduction to VBA included in the book download.

Rather than repeating what is in the Help files (and that varies from version to version), I teach the basics by creating a number of useful macros. My goal is to create something that may already do some of what you want to do, and to provide you with basic blocks of working code that you can copy into your own macros. You will learn by example and will end up with lots of useful working code. This gives you a great head start in writing your own macros.

First of all, you need to make sure that you make good use of formulas in custom fields. It does not make sense to write event code and a loop to calculate data for each task if a formula can do it for you without code. Module 01 in this section, therefore, deals with custom fields and writing formulas. Module 02 then delves into how Project VBA structures its objects (such as projects, tasks etc.) Finally, the fun starts as you learn to create productive macros in Project VBA! Unless otherwise stated, all VBA code works for all versions of Project and both Project Standard and Project Professional.

Adding the Developer Tab to the Project Ribbon

In Project 2010, to view your VBA code, work with add-ins and more, you need to use the *Developer* tab in the *Project* ribbon. By default, the *Developer* ribbon is hidden, so to display it:

1. Right-click any tab in the ribbon and select the *Customize the Ribbon* option.

2. In the right hand list of main tabs, select the *Developer* tab as shown in Figure S1 - 1:

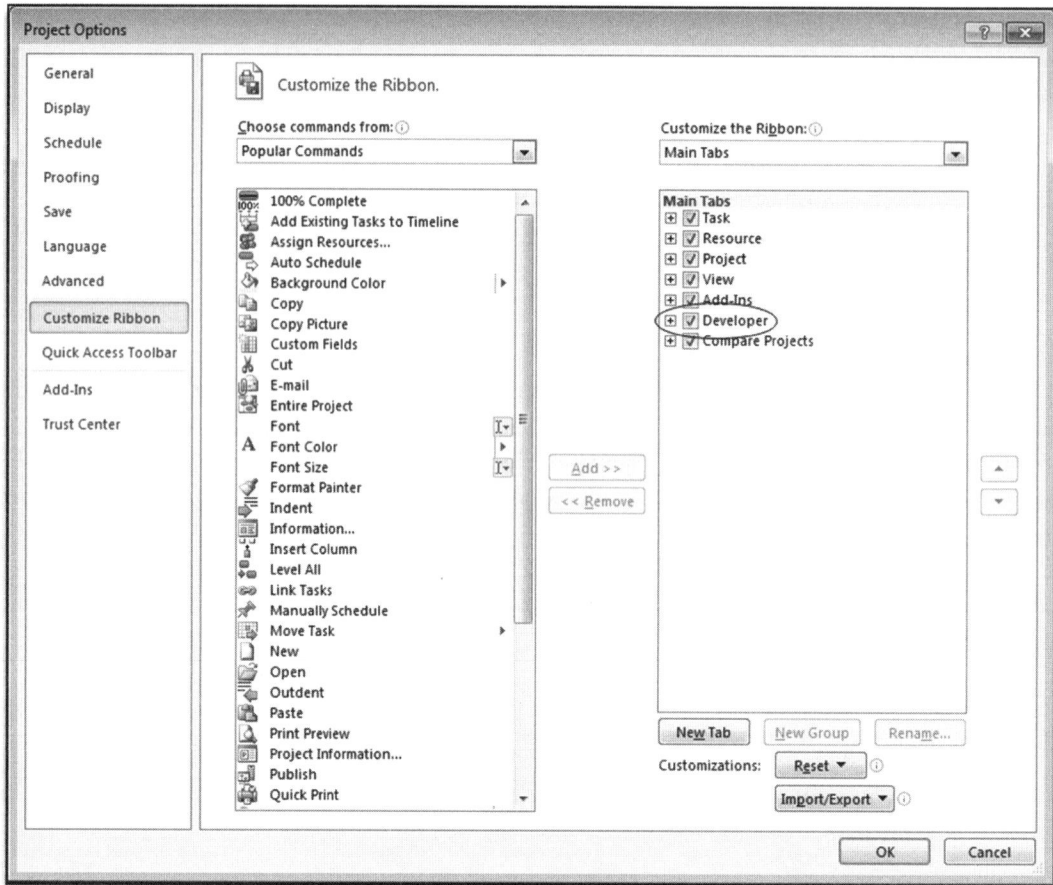

Figure S1 - 1: Displaying the Developer Tab

Sample Project Files

See the URL in the front of the book for the download site, which contains sample Microsoft Project files, with one file per module. These files contain all of the sample code in this workbook. Download all these sample files so they are available to you while you work through each module. The Project 2000-2003 file format is suitable for use with any recent version of Microsoft Project, from 2000 to 2010.

Note: Sample files are in Project 2000-2003 format, so if you have Project 2007 or later, open the files, then Save As into your version's format, especially if you want to use any code that is Project 2007 or 2010 specific.

> Note that in Project 2010, if the file format is Project 2007 or earlier, you cannot use 2010 features such as Manual Scheduling. Re-saving the file in Project 2010 format enables all 2010 features.

If Project will not open the files, enable opening legacy files by following the instructions in Table S1 - 1:

Step	Project 2010	Project 2003 SP3 and 2007
1) Open Options	Task Ribbon ➢ Options	Tools ➢ Options
2) Show security options	Trust Center tab ➢ Trust Center Settings button ➢ Legacy Formats tab	Security tab
3) Select *Legacy file* option	Select the *Allow loading files with legacy or non default file formats* option	Select the *Allow loading files with legacy or non default file formats* option

Table S1 - 1: Instructions to allow opening of older file formats

Module 01

Defining and Using Custom Fields

Lesson Objectives

After completing this module, you will be able to:

- Use formulas in custom fields to complement Microsoft Project VBA macros
- Define custom fields and outline codes to track task and resource information
- Define custom fields using value lists, formulas, and graphical indicators
- Create custom views, tables, and filters using custom fields
- Use AutoFilter to easily create custom filters

Inside Module 01

Overview of Custom Fields

Microsoft Project offers custom fields to store your unique project data. As Project users find more uses for custom fields and demand extra capacity, Microsoft has steadily increased the number of fields and field types available. Microsoft introduced an unlimited number of enterprise custom fields in Project Server 2007 that Project Web App manages.

For Project Server 2003 and earlier, Project Professional has built-in enterprise custom fields such as *Enterprise Text1*, etc. Table 1 - 1 lists the local custom fields available in Microsoft Project 2003 and later (earlier versions have fewer than those shown in Table 1 - 1). Project 2007 has an unlimited number of *Enterprise* custom fields.

Field Type	Number Available	Data Type
Cost	30 (10 task, 10 resource, and 10 assignment fields)	Cost data formatted in local currency, for example: $#,##0.00
Date	30 (10 task, 10 resource, and 10 assignment fields)	Date data formatted using the formatting specified in the *Options* dialog
Duration	30 (10 task, 10 resource, and 10 assignment fields)	Duration data formatted in Days
Finish	30 (10 task, 10 resource, and 10 assignment fields)	Date data formatted using the formatting specified in the *Options* dialog
Flag	60 (20 task, 20 resource, and 20 assignment fields)	*Yes* or *No* only
Number	60 (20 task, 20 resource, and 20 assignment fields)	Unformatted number data
Start	30 (10 task, 10 resource, and 10 assignment fields)	Date data formatted using the formatting specified in the *Options* dialog
Text	90 (30 task, 30 resource, and 30 assignment fields)	Unformatted text data
Outline Code	20 (10 task and 10 resource fields only)	Outline data formatted using an Outline Code definition

Table 1 - 1: Custom fields available in Microsoft Project 2003 and later

In addition to the custom fields listed in Table 1-1, Microsoft Project Professional 2002 or newer, when connected to Project Server, offers additional enterprise custom fields. Enterprise fields come in three types: *Task, Resource*, and *Project*. While many standard (non-enterprise) custom task fields carry a discrete value at the assignment level, *Enterprise* task-level fields cannot contain unique values at the assignment level. The system stores enterprise field definitions in the Enterprise Global file and only Project Server administrators can create and edit these field definitions.

Microsoft Project displays fields as data columns in *Task* and *Resource* tables. The software includes user-defined custom fields in only a few of the default tables. For example, the PERT Analysis data stores user-defined *Duration, Start,* and *Finish* fields. The software provides the remaining custom fields for your personal project management use.

To become truly knowledgeable about Microsoft Project, Rod Gill recommends that you learn as much as you can about default and custom fields. Gaining more knowledge about fields also increases your knowledge about views, tables, filters, groups, and reports.

Microsoft Project manages data in both standard and custom fields in one of three ways:

- **Calculated** – Microsoft Project calculates the values in the field and you cannot change the value.

- **Entered** – You must manually enter the values in the field.

- **Calculated/Entered** – Microsoft Project calculates the values in the field, but allows you to edit or enter a value as well.

The *Duration* field is a good example of a standard *Calculated/Entered* field. The software calculates the duration of a task when you assign resources to a task using *Units* and *Work* values for the assignment. On the other hand, you can enter your own *Duration* value for the task forcing the software to recalculate either *Units* or *Work*.

For the most part, data in custom fields is user-entered. The fields in the *PERT Analysis* tables (Project 2007 and earlier only) and the *Rollup* table are the only exceptions to this rule of thumb as they get automatically filled by Project.

Using Formulas to Support Project VBA Macros

You can use formulas in custom fields to replace or complement Project VBA macros. For example, if you want to use a *Text* field to display a *Duration* value converted to 8 hour working days, then use the following formula:

    Format([Duration]/60/8,"0\d")

The preceding formula does everything you need, eliminating the need for a macro. To make the formula more flexible, use the active project's conversion rate to minutes as follows:

Format([Duration]/[Minutes Per Day],"0\d")

Use a combination of a custom field and a macro when you need to report on a subset of tasks for different management reports by completing the following steps:

1. Create a custom *Flag* field for each report, such as the *Flag1* field, and set it to *Yes* for each task you want to include in the report.

2. Write your VBA macro code to do the following:

   • Create a filter for the *Flag* field used with the report

   • Apply the filter

   • Print the report

If you want a result displayed in a custom field and the result uses data for only the current task, then a formula gets the job done immediately without needing to run a macro. If you need to read data across tasks, such as predecessors and successors then you have to use VBA code. Custom fields can often act as very useful intermediary steps. The simplest solution to a reporting problem might include both a formula and VBA code.

> To discover how to write VBA code to add formulas to a field, simply record a macro while you manually create a formula in a custom field.

Defining Custom Fields

Before you define any custom fields, you must understand your organizational reporting needs. Based on your knowledge of project stakeholders, you can define custom fields for use in the reporting process through custom views, tables, filters, groups, and reports. Table 1 - 2 shows you the different steps you need to use based on your version of the software.

Step	Project 2010	Project 2007 and earlier
Show *Custom Fields* dialog for active project	Project Tab ➤ Custom Fields	Tools ➤ Customize ➤ Fields

Table 1 - 2: Displaying the Custom Fields dialog

To define a custom field, open a project and then click Tools ➢ Customize ➢ Fields. The *Custom Fields* dialog opens as shown in Figure 1 - 1.

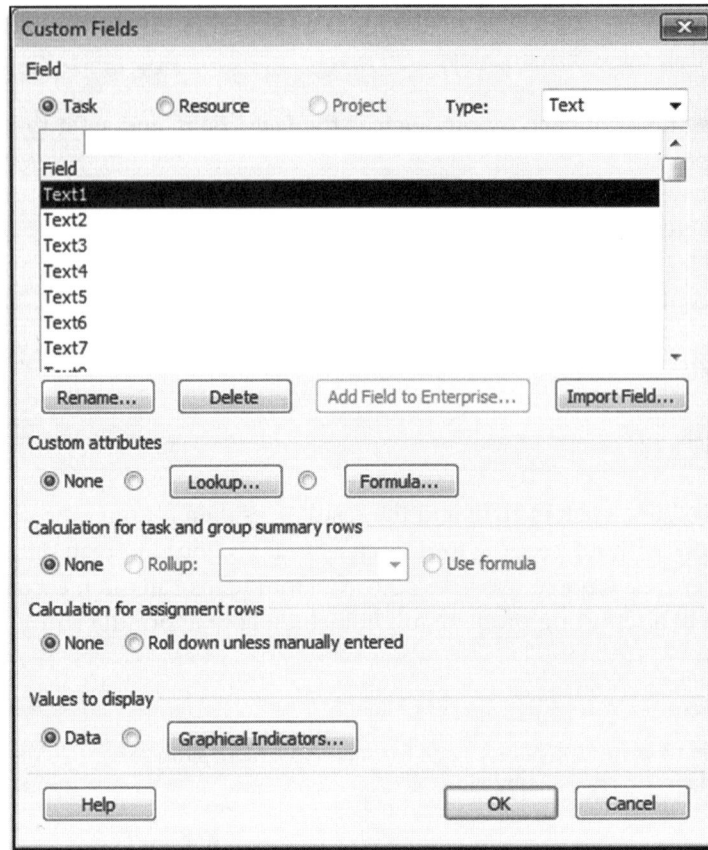

Figure 1 - 1: Custom Fields dialog

Figure 1 - 1 shows that each field has its own set of custom attributes, including value lists, formulas, and graphical indicators. Assume that as a part of your organization's project management methodologies, you must assign a *Cost Center* number to each task in every project. To create a custom field to capture this information, complete the following steps:

1. Select the *Task* option at the top of the dialog.

2. Click the *Type* pick list and select the *Text* field type.

3. Select an unused *Text* field, which is the *Text1* field in this example. Renaming fields as done in step 4 makes finding an unused field much easier and helps prevent using the same field for more than one set of data.

4. Click the *Rename* button. The system displays the *Rename Field* dialog shown in Figure 1 - 2.

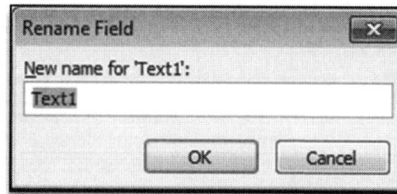

Figure 1 - 2: Rename Field dialog

5. Enter the name *Cost Center* in the *Rename Field* dialog and click the *OK* button.

Figure 1 - 3 shows the *Custom Fields* dialog after renaming the new *Cost Center* field.

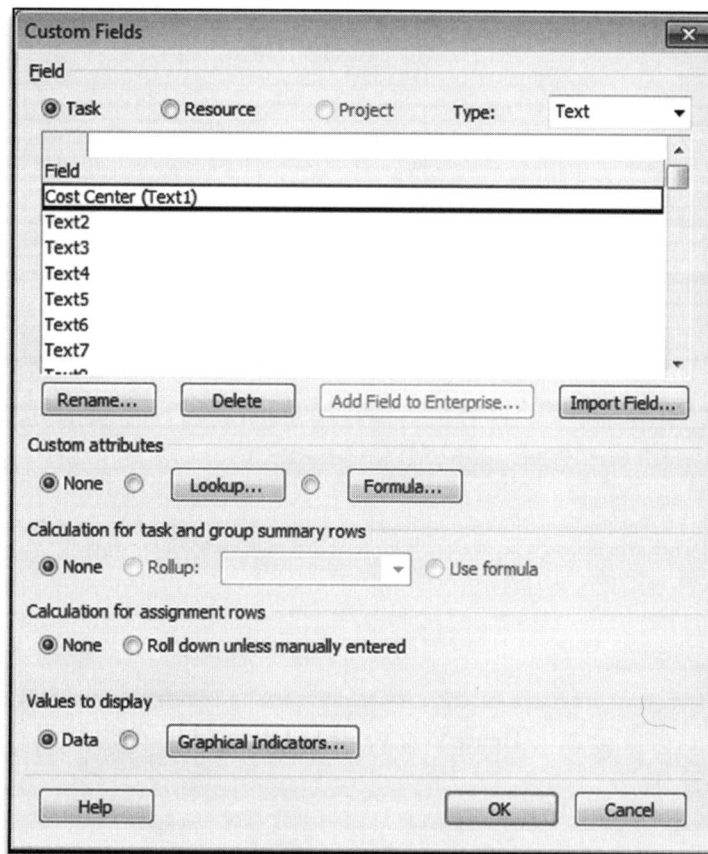

**Figure 1 - 3: Custom Fields dialog
shows custom Cost Center field**

Using a Value List in a Custom Field

Assume that as a part of your organization's project management methodologies, you must categorize the date slippage risk as *High, Medium,* or *Low* for each task in every project. Assume also that the default risk on every task is *Low* unless you specify otherwise. To create a custom task *Text* field with a value list, complete the following steps:

1. In the *Custom Fields* dialog, select the *Text2* field and rename the field *Risk*.

2. Click the *Lookup* button.

The software opens the *Edit Lookup Table* dialog shown in Figure **1 - 4**.

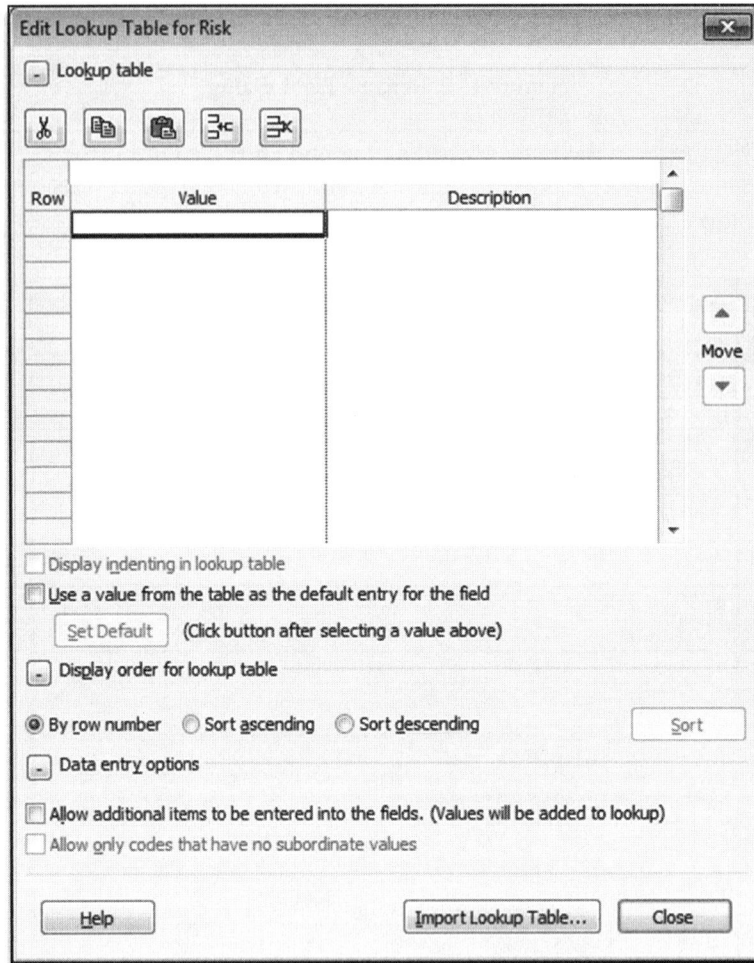

Figure 1 - 4: Value List dialog

3.   Enter *High, Medium,* and *Low* values in the *Value* column.

4.   Enter an optional description for each value in the *Description* column.

5.   Select the *Use a value from the table as the default entry for the field* option.

6.   Select the *Low* value and click the *Set Default* button.

7.   Select the *By row number* option in the *Display Order for lookup table* section.

8.   I leave the *Allow additional items to be entered into the fields* option unchecked in the *Data entry options* section.

i

Project 2003 and earlier have a *Restrict field to items in the value list* option so by default you can enter new values, a different behavior than Project 2007 onwards which have the *Allow additional items* option instead.

The *Risk* custom field now has a drop down list containing *High*, *Medium*, and *Low* values. *Low* is the default choice and once shown, the software sorts the drop down list in the order the values were entered. You cannot type any additional values into the *Risk* field.

Click the *Help* button for further information on how to use the different options for your version of Project.

When you define a new field and want to use a value list from an existing field, click the *Import Lookup Table* button at the bottom of the *Edit Lookup Table* dialog. The system displays the *Import Lookup Table* dialog shown in Figure 1 - 5.

Figure 1 - 5: Import Lookup Table dialog

Click the *Project* pick list button and select one of the project files that you currently have open. Select the *Field type* for the field containing the value list. Click the *Field* pick list button and select the field containing the value list you want to import. Click the *OK* button to complete importing the existing value list into your current field.

In the case of the *Risk* field, there is no need to import a value list, so click the *OK* button in the *Import Lookup Table* dialog. The software displays a warning message shown in Figure 1 - 6.

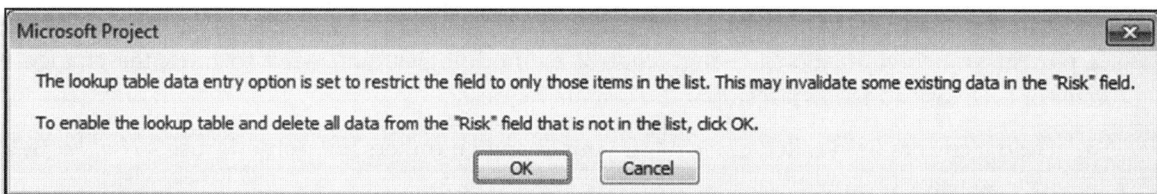

Figure 1 - 6: Warning dialog

The software warns you that if you previously entered values in this field before defining the value list, it may invalidate any or all of those pre-existing values. Click the *OK* button to return to the *Custom Fields* dialog shown in Figure 1 - 7.

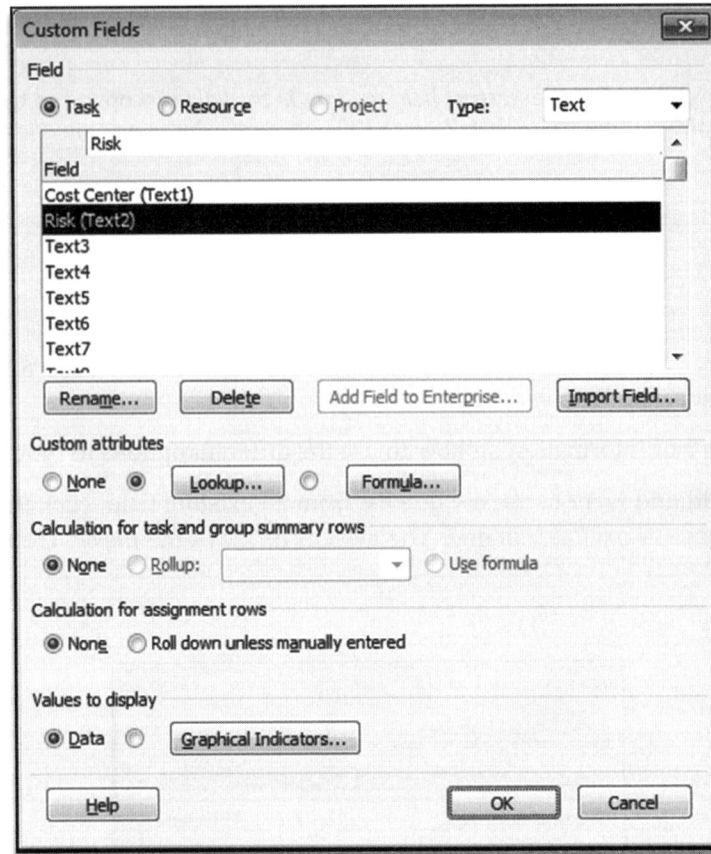

Figure 1 - 7: Custom Fields dialog after creating the Cost Center and Risk fields

Hands On Exercise

Exercise 1-1

As a part of your organization's change control methodologies, you need to track the change request number of each task added as a result of the change request.

1. Add a custom field called *Change #*. If your change numbers are numeric, use a *Number* field, otherwise use a *Text* field.

2. Close the *Custom Fields* dialog.

3. Insert the custom field you created in step #1 to the *Gantt Chart* view of any project.

4. Enter some *Change* numbers against some tasks that have resources assigned.

5. From the *View* ribbon, click the *Group* pick list and select the *More Groups* item and then create a new Group that groups by the *Change #* custom field.

6. Apply the *Work* table then apply your new custom group to see subtotals for extra work added by each change.

Exercise Note: For work changed or removed by a change, you can use a custom *Number* field to hold the *Work* value before you apply the change. Use a formula in another custom field to calculate the difference between the original work (zero for new tasks for the change) and current work. Group totals for this difference field will then reflect changes to work, not just additions.

Using a Formula in a Custom Field

Assume that as part of your organization's project management methodologies, you must show the percentage of cost over budget for every task in each project. This requires a custom *Number* field containing a formula. To define this custom field, complete the following steps:

1. In the *Custom Fields* dialog, click the *Type* pick list and select the *Number* field.

2. Select an available *Number* field and rename it *Percent Over Budget*.

3. Click the *Formula* button.

> Microsoft introduced the use of formulas in custom fields in Project 2000; therefore, Project 98 does not allow you to use formulas.

The software opens the *Formula* dialog shown in Figure 1 - 8.

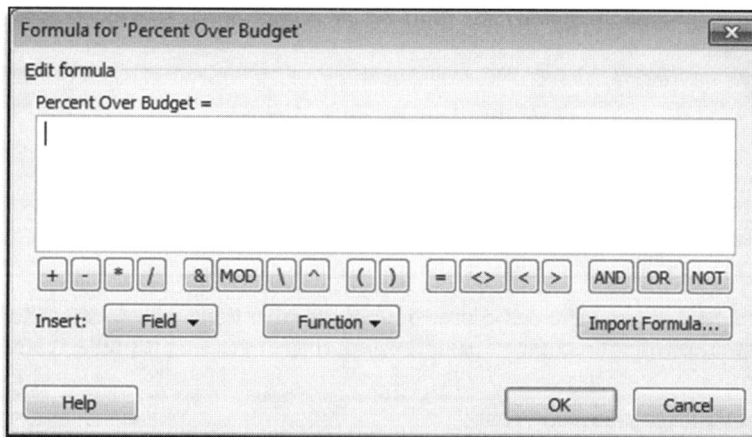

Figure 1 - 8: Formula dialog

The *Formula* dialog provides graphical tools for building formulas. You can use the *Field, Function,* and various *operand* buttons to build your formula or you can type your formula manually. The software displays the resulting formula in the text area of the dialog.

4. Using the *Field* pick list button and *operand* buttons, create the following formula to calculate the percent of cost variance:

```
IIf([Baseline Cost]=0, 0 ,[Cost Variance]/[Baseline Cost])
```

Notice that the formula for the percentage of cost over budget is simply the **Cost Variance** divided by the **Baseline Cost**. If the current Cost for a task is $50,000 when the Baseline Cost is only $45,000, then the Cost Variance is $5,000 (Cost – Baseline Cost). Applying the percentage of cost over budget formula, the task is 10% over budget ($5,000 ÷ $50,000).

> **i** If you created a formula in another field, you can import it into the current field by clicking the *Import Formula* button. The formula can be in a field in the active project, or in another project; but the project containing the formula must be open before you can import it.

5. Click the *OK* button.

The software displays the warning message shown in Figure 1 - 9. The warning indicates that, upon acceptance, the software deletes any pre-existing values in the *Percent Over Budget* field because a formula now calculates the values.

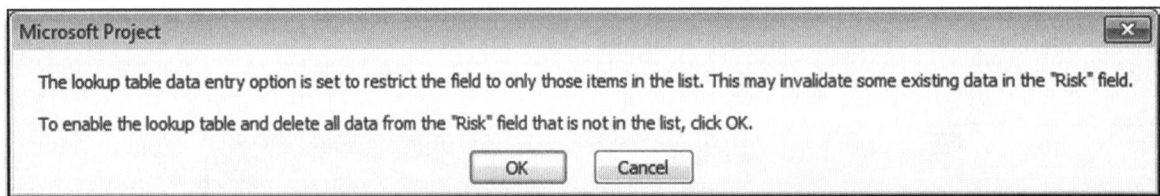

Microsoft Project

The lookup table data entry option is set to restrict the field to only those items in the list. This may invalidate some existing data in the "Risk" field.

To enable the lookup table and delete all data from the "Risk" field that is not in the list, click OK.

[OK]   [Cancel]

Figure 1 - 9: Warning dialog

6. Click the *OK* button to close the *Warning* dialog.

> **i** Microsoft Project formats all values in user-defined *Number* fields as a decimal. To display the *% Over Budget* field values with percentage formatting, enter the following formula in any user-defined *Text* field:
>
> Format([Cost Variance]/[Baseline Cost],"0%")
>
> The *Format* function takes a number and formats it as a text string just like the VBA *Format* function.

Figure 1 - 10 shows the *Custom Fields* dialog with the new custom field containing the formula.

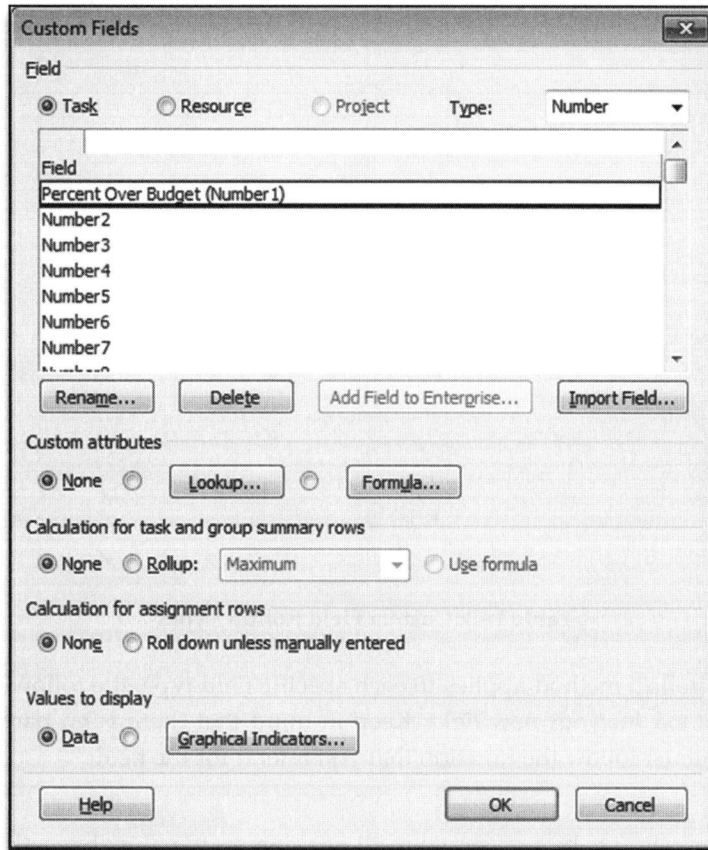

Figure 1 - 10: Custom Fields dialog

When you define a custom field with a formula, you must determine how the software uses the formula for summary tasks and group summary rows by selecting options in the *Calculation for task and group summary rows* section of the dialog. If you want Microsoft Project to apply the formula directly to both summary tasks and group summary rows, select the *Use formula* option. For the *Percent Over Budget* field, select the *Use formula* option to apply the formula to all summary tasks and subtasks in the project.

If you want to apply the formula in a different manner, select the *Rollup* option and then select a rollup value from the pick list. *Rollup* options apply to all custom fields except *Text* fields. Table 1 - 3 lists the field types and their rollup capabilities.

Rollup Type	Cost	Date	Duration	Flag	Number
Average	✓		✓		✓
Average First Sublevel	✓		✓		✓

Rollup Type	Cost	Date	Duration	Flag	Number
Count All					✓
Count First Sublevel					✓
Count Nonsummaries					✓
Maⓞimum	✓	✓	✓		✓
Minimum	✓	✓	✓		✓
Sum	✓		✓		✓
And				✓	
Or				✓	

Table 1 - 3: Custom Field Rollup Types

Now that you know which rollup method applies to each specific field type, the following explanations help you choose the appropriate method for your new field. Keep in mind that there is no particular right or wrong answer. The choice you make must follow the function that you intend for the field.

- **Average**: Causes the rollup to be an average of all non-summary values beneath the summary row.

- **Average First Sublevel**: Causes the rollup to be an average of both the non-summary and summary values on just the first level of subtasks or grouped tasks.

- **Count All**: Causes the rollup to be a count of all summary and non-summary items beneath the summary row.

- **Count First Sublevel**: Causes the rollup to be a count of both the summary and non-summary tasks on only the first level beneath the summary row.

- **Maximum**: The rolled up value is the maximum value of values beneath the summary row.

- **Minimum**: The rolled up value is the minimum value of all values beneath the summary row.

- **Sum**: The rolled up value is the sum of all non-summary values beneath the summary row.

- **AND**: The rolled up value is the logical AND of all the flag values appearing beneath the summary row. If all flags in the subtasks are set to *Yes*, then the rollup in the summary task is *Yes*. If any flags in the subtasks are set to *No*, then the rollup in the summary task is *No*.

- **OR**: The rolled up value is the logical OR of all flag values appearing beneath the summary row. If any flags in the subtasks are set to *Yes*, then the rollup is *Yes*.

Testing for an NA Date Value

When there is no date in a *Date* field such as *Baseline Start*, then Microsoft Project displays an *NA* value in the field. The system stores the *NA* value internally as the largest possible number the *Date* field can hold. One test for an *NA* date value is to test for the date being a large number; however this method does not obviously explain what's happening.

A more readable and easier to support method is to test for the value returned by using the *ProjDateValue("NA")* function. For example, to use the *Text1* field to display whether a date exists in the *Baseline Date* field, use the following formula:

IIf([Baseline Start]=ProjDateValue("NA"),"No Date",[Baseline Start])

Using Graphical Indicators in a Custom Field

Using graphical indicators with a custom field offers you the ability to create a graphical presentation of the data in the field. It is easiest to apply graphical indicators to a field that already contains a value list or a formula.

Assume that as a part of your organization's project management methodologies, you must use stoplight indicators to display the data in the *Percent Over Budget* field. Assume your organization's criteria for displaying stoplight indicators in the *Percent Over Budget* field are as follows:

- If the *% Over Budget* is less than 5%, then display a green smiley face icon.

- If the *% Over Budget* is greater than or equal to 5% but less than 10%, then display a yellow neutral face icon.

- If the *% Over Budget* is greater than or equal to 10%, then display a red unhappy face icon.

In addition, you want to see the underlying value in this field for any task by floating the mouse pointer over the graphical indicator while in a task view. To define graphical indicators in the *Percent Over Budget* field, complete the following steps:

1. In the *Custom Fields* dialog, select the *Percent Over Budget* field.

2. Click the *Graphical Indicators* button.

The system opens the *Graphical Indicators* dialog shown in Figure 1 - 11. Notice in the *Indicator criteria for* section of the dialog, the system accepts the criteria for displaying graphical indicators for three types of tasks: *Nonsummary* tasks (subtasks), *Summary* tasks, and the *Project summary* tasks (Row 0). Because of this, you can set completely different criteria for each of the three types of tasks, and define whether the summary rows inherit criteria from the non-summary rows.

21

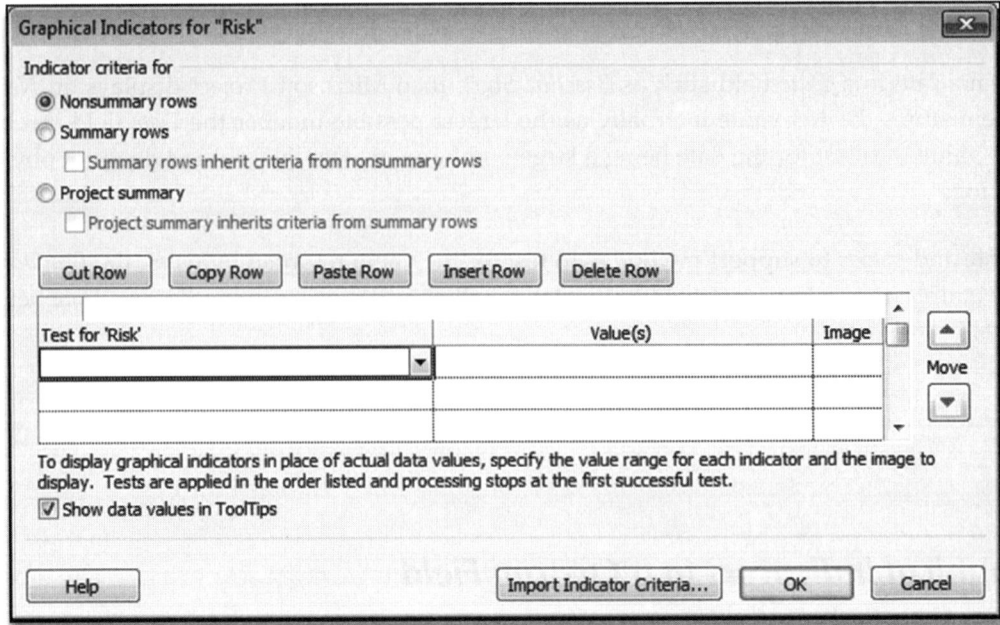

Figure 1 - 11: Graphical Indicators dialog

3. Select the *Nonsummary rows* option.

4. Set the *Test, Value(s),* and *Image* values (Project evaluates from the top, using the image for the first test that returns true) as follows:

Test	Value(s)	Image
Is greater than or equal to	.10	Red unhappy face
Is greater than or equal to	.05	Yellow neutral face
Is less than	.05	Green happy face

5. Click the *OK* button.

In Figure 1-11 the *Show data values in ToolTips* option is located in the lower left corner of the *Graphical Indicators* dialog. When you select this option, the software displays the underlying value in the field as a tooltip when you float the mouse pointer over the graphical indicator.

If you previously created graphical indicators in a field, you can import them into the current field by clicking the *Import Indicator Criteria* button. The indicator criteria can be in a field in the active project, or in another project, but the project containing the indicator criteria must be open before you can import them.

To set the criteria used to determine the graphical indicator for each task, you must specify multiple tests using the available pick lists in the grid. The *Test* column offers the following tests:

- Equals

- Does not equal

- Is greater than

- Is greater than or equal to

- Is less than

- Is less than or equal to

- Is within

- Is not within

- Contains

- Does not contain

- Contains exactly

- Is any value

The "Is any value" test yields a positive result in all cases. This makes it useful as a "catch all" test to include at the bottom of the criteria list, as it will display an indicator to represent any value not otherwise defined.

The tests you select in the *Test* field apply to the values you select or enter in the *Value(s)* field. In the *Value(s)* field, you can select any standard or custom field, or you can enter a literal value. In the *Image* field, select a graphical indicator for each test.

Table 1 - 4 shows the types of multi-colored graphical images available and the number of each type of image.

Image Type	Number
Blank indicator	1
Stoplights	13
Flags	8
Solid color squares	5
Plus signs	5
Minus signs	6
Solid color diamonds	3
Blue arrows	5
Semaphores	7
Light bulbs	2
Miscellaneous	5
"Smiley face" icons	6

Table 1 - 4: Graphical Images

How does Microsoft Project determine which graphical indicator to display for each task? The software processes the graphical indicator test criteria from the top down. If the first test results in a "False" condition, the system processes the second test, and continues processing each test in the list until a test results in a "True" condition. The software displays the graphical indicator for the first test that results in a "True" condition and then stops processing the list of tests. If none of the tests results in a "True" condition, the system does not display a graphical indicator for that task. You should keep this in mind while structuring your tests and, at the same time, use it to your advantage.

Microsoft Project displays a blank graphical indicator in any cell in which a formula generates an error, such as when the software generates a division by 0 error.

Hands On Exercise

Exercise 1-2

As a part of your organization's project management methodologies, you need to define a custom field to calculate the percentage of work that exceeds your original Baseline Work budget for every task in your project.

1. Open any project file you have baselined that contains tasks, resources, and assignments.
2. Click Tools ➤ Customize ➤ Fields.
3. Select the task *Number1* field and rename it *Percent Work Over Budget*.
4. Create a formula in the field that calculates the percentage of work in excess of your original Baseline Work budget.
5. Apply the formula to every task in the project, including summary tasks and group summary rows.
6. In the *% Work Over Budget* custom field, display graphical indicators according to the following criteria:

   • If the task is on or below its original Baseline Work budget, display a green smiley face indicator.

   • If the task is greater than 0% and less than or equal to 5% over its original Baseline Work budget, display a green indicator.

   • If the task is greater than 5% and less than or equal to 15% over its original Baseline Work budget, display a yellow indicator.

   • If the task is greater than 15% and less than or equal to 25% over its original Baseline Work budget, display a red indicator.

   • If the task is greater than 25% over its original Baseline Work budget, display a black indicator.

7. Close the *Custom Fields* dialog.
8. Save and close your project file.

Defining Custom Outline Codes

Custom outline codes differ significantly from custom fields in the following ways:

• Outline codes can accommodate either a flat value list or hierarchical outline structure.

• Outline codes do not contain formulas or graphical indicators.

- For Project 2007 and later the code mask is optional. However, when defining a custom outline code in Microsoft Project 2003 or earlier you must first define a code mask that determines the allowable structure of an outline code value.

Assume that as a part of your organization's resource management information, you need to track each resource's primary job skill. To create a custom resource outline code for this purpose, complete the following steps:

1. In the *Custom Fields* dialog, click the *Type* pick list and select the *Outline Code* item from the list of choices (in Project 2003 or earlier select the *Custom Outline Codes* tab).

Figure 1 - 12 shows the *Custom Outline Codes* page of the *Custom Fields* dialog for Project 2007 and later.

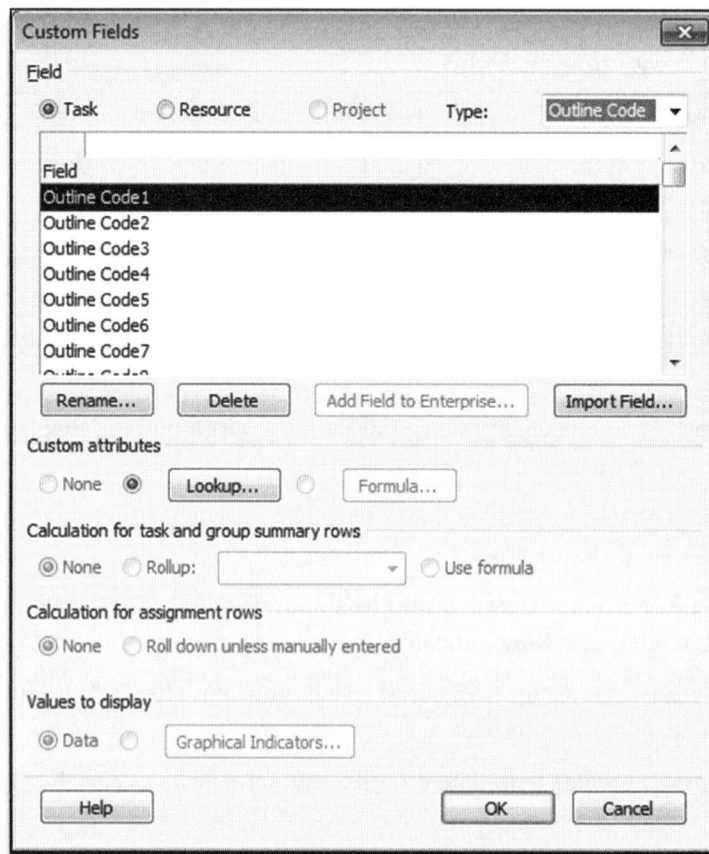

Figure 1 - 12: Custom Outline Codes page

2. Select the *Resource* option.

3. Select the *Outline Code1* field and rename it *Primary Skill*.

4. Click the *Lookup* button.

The software opens the *Edit Lookup Table* dialog shown in Figure 1 - 13.

5. Expand the *Code mask* option.

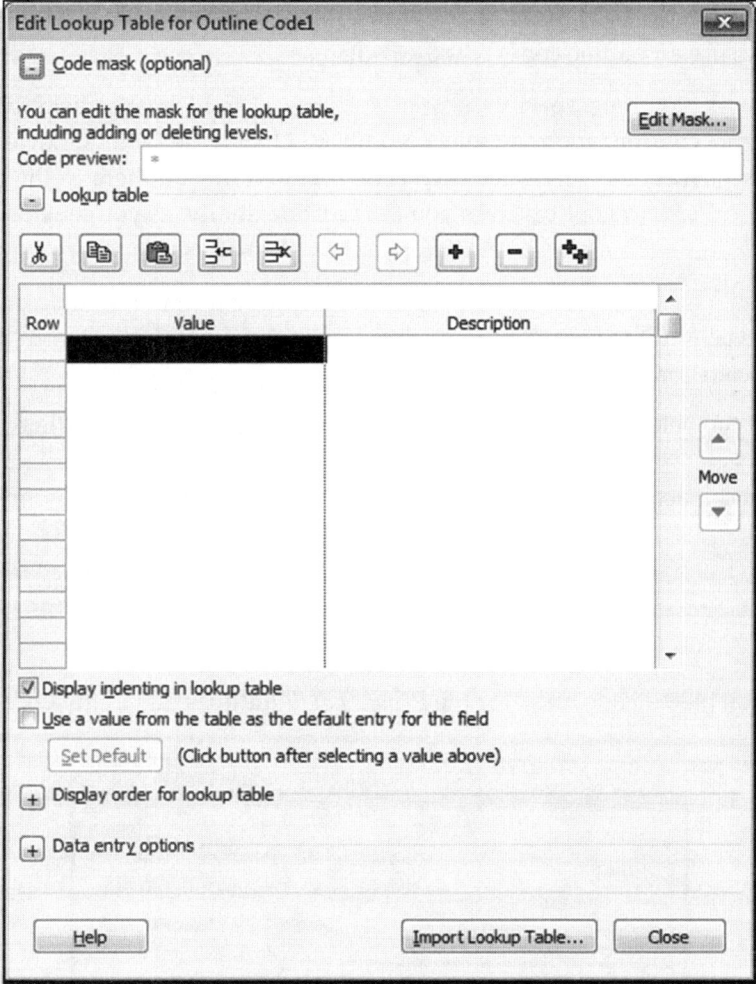

Figure 1 - 13: Edit Lookup Table dialog

6. Click the *Edit Mask* button. The software displays the *Code Mask Definition* dialog shown in Figure 1 - 14.

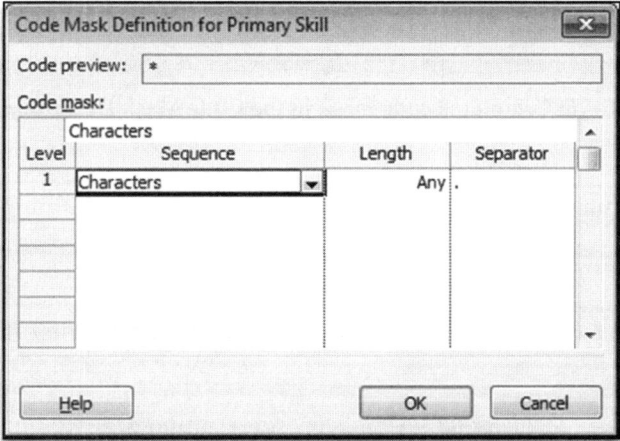

Figure 1 - 14: Code Mask Definition dialog

By default, a character mask that allows any characters in a single level (no indents allowed) is in place. Microsoft Project allows you to indent a row in the *Lookup* table to create a second outline level; but highlights the entry in red to show it does not match the code mask. If you do want more than one level of outline code (which is presumably why you want to use an outline code) edit the code mask.

To edit an outline code mask, you must specify the *Sequence, Length,* and *Separator* field values for each level of the outline code. In the *Sequence* column, you may select Numbers, Uppercase Letters, Lowercase Letters, or Characters. When you select a sequence, the values for each code segment must adhere to the type of data specified in the sequence. Selecting the *Characters* option gives you the most flexibility, as you may use any character to define your values.

In the *Length* column, you have the choice of limiting the segment to a number value on the list (between 1 and 10) or to a number you type into the field. You may also choose the *Any* selection from the pick list to allow any number of defined characters for the outline code segment.

In the *Separator* column, you select the character used as the separator between outline code segments. You can use a period, dash, plus sign, or a forward slash as the separator for each code segment. The system also allows you to enter other special characters, such as those found above the number keys on your keyboard.

7.   Define a two-level code mask, set the sequence to *Characters*, set the length to *Any*, and set the separator to *periods*.

Figure 1 - 15 shows the completed code mask for the *Primary Skill* outline code in the *Code Mask Definition* dialog.

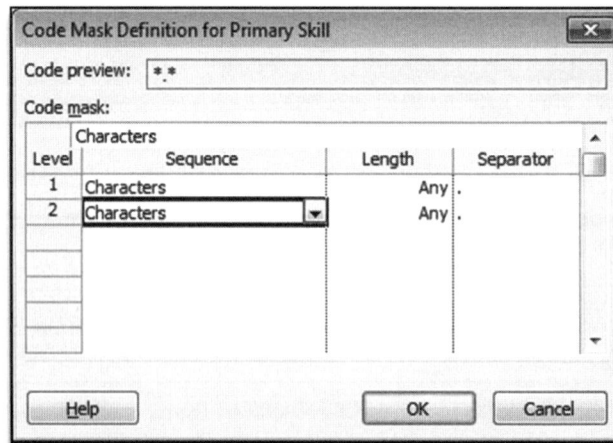

Figure 1 - 15: Completed code mask in the Code Mask Definition dialog

Back in the *Edit Lookup Table* dialog, there are two additional options for defining the behavior of your custom outline code:

- Select the *Allow additional items to be entered into the fields* option to enter items not already in the *Lookup* table.

- Select the *Allow only codes that have no subordinate values* option to force only the selection of values at the lowest outline level.

Warning: Microsoft Project 2003 and earlier allows ad hoc entry of *any type* of additional code values that do not conform to the code mask *unless* you restrict this by selecting one of these two additional options.

8. Enter the outline code information for each segment in the *Outline Code* column, using the *Indent* and *Outdent* buttons as necessary to build the outline code structure.

You can enter an optional description for each outline code segment in the *Description* column.

Figure 1 - 16 shows the completed outline code structure for the resource *Primary Skill* outline code.

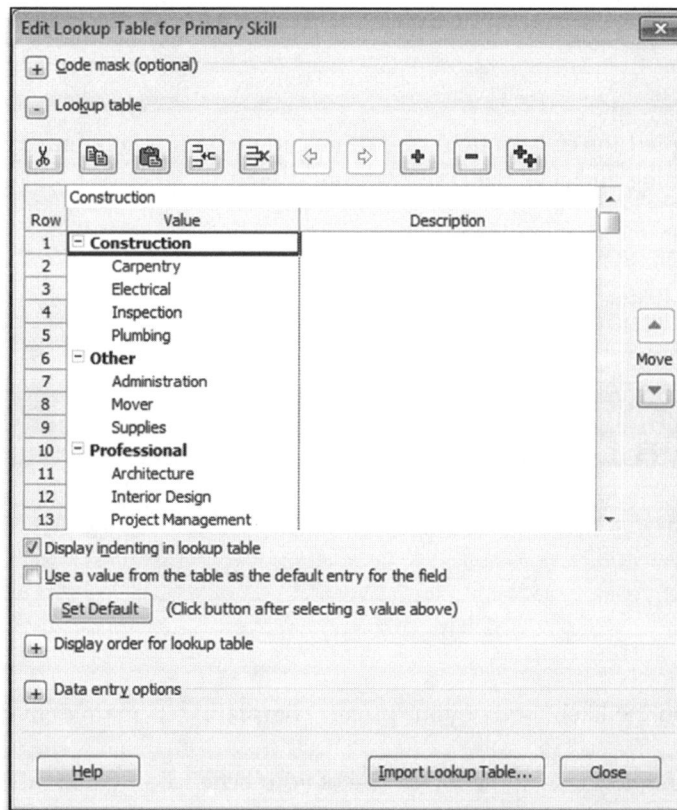

Figure 1 - 16: Completed outline code

Figure 1 - 16 shows that you can display indenting by selecting or deselecting the *Display indenting in lookup table* option towards the lower left hand corner of the dialog.

Tip: Although you can select a sort order for custom fields, if you want the system to display an outline in a specific order, prefix your codes with numbers, or with alphabetic characters such as "a-," "b-," etc.

9. Click the *OK* button to return to the *Custom Fields* dialog.

Deleting a Custom Field or Outline Code

One way to delete a custom field or outline code is to use the *Organizer* tool to complete the following steps:

1. Open a project containing the custom field or outline code.
2. Click Tools ➤ Organizer to display the *Organizer* dialog.
3. Select the *Fields* tab.
4. In the list of custom fields on the right side of the dialog, select the custom field or outline code you wish to delete.
5. Click the *Delete* button.
6. If you previously copied the custom field or outline code to your Global.mpt file, select it from the list on the left side of the dialog and click the *Delete* button.
7. Click the *Close* button.
8. Save the project.

Hands On Exercise

Exercise 1-3

You need to report on the likelihood of your project completing its main deliverables on time.

1. Include a summary task at the top of one of your schedules with a milestone to represent every deliverable in your project.
2. Link those deliverable milestones to the last task that completes them.

3. Double-click each milestone, click the *Advanced* tab, and enter a deadline for its delivery date in the *Deadline* field.

> To add deadline dates to your tasks, you can also insert the *Deadline* column temporarily in any *Task* view.

When you add a deadline date for a task, the system displays a hollow green arrow on the Gantt chart representing the deadline date for each task. If the task slips past its deadline date, the system displays a red diamond in the *Indicator* column.

4. Create a custom *Text* field and name it *RAG* (RAG stands for Red, Amber and Green).

5. Create a formula in the *RAG* field to do the following:

- Display a G if the task's *Finish* date is 5 working days ahead of the deadline date.

- Display an A if the task's *Finish* date is less than 5 days ahead.

- Display an R if the task's *Finish* date is later than the deadline date.

- Display a blank value if there is no deadline date on the task.

Module 02

Using Objects, Methods, and Properties

Learning Objectives

After completing this module, you will be able to:

- Understand and use Microsoft Project Objects, Methods, and Properties
- Use the Object Browser to find different Objects, Methods, and Properties in Project

Inside Module 02

Understanding the Microsoft Project Object Model

The Object Model is at the heart of VBA for Microsoft Project. Because there are hundreds of objects, properties and methods, I describe only the ones most commonly used in this book. However, pay close attention to the **Using the Object Browser to Locate an Object, Method, or Property** section of this module to learn ways of finding the information you need to write that extra little bit of code.

To see a diagram in Project Help on all objects in Project VBA, complete the following steps as outlined below in Table 2 - 1:

Step	Project 2003 and later	Project 2003 and earlier
1) Open Visual Basic Editor	Press **Alt+F11**	Press **Alt+F11**
2) Open Help	Press **F1** or click Help ➢ Microsoft Visual Basic Help	Press **F1** or click Help ➢ Microsoft Visual Basic Help
3) Show Project object model	1) If the Table of Contents section is not visible, display it by clicking on the closed book icon 2) Click the *Project Object Model Reference* link 3) Click the *Object Model Maps* link 4) Click the *Application and Project Objects Map* link to see the Object model, as shown in Figure 2 - 1	1) Click the *Microsoft Office Project Visual Basic Reference* book 2) Click the *Microsoft Office Project Object Model* link

**Table 2 - 1: How to find Microsoft Project Object
model in VBA Help**

Click any yellow or blue box to get help on that object. Objects are in hierarchies and the topmost object is the *Application* object. Figure 2 - 1 shows the Project 2010 Object Model.

> In Project 2003 and earlier, there are small red triangles next to some objects. Click on them to expand that branch of the hierarchy. For example the *Tasks* object has an arrow and expanding it shows all objects below it.
>
> In Project 2007 and later, red asterisks represent new objects or collections of objects.

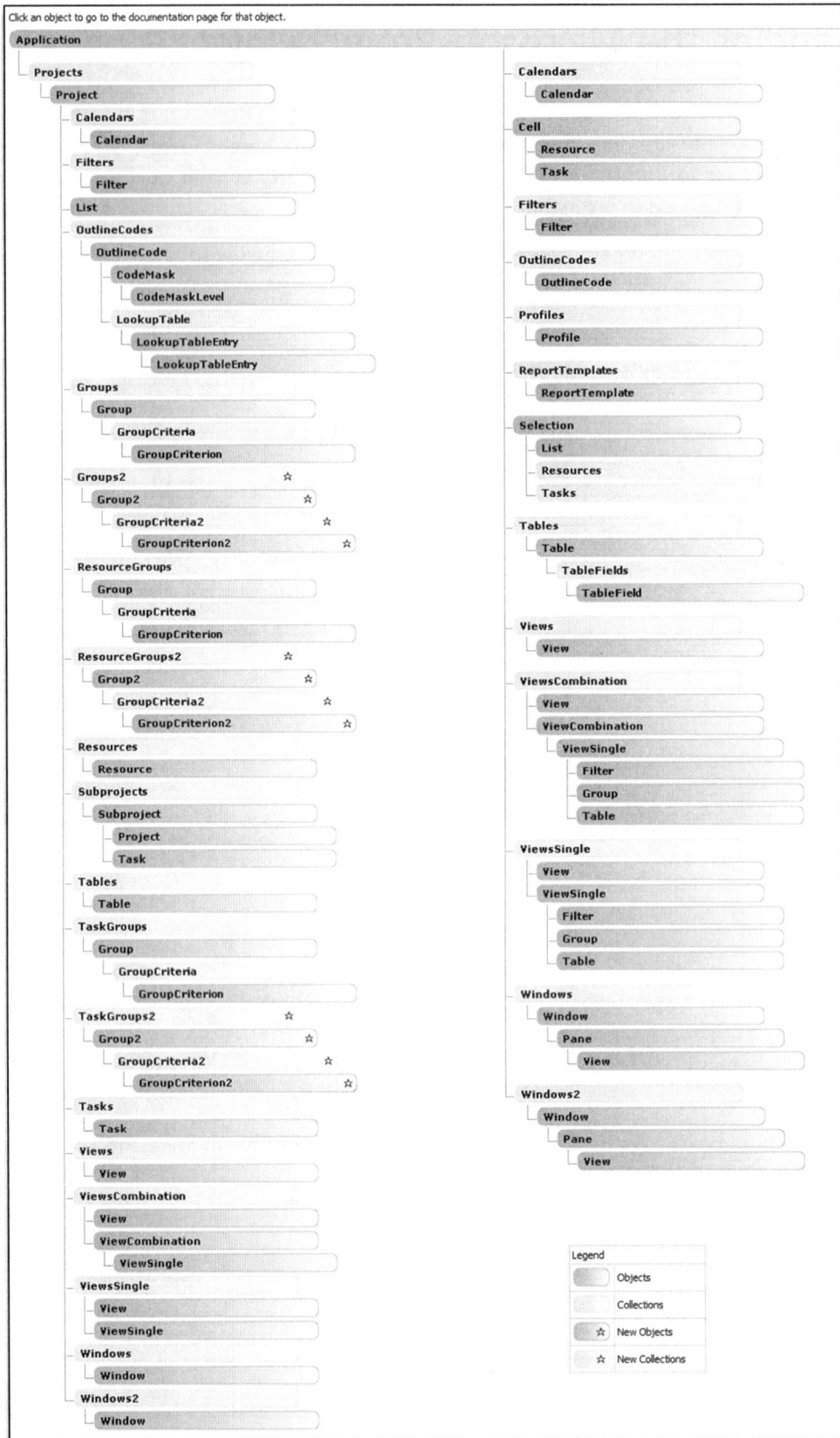

Figure 2 - 1: Project 2010 Object Model

Explaining Objects, Methods and Properties

In Figure 2 - 1 the darker boxes (in Help the darker boxes are blue) are objects, such as project, task, resource, etc. The lighter color boxes (in Help the lighter boxes are yellow) are collections of objects. A *Task* object is a single object, representing a single row in your Gantt chart. A tasks collection is a group of tasks; for example, all tasks in a project or all selected tasks.

Collections of objects and objects (singular) have methods and properties. A method is an action like *Add* or *Delete*. A property describes or defines something about an object. For example, the *Count* property reports how many objects there are in a collection. The *ActiveProject.Tasks.Count* object tells you how many tasks there are in the active project. Some properties like *Count* are "read only" (it is only changed after you add or delete an item to the collection), some are write only (you can only set them, not read them. An example is the *Font* method) while others like work are "read and write".

Using Application-Related Objects, Methods, and Properties

The *Application* object represents Microsoft Project itself, so anything that you want to do with the application rather than with a project belongs to the *Application* object. Commonly used methods for the *Application* object are **FileOpen**, **FileClose**, and **SaveBaseline**. All of these actions are independent of a project or you can perform them only on the active project, so they belong to the *Application* object.

The following code opens a project, sets the header to the project name and the current date, turns off the *Legend* section, and then displays a print preview for tasks for the next two weeks. Finally, it closes and saves the project so the header settings are preserved.

```
Sub PrintProject()
Const DaysToPrint = 14
     FileOpen "C:\My Schedule.mpp"
   'Set header to the project's title and hide the Legend
     FilePageSetupHeader Text:="&[Project Title] - &[Date] "
     FilePageSetupLegend LegendOn:=False

   'Print Tasks for next 14 days
     FilePrint FromDate:=Date, ToDate:=Date + DaysToPrint, Preview:=True
     FileClose pjSave  'Save project to preserve Header and Legend changes
End Sub
```

Note I use comments in the code to describe what should be happening. This makes understanding and maintaining the code much easier and quicker. Four important objects belong to the *Application* object: *ActiveCell, ActiveProject, ActiveSelection*, and *ActiveWindow*. Use them as follows:

- **ActiveCell** provides a pointer to the active cell in the current view. You typically use this object to reference the current task or resource currently selected by the cursor. The following code displays the name of the currently selected task in a *Task* view such as the Gantt chart:

```
MsgBox    "Current    Task's    Name    is:    "    &    ActiveCell.Task.Name,    _
vbInformation + vbOkOnly
```

The *ActiveCell.Task* object returns the *Task* object for the selected task on *Task* views and the *ActiveCell.Resource* object returns the *Resource* object for the selected resource in *Resource* views.

- **ActiveProject** returns an object for the current project. Use this object when you want to refer to the current project rather than a named project. Macros that use the *ActiveProject* object work with the currently active project. The following code sets an object variable for the active project, opens a new project then reselects the original one.

```
Sub ActiveProjectSample()
Dim FirstProject As Project
Dim SecondProject As Project
    Set FirstProject = ActiveProject
    FileOpen "Second Project.mpp"
    Set SecondProject = ActiveProject
    FirstProject.Activate
End Sub
```

> In the preceding code sample, notice that I must use the *Set* statement when setting an object variable to point to an object.

I can use the objects *FirstProject* or *SecondProject* (instead of *ActiveProject*) to access any task in either project without first making them active, and without moving the cursor.

- **ActiveSelection** is a collection of all tasks or resources currently selected. Use it for macros that need to operate on selected cells only in *Task* or *Resource* views. The *ActiveSelection.Tasks* object only works when a *Task* view is active and returns a *Task* collection containing all selected tasks. You do not need to select the whole task by clicking its row ID number; selecting only one cell is enough. The following code displays the number of tasks selected:

```
MsgBox "Number of tasks selected is: " & ActiveSelection.Tasks.Count
```

- **ActiveWindow** returns a *Window* object and you mostly use it to select, close, or refresh the current window.

The following list contains other useful application level objects and methods:

- **Projects** is a collection of *Project* objects that point to all open projects.

- **FileOpen**, **FileClose**, and **FileSave** are methods that do the same as their namesakes under the *File* menu.

- **Select Methods** – The system provides a variety of *Select* methods, such as the *SelectCellDown* method, that move the cursor. However, you do not need to move the cursor when you work with tasks. Preferred practice is not to use these *Select* methods unless you want to leave the cursor in a specific place at the end of your macro.

- **EditGoto** duplicates the *F5 Go To (or Ctrl+G)* functionality in Microsoft Project. This method can accept a task ID number; or in a view with a timescale, you can pass a date to scroll the timescale.

- **ViewApply**, **TableApply**, and **FilterApply** do the same as selecting a view, table, or filter from the *View* menu or the *Project* menu.

In the *Immediate* window, type *Application* followed by a period character. IntelliSense displays a list of all objects, properties, and methods that belong to the *Application* window. To learn more about each one, select it and then press the **F1** key for Help.

To be precise, your code should use the *Application.ActiveProject* object. However, if you search Help for the *ActiveProject* object (or many other objects and methods), you will note that Help either says the parent object (in this case *Application*) is optional, or the example does not use the *Application.Object* object. Instead, it just uses the object. There is no best practice here. You may either write the *Application.ActiveProject* object or just the *ActiveProject* object, whichever is easier for you and your team to read and understand, but be consistent.

Using Project-Related Objects, Methods, and Properties

You use a *Project* object in most macros, most often as the *ActiveProject* object. If your macro always works with the *ActiveProject* object rather than using *Projects*("My Project") to select a specific project, then your macro will work for any active project. This obviously makes your code much more flexible.

The following sections explain the more useful objects, methods, and properties belonging to the *Project* object.

Using Project Objects

Tasks and *Resources* are two very important collections of objects that belong to the *Project* object. Module 04 describes how to iterate through all tasks and resources in your project file using *Project* objects.

The Project Summary Task (row zero in a Gantt chart) shows totals and other summarized data for the whole project. To show the Project Summary Task do the following as outlined below in Table 2 - 2 :

Step	Project 2010	Project 2007 and earlier
1) Find the option	Click the *Format* tab in the ribbon	Click Tools ➢ Options
2) Show the Project Summary Task	In the *Show/Hide* section of the ribbon select the *Project Summary Task* option	Click the *View* tab then select the *Show Project Summary Task* option

Table 2 - 2: How to Display the Project Summary Task

The *ActiveProject.ProjectSummaryTask* object is a *Task* object that represents the Project Summary Task (row zero). You can use it to read summarized project totals, as shown in the following example:

```
MsgBox    "Total    Work    for    Active    Project    is:    "    &    _
ActiveProject.ProjectSummaryTask.Work / 60 / ActiveProject.HoursPerDay & " days"
```

The preceding code displays the total work for the project, expressed in *Days*. The *Work* property returns the amount of work in *Minutes*, so dividing by 60 returns *Hours*. The *HoursPerDay* property returns the current *Hours Per Day* option setting, accessed in Project 2010 by File tab ➢ Options then looking under the *Schedule* tab and in Project 2007 and earlier by clicking Tools ➢ Options and then selecting the *Calendar* tab.

The *ActiveProject.BuiltInDocumentProperties* object returns a collection of *Document* properties. Use them to access the values in the *Project Properties* dialog. To display a project's properties do the following as outlined below in Table 2 - 3:

Step	Project 2010	Project 2007 and earlier
View Properties	1) File tab ➢ Info 2) Click the *Project Information* pick list 3) Select *Advanced Properties*	File ➢ Properties

Table 2 - 3: How to view the Project Properties dialog

Figure 2 - 2 shows the Project 2010 Information pick list:

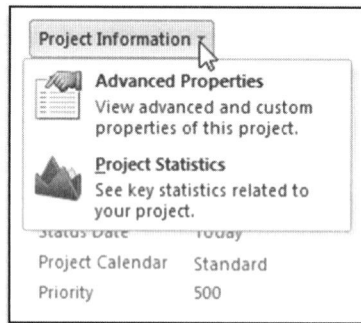

Figure 2 - 2: The Project Information picklist

For example, the following code displays the *Author* name in a pop-up messages dialog:

```
MsgBox "Author: " & _
    ActiveProject.BuiltInDocumentProperties("Author")
```

The final collection of *Project* objects is the *Calendars* collection which includes the *Standard* and other built-in and custom base calendars. A common use for the *Calendars* collection is to reference the *Standard* calendar and set company holidays. I offer sample code to do this in Module 16.

Using Project Methods

Methods do things; and they are the "verbs" of the VBA language. *Activate* and *SaveAs* are the two most commonly used methods for the project object:

- **Activate** – If you have several project files open, then you can use the following code to activate a specific open project:

```
Projects("Any open Project file name").Activate
```

- **SaveAs** – Use to save a project that is not active as shown in the following example or with ActiveProject:

```
Projects("My Other Project").SaveAs "My Other Project Backup"
```

Using Project Properties

Unlike *Project* methods, there are many *Project* properties. The previous example for *Project* objects used the *HoursPerDay* property. Many properties are read-only, but the rest are read/write, like the *HoursPerDay* property. VBA Help will tell you which properties are read-only and which are read/write. To force the the *ActiveProject* object to its default of 8 hours per day, for example, use the following code:

```
ActiveProject.HoursPerDay = 8
```

There is a batch of properties starting with "Current" that let you read the currently-applied view, table, filter, or group. The following code stores the current task and view name then returns to them after some other code executes, and presumably has changed them:

```
Sub CurrentViewExample()
Dim Tsk As Task
Dim strView As String
    Set Tsk = ActiveCell.Task
    'Save name of current View, then  work with a different View
    strView = ActiveProject.CurrentView
    'Code that changes the Task and View
    'Restore original View and goo originally selected task
    ViewApply strView
    EditGoTo ID:=Tsk.ID
End Sub
```

In the preceding example, I use the *strView* variable name to emphasize that it holds the string name of the view and is not a *View* object. I also used the *EditGoto* method to reselect the original task.

Two very useful *Project Object* properties are **Name** and **FullName**. The *Name* property contains the file name only while the *FullName* property includes the full path of the .mpp file, once saved.

You can read and set many of the properties editable in the *Options* dialog through VBA. The *HoursPerDay* property is just one example. Follow the instructions on the Object Browser at the end of this module to find the correct property name and then in Help to determine whether the property is read-only, read/write or write-only.

Using Task-Related Objects, Methods, and Properties

Task objects are most often part of a task collection, such as the *ActiveProject.Tasks* collection. To access any *Task* object within a *Task* collection, you can take three basic approaches:

- Refer to the task by its index: ActiveProject.Tasks(1) – Returns a *Task* object for the first task (row 1).

- Refer to the task by its name: ActiveProject.Tasks("My First Task") – Returns the task named *My First Task*.

- Refer to the task by its Unique ID: ActiveProject.Tasks.UniqueID(1) – Returns the task whose Unique ID is 1.

In the preceding three examples, an error occurs if there are no tasks in the schedule, no task called *My First Task*, or no task with a Unique ID of 1 (such as when it has been deleted because Unique IDs are never re-used within a project). To check whether your task collection has any tasks in it, use:

```
If ActiveProject.Tasks.Count>0 Then
```

or

```
If Not ActiveSelection.Tasks is Nothing Then
```

There is always a *Tasks* collection for a project, even if there are no tasks yet. If one or more blank cells are selected, the *ActiveSelection.Tasks* collection has the *Nothing* value.

A task contains three properties that return three important collections of objects:

- **Assignments** – A collection of all resource assignments for the task.

- **TaskDependencies** – A collection of all predecessors and successors for the task.

> Module 10 describes a macro that works with the TaskDependencies Object to show all tasks linked to the selected task.

- **TimeScaleData** - Returns the data you see in the *Task Usage* view in the timephased grid on the right side of the view.

> I explain the use of the TimeScaleData Collection Object with sample code in Module 09.

Task objects also contain a few methods, including:

- **Delete** – To delete the task.

- **Add** – To add a task (Add belongs only to the *Tasks* collection, not to an individual *Task* object).

Each task has hundreds of properties. For example, there is a property for every *Task* field, including those added in the enterprise versions.

The *Unique ID* field is a little-known field in Project that guarantees to provide a *Unique ID* number for every task, resource, and assignment in a project. Unlike ID numbers that change whenever you delete or add rows or apply sorting, *Unique ID* numbers never change. Therefore, to guarantee that your code can find a specific task, resource, or assignment, save its Unique ID for later use.

The following code examples show how to read and write to *Task* fields:

```
'Set a task flag
ActiveProject.Tasks("My Task").Flag1 = True

'read the task duration and display it in a message box with units of hours
MsgBox "Duration = " & ActiveProject.Tasks(1).Duration / 60 & "h"

'Set the duration of the task with unique ID = 1 to 1 day duration
ActiveProject.Tasks.UniqueID(1).Duration = 8 * 60
```

Note that duration and work are always stored in minutes.

Using Resource-Related Objects, Methods, and Properties

Working with resources in VBA is very similar to working with tasks; you access them in exactly the same way as tasks. *Resource* objects come in collections. The most commonly used resource collection is *ActiveProject.Resources*. The system provides you with three ways to access any one *Resource* object within a *Resource* collection:

- ActiveProject.Resources(1) – Returns a *Resource* object for the first resource (row 1).

- ActiveProject.Resources("My First Resource") – Returns the resource named *My First Resource*.

- ActiveProject.Resources.UniqueID(1) – Returns the resource whose Unique ID is 1.

As with tasks, if no object meets any of the three criteria above, the system generates an error. Resource names rarely change (unlike task names) so the *Resources("Resource Name")* name is a good way to refer to a specific resource. However, for tasks and assignments, the most reliable access uses their Unique ID.

Each resource also has three properties this time returning two important collections of objects and one single object:

- **Assignments** – All assignments for the resource.

- **TimeScaleData** - Returns data you see in the *Resource Usage* view.

- **Calendar** – Returns an object for the resource's calendar.

Likewise, resources have only a few methods, including the following:

- **Delete** – To delete the resource.

- **Add** – To create a new resource (*Add* only belongs to the *Resources* collection).

As with tasks, there are hundreds of properties for each resource, such as a property for every *Resource* field, including the additional fields added in the enterprise version.

> **Important Note:** If you Copy/Cut and then Paste a task or resource, the newly-pasted task or resource gets a new Unique ID number. This is not a recommended practice when working with Enterprise Projects saved in a Project Server database, especially if you use Project Server timesheets.

> **Tip:** If you want to update task or resource tracking status in another system, you must export current task and resource Unique ID's to that system to track data linked to the Unique ID's. This guarantees that you can find the appropriate task or resource in your update code, even if the task or resource name or row number has changed.

Using Assignment-Related Objects, Methods, and Properties

Assignments belong to tasks and resources. The *Assignments* collection for a task is all resources assigned to that task. An *Assignments* collection for a resource is all tasks assigned to that resource. Each assignment is unique, but it appears in both the *Tasks* collection and *Resource Assignments* collection.

An assignment has only one object, the **TimeScaleData** object, which returns the data you see in the *Usage* views. *Assignment* objects have several methods, including the following:

- **Delete** – To delete the resource assignment.

- **Add** – To create a new assignment (Add belongs only to the *Assignments* collection).

As with tasks and resources, the system provides more than a hundred properties for each assignment, including a property for every *Assignment* field, plus those properties added in the enterprise version.

Using the Object Browser

A common dilemma when writing code is determining the name of a particular property and determining the object to which it belongs. This is especially true when you reference another program such as Excel and you need to find something in Excel VBA. There are two approaches that work well in resolving this challenge:

- Record a macro (in Project or Excel) and examine the recorded code.

- Use the Object Browser.

The Object Browser provides a complete list of all objects, methods, properties, and constants available in any of the linked libraries for your code. To see all the linked libraries, complete these steps:

1. In the Visual Basic Editor (VBE), click Tools ➤ References.

The checked libraries (located at the top of the list) are the ones you selected, along with some default libraries such as Office and Project, as shown in Figure 2 - 3.

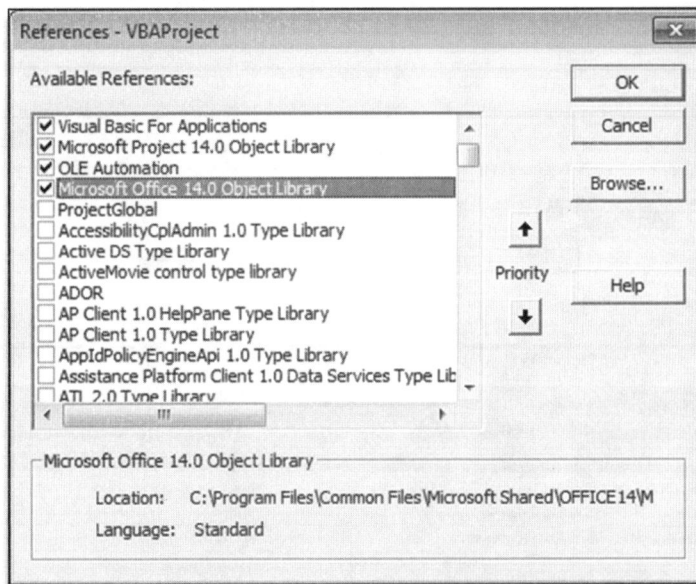

Figure 2 - 3: References dialog shows selected libraries

2. Click the *OK* button to close the *References* dialog.

3. Click View ➤ Object Browser (or press the function key F2) as show in Figure 2 - 4.

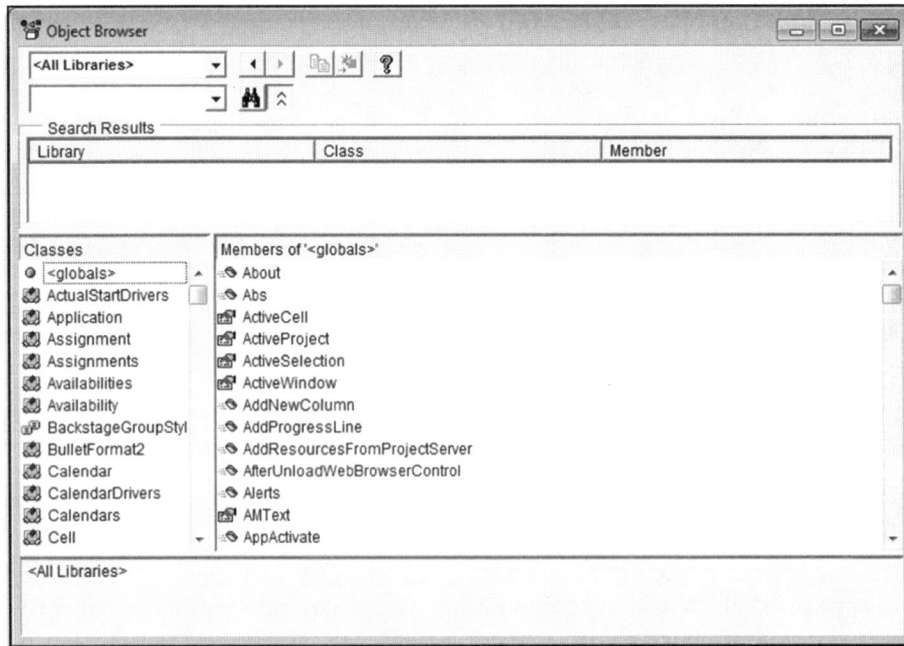

Figure 2 - 4: Object Browser window

4. In the upper left corner of the *Object Browser* window, click the *Project/Library* pick list button and select the *MSProject* option, as shown in Figure 2 - 5.

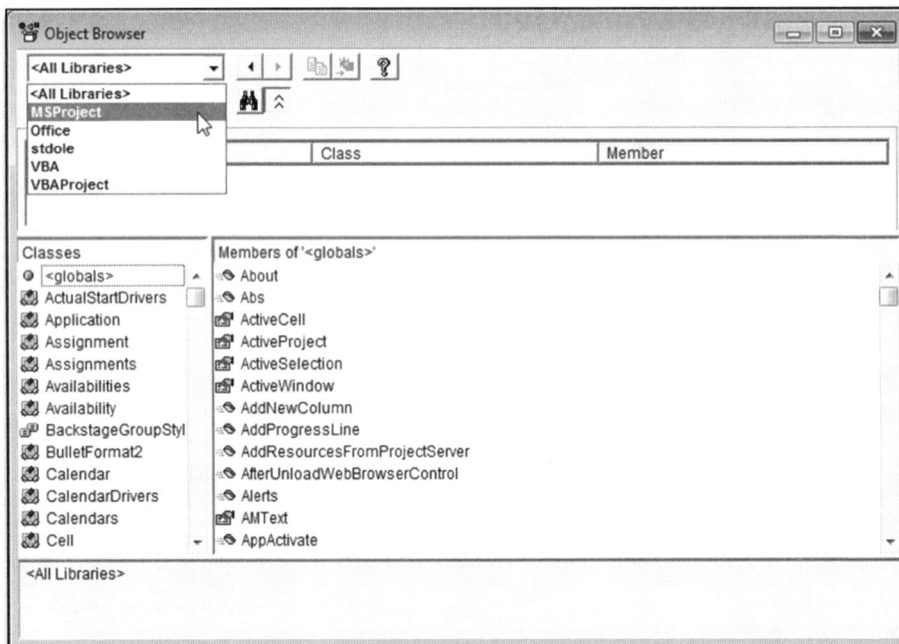

Figure 2 - 5: Object Browser window
with MSProject library selected

The Object Browser now displays only the objects, methods and properties for Microsoft Project VBA.

5. In the upper left corner of the *Object Browser* window, enter text in the *Search Text* field and then click the *Search* button.

For example, if you want to find the *HoursPerDay* property for a project, you might type *Hours* into the *Search Text* field. The *Search Results* pane shows everything related to *Hours*. In fact, the *HoursPerDay* property is the first item on the list, as shown in Figure 2 - 6.

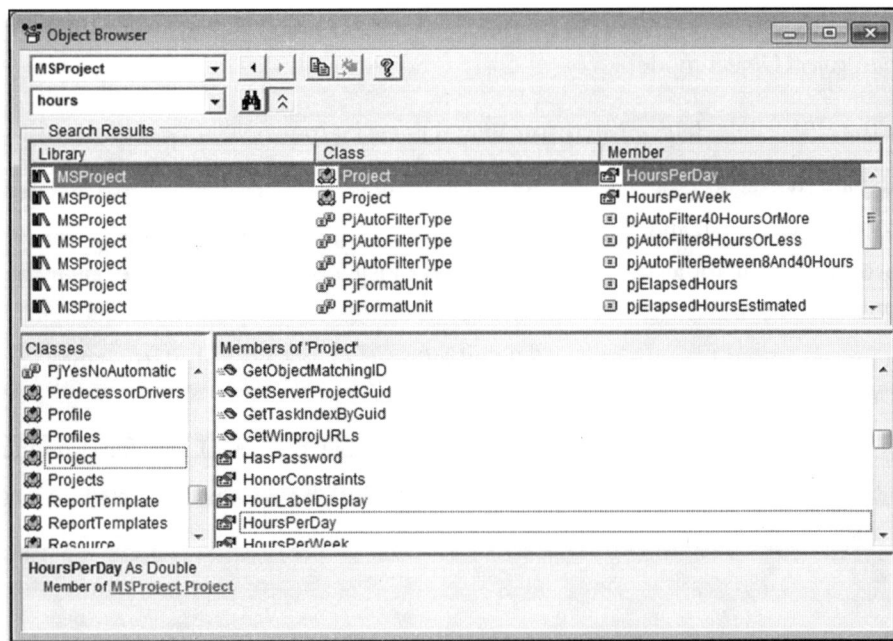

Figure 2 - 6: HoursPerDay Property in the Object Browser

6. Select an item in the upper pane to see class and other object members in the lower pane.

For example, click the *HoursPerDay* item in the upper pane and notice that the system selects the same item in the lower pane. You can also see that the main class is the *Project Object* class. Notice the *HoursPerWeek* property.

7. Select your item of interest and press **F1** to view the Help article on that item.

You should experiment with the Object Browser because it provides a great way to search for objects, methods, and properties within all linked libraries.

Hands On Exercise

Exercise 2-1

Explore the Project Object model.

1. In the VBE, click Help ➤ Microsoft Visual Basic Help.

2. Display the *Table of Contents* section, if necessary.

3. For Project 2010 click the *Object Model Maps* link in the table of contents. For Project 2007 and earlier, click the topic *Microsoft Office Project Visual Basic Reference* at or near the top of the table of contents.

4. In the expanded list is the *Microsoft Office Project Object Model* link (versions earlier than 2002 call it *Microsoft Project Object Model Overview*).

5. Explore the object model and click on different object boxes to see Help on what they do. Be sure to explore project, task, resource and assignment objects.

Exercise 2-2

Explore the Object Browser.

1. In the VBE, press the F2 function key to display the Object Browser.

2. In the upper left corner of the *Object Browser* window, click the *Project/Library* pick list button and select the *MSProject* option.

3. In the *Search Text* box enter the word "Current" (without the quotes) and then press the **Enter** key or click the *Search* button.

4. Browse the *Search Results* list to see the current properties.

5. Click the *CurrentView* property then click the *Help* button or press the F1 function key for Help to read about this property.

6. Search for other topics such as Task, HoursPerDay and Calendar to explore the Object Browser further.

Module 03

Recording Macros

Learning Objectives

After completing this module, you will be able to:

- Record a macro in Microsoft Project VBA
- Understand what types of macros are the most useful to record
- Understand macro recording limitations
- Modify recorded macros
- Store your VBA modules in your desired location
- Control file bloating
- Repair corrupted files

Inside Module 03

Understanding When to Record a Macro

With Microsoft Project, you can record macros, in addition to writing them. Recording a macro is useful when you want to create a macro to edit a table, but recording a macro definitely has its limits. For example, you cannot record a loop to do the same thing to all tasks, but you can record what to do to one task and then manually add loop code around your recorded code.

Recording a Macro

To record a macro, complete the steps outlined below in Table 3 - 1:

Step	Project 2010	Project 2007 and earlier
1. Start Recording	1. Click the *Developer* tab 2. Click the *Record Macro* button	1. Click Tools ➤ Macro ➤ Record New Macro. 2. Or press the keyboard shortcut of **Alt+T, M, R**.

Table 3 - 1: Steps to record a macro

The system displays the *Record Macro* dialog shown in Figure 3 - 1.

Figure 3 - 1: Record Macro dialog

2. In the *Macro Name* field, edit the name to give it a meaningful name.

3. Click the *Store macro in* pick list and select the *This Project* option. Do not save your macro in the Global.mpt file until you complete testing the macro and wish to share it with all projects.

4. Enter a description in the *Description* field to describe the function of your macro.

5. Click the *OK* button.

Recording macros works better if you execute your manual actions correctly; otherwise, your recorded code includes all your corrections and mistakes as well! To properly prepare for recording a macro, I recommend you do the following:

1. Practice the steps manually and write them down as you go to create a script.

2. If you want the macro to work on a new file, make sure the first recorded operation is to create the new file.

3. Start recording and follow the script.

4. Do not forget to stop recording at the end of the script as outlined below in Table 3 - 2:

Step	Project 2010	Project 2007 and earlier
Stop Recording	1. Click the *Developer* tab. 2. Click the *Stop Recording* button.	1. Click Tools ➢ Macro ➢ Stop Recording. 2. Or press the keyboard shortcut of **Alt+T, M, R**.

Table 3 - 2: Steps to stop recording a macro

Shortcut for Recording a Macro in Project 2010

On the status bar, right click any of the *View* icons. In the list that appears, select the *Macro Recording* option as shown in Figure 3 - 2.

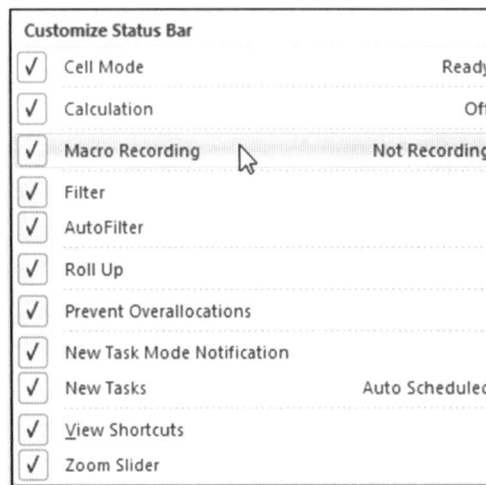

Figure 3 - 2: The Customize Status Bar list

In the bottom left corner of your screen, you will now see a *Record macro* button as shown in Figure 3 - 3. While recording, this button becomes a *Stop recording* button.

Ready | 🗐 | 🗦 New Tasks : Auto Scheduled

Figure 3 - 3: The Record macro button

Hands On Exercise

Exercise 3-1

Assume that you need to record a macro to show all current tasks for the next two weeks. By our definition, current tasks meet the following criteria:

- Progress < 100%
- Start Date < Today's date + 14d

Record a macro to create this new filter.

1. Open a project with at least one task that is not complete within the next 2 weeks.
2. Start recording a macro.
3. Change the name in the *Macro name* field to *CurrentTasks*.
4. Click the *Store Macro in* pick list and select the *This Project* item.
5. Click the *OK* button.

Record the following actions:

1. Create a new filter.
2. In the *Filter Definition* dialog, create a new filter to match the specifications displayed in Table 3 - 3 below:

Name	Current Tasks		Show in menu	Selected
And/Or	**Field Name**	**Test**	**Values**	
	% Complete	is less than	100	
And	Start	is less than or equal to	Enter a date 2 weeks into the future	
Show related summary rows	Selected			

Table 3 - 3: Current Tasks filter details

3. Click the *OK* button then click the *Apply* button.

4. Stop recording the macro.

To see VBA code for the macro you just recorded, complete the following steps:

1. Open the VBE (shortcut **Alt+F11**) and press **Ctrl+R** to activate the Project Explorer.

2. In the Project Explorer pane, expand the project in which you recorded the macro, expand the *Modules* folder, and locate the newest module (its name is likely to be *Module1* or *Module2*).

The code you see should be similar to the following:

```
FilterEdit Name:="Current Tasks", TaskFilter:=True, _
   Create:=True, OverwriteExisting:=True, FieldName:="% Complete", _
   Test:="is    less    than",    Value:="100%",    ShowInMenu:=True,    ShowSummary-
Tasks:=False
FilterEdit Name:="Current Tasks", TaskFilter:=True, FieldName:="", _
   NewFieldName:="Start", Test:="is less than or equal to", Value:="6/6/10", _
   Operation:="And", ShowSummaryTasks:=False
FilterApply Name:="Current Tasks"
```

There are a few points worth noting about this recorded code:

- The software records the code as one line per action. You can break the long lines up using the "space underscore" continuation characters (_) to read the code without needing to scroll horizontally. For example the first line would be easier to read by formatting it like this:

```
FilterEdit Name:="Current Tasks", _
   TaskFilter:=True, _
   Create:=True, _
   OverwriteExisting:=True, _
   FieldName:="% Complete", _
   Test:="is less than", _
   Value:="100%", _
   ShowInMenu:=True, _
   ShowSummaryTasks:=False
```

- Some parameters, such as the *OverwriteExisiting* parameter for which there were no options in the *Filter* window, will have no recorded values.

- You will need to modify the preceding recorded code to make it survives the test of time, and to be more readable and easier to maintain.

Modifying a Recorded Macro

If you run the recorded code from Exercise 3-1, it works as expected. If you run the code a day later, however, the results are incorrect because the Macro Recorder hard coded today's date into the macro (6/6/10 in the previous code example). This problem is inherent when recording macros, but luckily it is easy to fix.

To change the macro so that it will always work with a date 14 days from today, you need to edit the *6/6/10* date value to become a *Date + a constant value*. In this case we define a *DeliveryPeriod* constant and set the value to *14 days*.

The final code from Exercise 3-1 (including indenting for readability) should appear as follows:

```
Sub CurrentTasks()
'set the constant for a two week window
Const DeliveryPeriod = 14

    FilterEdit Name:="Current Tasks", TaskFilter:=True, _
        Create:=True, OverwriteExisting:=True, _
        FieldName:="% Complete", test:="is less than", _
        Value:="100%", ShowInMenu:=True, ShowSummaryTasks:=False
    FilterEdit Name:=" Current Tasks ", TaskFilter:=True, _
        FieldName:="", NewFieldName:="Start", Test:="is less than or equal to", _
        Value:=Date + DeliveryPeriod, Operation:="And", ShowSummaryTasks:=False
    FilterApply Name:="Current Tasks"
End Sub
```

> **Tip:** Always indent any continued lines. It makes them much more readable and easier to understand and maintain.

The good news with recorded macros is that they automatically include parameter names (such as *Name*), making the code easy to understand and modify.

Recording macros can be very useful and can save you a lot of time when you do not know how to write the required code in Project VBA. With a little bit of editing, you can create very useable and efficient code.

The most important manual action **not to record** is moving the cursor from task to task because your schedules change over time and you cannot predict future task sequencing. If you record cursor movements, delete them. Replace them with *Task* objects pointing to your tasks, and then work with those objects.

Hands On Exercise

Exercise 3-2

Modify a recorded macro.

1. In a new project, record a macro to create and apply a new table in an existing project.

2. Break up long lines of code using the underscore character so that all code is visible without needing to scroll.

Storing Your VBA Code

Typically, the system stores VBA macros in the .mpp file where you first create them and most can easily stay there. However, if you want a macro to work in all projects without needing the original .mpp file, then do one of the following:

- Copy or move the module into the Global.mpt file.

- If your organization uses Microsoft Project Server, ask your Project Server administrator to copy or move the module into the Enterprise Global file, making your macro available to all Project Server users.

The Global.mpt file stores all default objects that ship with Microsoft Project, including views, tables, filters, groups, macros, etc. Should you desire, you can also use the Global.mpt file to store your custom personal objects, including any macros you write or record. To copy modules to and from your Global.mpt file, or between any open files, or to rename or delete modules, follow the steps in Table 3 - 4.

Step	Project 2010	Project 2007 and earlier
1. Open the Organizer	Click the *File* tab Click the *Info* tab Click the *Organizer* button in the main backstage area	Click Tools ➢ Organizer
2. Show all modules	Click the *Modules* tab	Click the *Modules* tab
3. Copy a module	Click the module you want to copy then click the *Copy* button	Click the module you want to copy then click the *Copy* button
4. Rename a module	Click the module you want to rename then click the *Rename* button	Click the module you want to rename then click the *Rename* button
5. Delete a module	Click the module you want to delete then click the *Delete* button	Click the module you want to delete then click the *Delete* button

Table 3 - 4: Steps to copy, rename or delete a module to the Global.mpt file

Figure 3 - 4 shows the *Organizer* dialog in Project 2010 and Figure 3 - 5, **Error! Reference source not found.**show the *Organizer* dialog in Project 2007 and earlier. For both versions, be sure to select the module in the correct file and note that the *available in* drop down box shows only open projects.

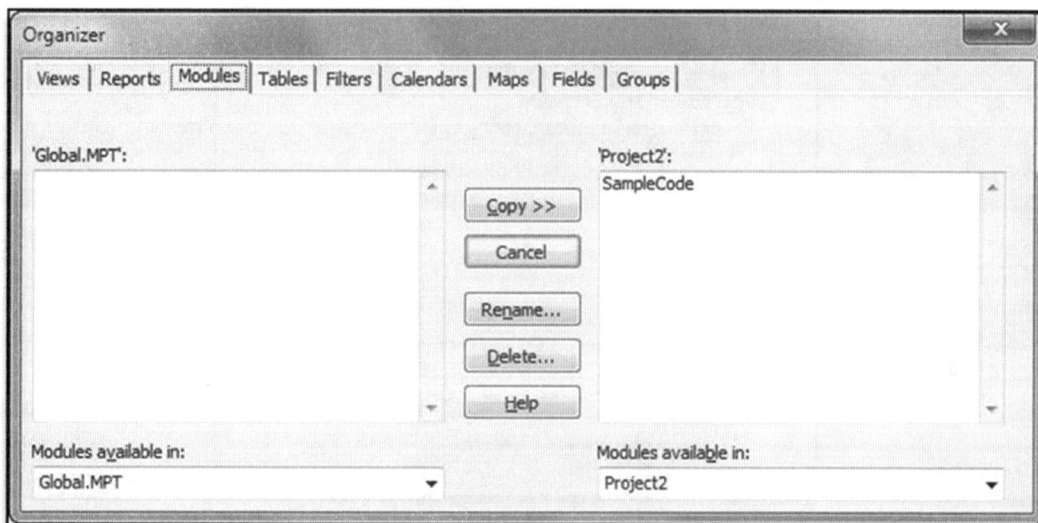

Figure 3 - 4: Organizer dialog in Project 2010

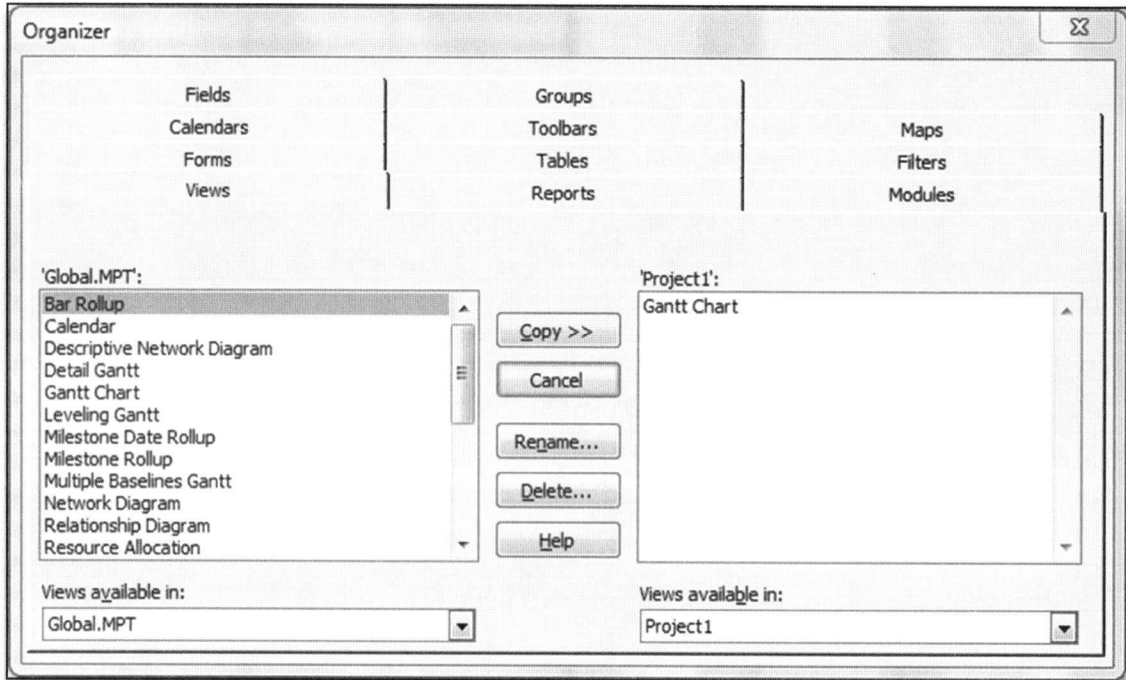

Figure 3 - 5: Organizer dialog in Project 2007 or earlier

To copy or rename modules you can also use the Project Explorer by completing the following steps:

1. Open the VBE then press **Ctrl+R** to open and activate the Project Explorer.

2. Expand all the folders for the open projects and for the Global.mpt file. You should see something similar to Figure 3 - 6 in Project 2007. Project 2010 does not ship with any built-in modules or forms.

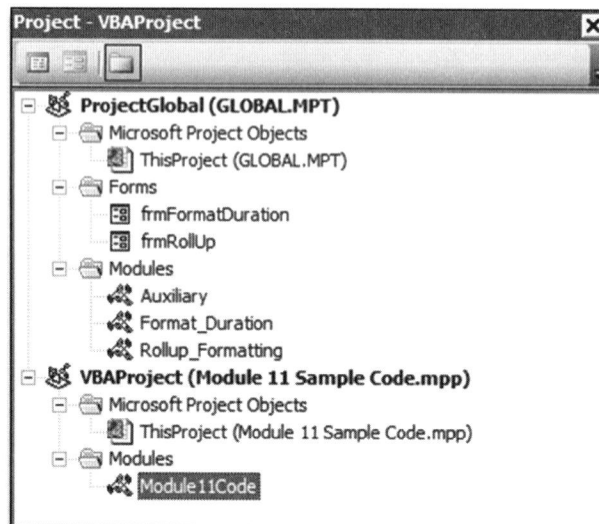

Figure 3 - 6: GLOBAL.MPT folders

3. To copy a module, click and drag a module from one file to another while holding down the *Ctrl* key, just as you do in Windows Explorer.

4. To copy a module, click and drag a module from one file to another, just as you do in Windows Explorer.

To rename a module using the Project Explorer, complete the following steps:

1. Select the module you want to rename.

2. Press the F4 function key to display the *Properties* window.

3. Edit the *Name* property and press the **Enter** key.

Notice that the default macros that ship with Microsoft Project 2007 and earlier are in the *Modules* folder of the Global.mpt file.

> The **ThisProject (Global.mpt)** file is very special. Store macro code here that needs to run automatically when certain events occur, such as when you open a file.

> Rod Gill recommends that you store macros in individual files if you intend to use the macros for one or two projects only. Use the Global.mpt file only for macros needed by many different projects. This keeps the Global.mpt file less cluttered and more manageable.

Controlling the Size of Project .MPP Files

If you do a lot of code editing, especially if you add and remove modules, or if the code adds and deletes a lot of tasks, your Project .mpp file size may bloat. The reason is because Microsoft Project keeps deleted material in the file to save time, and because Microsoft Project writes new tasks added into the project as new file sectors at the end of the file. The result is a fragmented and bloated file. To correct this problem, use the following steps:

1. Close the .mpp file.

2. Re-open the .mpp file.

3. Immediately save the file before performing any other action.

> Microsoft Project compacts a file only when you save the file immediately after opening it, or when you perform a Save As. The compacting process shrinks .mpp file sizes by removing blocks of data left over from deletions and by putting all tasks together sequentially, thus making the file smaller and more efficient.

Repairing Corrupted Files

Occasionally .mpp files become corrupt, especially if you have links between files, have linked master projects or resource pools, and you do one of the following to one of the linked files:

- Overwrite it

- Rename it

- Delete it

- Move it

Any of these actions will eventually cause a corruption. It is a question of when, not if. While developing VBA does not corrupt files, the intensive use of a file can show up symptoms of file corruption that might not be noticeable under normal usage. Symptoms of file corruption include:

- You cannot open the file.

- The file does not calculate properly.

- The file displays unusual behavior.

If you can open a file that you suspect is corrupt, one way to repair the corruption is to do the following:

1. Save the file with a different file type, preferably as an .mpd (versions 98 to 2003) or .xml file (2007 and later).

2. Close your project.

3. Reopen the project from the new file type.

4. Save the file as the original file type, preferably with a different name in case the process loses anything.

Tip: You will probably save many copies of your projects. To avoid breaking hyperlinks and links, never rename your master copy; only add dates to the names of master file **copies**.

Tip: If you want to create a temporary file, name it Delete Me.mpp so you know you can safely delete it when next you see it.

Module 04

Looping Through Your Schedule

Learning Objectives

After completing this module, you will be able to:

- Create code to loop through your schedule
- Prevent blank rows from interfering with looping through your project

Inside Module 04

Looping Through All Tasks in a Project

Looping through all tasks and performing some action on them is a common process in Project VBA macros. You might want to loop through all tasks setting a custom field. Usually looping works well, but there is one common problem that stops your macro "dead in its tracks" unless your code handles it. The problem is blank task rows in your project schedule.

It is a best practice to increase row height to create blank space in your project rather than using empty rows, but you must plan to handle blank rows in your VBA code nonetheless. In Project VBA, if you try to set a *Task* object to a blank row, it gets the special value: **Nothing**.

Nothing is a VBA value that refers to any object that has not been or cannot be initialized. Therefore, you should always test for blank rows, as the sample code below demonstrates.

To loop through all tasks and ignore blank rows use the VBA code in the following example:

```
'Example which loops through all tasks in the active project
Sub SimpleLoop()
Dim Tsk As Task
    For Each Tsk In ActiveProject.Tasks
            'Code to run on all tasks
    Next Tsk
End Sub

'example which adds a check for blank rows.
Sub SimpleLoop()
Dim Tsk As Task
    For Each Tsk In ActiveProject.Tasks
        If Not Tsk Is Nothing Then     'Test for blank row
            'Code to run on all tasks
        End If
    Next Tsk
End Sub
```

The same situation applies to all resources but there are no assignments with **Nothing** values. The following code copies the *Text1* field for each resource into the *Text1* field for each assignment:

```
Sub CopyResText1ToAssignments()
Dim Res As Resource
Dim Assgn As Assignment
    For Each Res In ActiveProject.Resources
        If Not Res Is Nothing Then 'Test for blank row
            For Each Assgn In Res.Assignments
                Assgn.Text1 = Res.Text1
            Next Assgn
        End If
    Next Res
    MsgBox "Assignment Text1 fields updated", vbInformation
End Sub
```

The *For Each* command is the easiest to use to loop through collections of objects. Use it to loop through objects such as *Tasks, Resources, Assignments, Calendars*, etc.

Clearing a Custom Field for Non-Summary Tasks

The following code is another example that loops through all tasks, and if the task is not a *Summary* task, it clears the *Text1* field. In addition, this code example only loops through all **selected** tasks (in Project before running the macro) using the *ActiveSelection.Tasks* collection.

```
Sub ClearText1()
Dim Tsk As Task
    For Each Tsk In ActiveSelection.Tasks
        If Not Tsk Is Nothing Then      'Test for blank row
            If Not Tsk.Summary Then         'If not a Summary Task
                Tsk.Text1 = ""
            End If
        End If
    Next Tsk
End Sub
```

This form of looping (For Each) does not affect the location of the cursor; but instead, points the *Tsk* task object to each task in turn. There is rarely any need to change the selected task. For performance and simplicity reasons, you should not loop through tasks by selecting each task in turn.

Technically, the tests for Nothing and for Summary Task can be combined. However when there are two or more tests in an IF statement, all tests are evaluated even if the first one fails. Tsk.Summary returns an error if the task object points to a blank row so the two tests must be separated into two IF statements as shown above. If the Nothing test fails, the test for Summary Task is not done avoiding an error.

Using Loops to Set Custom Field Values

There may come a time when you need to report the summary task name for every task. You can record this information for each task in a custom text field. To identify and ignore top level tasks (which have no parent task), use the *OutlineLevel* property of a task. The *OutlineParent* property of each task is a *Task* object of its *Summary* task, so you can use its *Property* name. Write the VBA code to copy *Summary Task* names as follows:

```
Sub SummaryNameCopy()
Dim Tsk As Task
    For Each Tsk In ActiveProject.Tasks
        If Not Tsk Is Nothing Then 'Test for blank row
            If Tsk.OutlineLevel = 1 Then
                Tsk.Text2 = ""      'No parent
            Else
                Tsk.Text2 = Tsk.OutlineParent.Name
            End If
        End If
    Next Tsk
End Sub
```

Note that the code does not move the selection on the screen, the code tests for blank rows, and if the task is at level 1 it clears the *Text2* value by setting it to an empty string (""), it does not assume the *Text2* value is already clear. By using the *ActiveProject Object* command, you have a procedure that works with any project, and is easy to copy and modify to perform a range of other tasks.

Hands On Exercise

Exercise 4-1

Module 4 Sample Code.mpp has some tasks with the *Number1* field set to be the required outline level for the tasks. Practice with this file to loop through all tasks in a project.

1. Write a macro to indent all tasks until their *OutlineLevel* property equals the value in the *Number1* field.

2. Write code to do one loop through all tasks and then do a second loop to keep indenting the task until its *OutlineLevel* property equals the value in the *Number 2* field.

You need to use this code if you want to import tasks and their outline level from a database or from a Microsoft Excel workbook. Given the required outline level, you can then indent tasks using the *OutlineIndent* method.

The solution for this exercise is in the Module 4 Sample Code.mpp file as shown in Figure 4 - 1.

Task Name	Number1
Module 04 Sample Code - Looping Thru your Sch	0
Planning and Control	1
Business plan identifying project opportunity	2
Define project objective and information needs	3
Identify industry standards for project objectives	2
Develop preliminary conceptual schedule and staffing	2
Initial planning complete	2
Develop appropriation strategy	3
Develop management model and staff plan	2
Site Assessment	1
Identify potential sites	2
Define infrastructure requirements	2
Define utility needs	2
Identify project site	3
Assess regulatory and environmental impacts	3
Identify permitting requirements	2
Recommend site	2
Site and planning review	2

**Figure 4 - 1: Test tasks for
Exercise 4-1**

Module 05

Creating New Objects in Microsoft Project

Learning Objectives

After completing this module, you will be able to:

- Understand how to create new Microsoft Project objects, such as custom views, tables, and filters
- Write code to create new toolbars and menus

Inside Module 05

Safely Creating New Objects

In Module 04 you learned that recording a macro is a powerful way to generate base code for your macro projects. It is always a good practice to assume that the custom view, table or filter that you need to reference in your macro does not exist or that the user has changed it. To guarantee that objects such as tables, filters, and views exist when you want them, always re-create them before applying them.

> **i** The exception to this rule is when you work in the Project Server environment where views, tables and filters in Project Server can be changed only by the Project Server administrator.

Creating New Views, Tables, and Filters

The simple way to create new filters and tables is to record a macro while creating them manually. To avoid adding these to lists of tables and filters available in Project, do not select the *Show in Menu* option (remember that every table always appears in the *More Tables* dialog and every filter always appears in the *More Filters* dialog).

When you create a new table or filter, use meaningful names, such as *Weekly Report – Milestones*. You can use the same name for a filter and a table, so the following code will work well for a weekly report:

> **i** Precede each name with an underscore (_) or initials of your organization. This will group all your custom objects together and make them easy to identify.

```
Sub WeeklyReport
    ViewApply "Weekly Report - Milestones"
    TableApply "Weekly Report - Milestones"
    FilterApply "Weekly Report - Milestones"
    FilePrintPreview
End Sub
```

By forcing the application of the view, table, and filter in the preceding code, you know exactly what you will get as a result. Better still, if your code re-creates the view, table, and filter first, you can be certain that no one changed it previously, thus guaranteeing the results.

Creating a New Toolbar

Recording a macro while you manually create a toolbar is the easiest way to get started using VBA to create new toolbars. There are two basic objects with which you work to create a new toolbar: **CommandBars** and **Command-BarButtons**. A *CommandBar* toolbar appears in *Toolbar* lists. A *CommandBarButton* is a button on the toolbar to which you can add a picture or text, and to which you can assign an action that the button performs. *CommandBars* can also refer to menus and *CommandBarButtons* to menu items.

The following code creates a toolbar with one button. When a user clicks the button, the *RunMyMacro* macro runs:

```
Sub AddToolbar()
Dim MyBar As CommandBar
Dim MyButton As CommandBarButton
    On Error Resume Next
    Set MyBar = CommandBars("My Bar")
    If MyBar Is Nothing Then
        Set MyBar = CommandBars.Add(Name:="My Bar", _
            Position:=msoBarFloating, Temporary:=True)
        MyBar.Visible = True
    End If

    Set MyButton = MyBar.Controls("MyButton")
    If MyButton Is Nothing Then
        Set MyButton = MyBar.Controls.Add(Type:=msoControlButton)
        With MyButton
            .Style = msoButtonCaption
            .Caption = "My Macro"
            .OnAction = "Macro ""RunMyMacro"""
        End With
    End If
End Sub
```

Run this code either as an individual macro, or in the *Project_Open* event. (Refer to Module 08 to learn how to automatically run code when you open a project.)

> In Project 2003 or earlier, the code:
> .OnAction = "RunMyMacro" works.
>
> From version 2007 onwards you have to include the *Macro* command as in:
> .OnAction ="Macro ""RunMyMacro""".

The preceding code introduces you to some basic error handling. The intent is that if the *MyBar Commandbar* variable does not exist, then the error does not stop the code. Instead, the next statement tests whether the *MyBar* variable has been set up correctly. If not, then the *MyBar* variable equals the special value *Nothing*. If the *MyBar* variable is *Nothing* equates to *True*, then the bar does not exist, so the code creates it. The *MyButton* variable is then tested the same way and if it is *Nothing*, the code creates it as well.

Rod Gill recommends that you never assume that views, tables, filters, toolbars, and buttons exist in a project. Make sure your code always tests for their existence or always recreates them.

Creating a New Menu

One way to make your macros accessible to end users and to make the macros easy to run is to add them to a menu. Menus are very effective when used with longer and more descriptive text. Toolbar buttons are more effective when just icons are used. The following code creates a menu with three items on it:

```
Sub AddMenu()
Dim MyMenu As CommandBarControl
Dim MyButton As CommandBarButton
    On Error Resume Next
    Set MyMenu = CommandBars("Menu Bar").Controls("My Menu")
    If MyMenu Is Nothing Then
        Set MyMenu = CommandBars("Menu Bar").Controls.Add(Type:=msoControlPopup, _
            ID:=1, Before:=9, Temporary:=True)
        MyMenu.Caption = "My Menu"

        Set MyButton = MyMenu.Controls.Add( _
            Type:=msoControlButton, ID:=1, Before:=1)
        With MyButton
            .OnAction = " Macro ""AddToolbar"""
            .Style = msoButtonCaption
            .Caption = "Add Toolbar"
        End With

        Set MyButton = MyMenu.Controls.Add( _
            Type:=msoControlButton, ID:=1, Before:=2)
        With MyButton
            .OnAction = " Macro ""DeleteBar"""
            .Style = msoButtonCaption
            .Caption = "Delete Toolbar"
        End With

        Set MyButton = MyMenu.Controls.Add( _
            Type:=msoControlButton, ID:=1, Before:=3)
        With MyButton
            .OnAction = " Macro ""DeleteMenu"""
            .Style = msoButtonCaption
            .Caption = "Delete Menu"
        End With
    End If
End Sub
```

The preceding code is similar to the code that creates a toolbar, but uses a *CommandBarControl* variable instead of a *CommandBar* variable. The menu bar is a standard *CommandBar* that always represents the main menu.

In Microsoft Project, the ninth menu from the left is the *Window* menu, therefore the *Before:=9* parameter inserts the *My Menu* variable immediately to the left of the *Window* menu. In Project 2010 the menu is automatically added to the *Add-Ins* tab. Another routine you need is the *DeleteMenu* macro code as shown below:

```
Sub DeleteMenu()
    On Error Resume Next
    CommandBars("Menu Bar").Controls("My Menu").Delete
End Sub
```

The following code includes one procedure to add a toolbar with one button on it and a separate procedure to delete the bar:

```
Sub AddToolbar()
Dim MyBar As CommandBar
Dim MyButton As CommandBarButton
    On Error Resume Next
    Set MyBar = CommandBars("My Bar")
    If MyBar Is Nothing Then
        Set MyBar = CommandBars.Add(Name:="My Bar", _
            Position:=msoBarFloating, Temporary:=True)
        MyBar.Visible = True
    End If

    Set MyButton = MyBar.Controls("MyButton")
    If MyButton Is Nothing Then
        Set MyButton = MyBar.Controls.Add( _
            Type:=msoControlButton)

        With MyButton
            .Style = msoButtonCaption
            .Caption = "My Macro"
            .OnAction = "Macro ""DeleteBar"""
        End With
    End If
End Sub

Sub DeleteBar()
    On Error Resume Next
    CommandBars("My Bar").Delete
End Sub
```

These examples should provide enough foundation for you to create the toolbars and menus you need. When you run this code in Project 2010, custom menus and toolbars appear in the *Add-ins* tab.

Rod Gill recommends you add code to delete menus and toolbars when the project file containing the macros referenced by the menus or toolbars closes. No toolbar or menu should be visible if the macros they run are not available just because the user closed the file containing the macros.

The new Project 2010 ribbon and menus

Project 2010 has the Office ribbon. Any new menus or commandbars created in VBA for Project 2007 or earlier will not work as expected. Instead, after running code to add a new menu or commandbar, your toolbars and menus appear in a new tab called *Add-Ins* on the Project ribbon.

The new *Add-Ins* tab is in two sections, one for *Menu Commands* and one for *Custom Toolbars*. Figure 5 - 1 shows the *Add-Ins* tab after running the macros in Module 05.

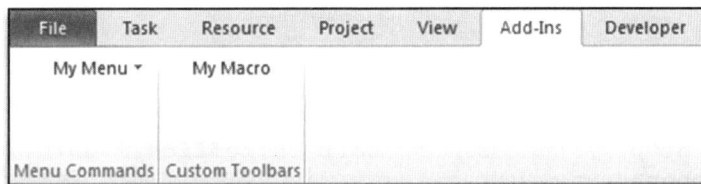

Figure 5 - 1: The Add-Ins tab after running the code in Module 05.

Full details of how to modify the ribbon are on the web at http://msproj.com/1000

Briefly, to modify or add icons to the ribbon:

1. Create the required xml string. From the above link an xml sample is:

```
<mso:customUI xmlns:mso="http:="//schemas.microsoft.com/office/2009/07/customui">
  <mso:ribbon>
   <mso:qat/>
   <mso:tabs>
     <mso:tab id="RodGillTab" label="Highlight=" insertBeforeQ="mso:TabFormat">
      <mso:group id="testGroup" label="Test" autoScale="true=">
        <mso:button id="highlightManualTasks" label="Delete the Custom Menu"
              imageMso="DiagramTargetInsertClassic="
              onAction="DeleteMenu="/>
      </mso:group>
     </mso:tab>
   </mso:tabs>
  </mso:ribbon>
</mso:customUI>
```

Your xml code is more easily formatted in Visual Studio if you have it, otherwise use Notepad. The indenting is only important for presentation purposes. It works just as well all in one line!

The *<mso:qat/>* code is used for the Quick Access Toolbar. The link near the beginning of this topic and the mostly self-explanatory nature of the xml should make it possible for you to experiment with various options.

> ✖ **Your xml code must include every customization as all previous changes are replaced by the changes in the new xml file.** Therefore, you cannot call SetCustomUI to add just one change.

2. Now create a macro to pass the xml code to Project. The entire xml needs to be copied into a string and passed using the *SetCustomUI* method. The code is:

```
Sub AddCustomUI()
Dim customUiXml As String

    customUiXml = "<mso:customUI xmlns:mso=" _
            & """http://schemas.microsoft.com/office/2009/07/customui"">" _
        & "<mso:ribbon>" _
          & "<mso:tabs>" _
            & "<mso:tab id=""myTab"" label=""Rod Gill Tab""  " _
                    & "insertBeforeQ=""mso:TabView"">" _
            & "<mso:group id=""group1"" label=""Test Group"">" _
              & "<mso:button id=""button1"" label=""Test Button"" " _
                    &"size=""large"" " _
                    & "imageMso=""GetExternalDataFromText"" " _
                    & "onAction=""RemoveCustomUI"">" _
              & "</mso:button>" _
            & "</mso:group>" _
            & "</mso:tab>" _
          & "</mso:tabs>" _
        & "</mso:ribbon>" _
    & "</mso:customUI>"

    ActiveProject.SetCustomUI (customUiXml)
End Sub
```

A double-quote is used to delimit a string and to include a double-quote within a string you need two of them. It is useful to maintain indents in the xml code to help denote the beginning and end of a tag, as in the tags above. This makes the code more readable and easier to understand and modify later.

To remove all ribbon customization, run the following code:

```
Sub RemoveCustomUI()
Dim customXml As String
    customXml = "<mso:customUI xmlns:mso=" _
                & """http://schemas.microsoft.com/office/2009/07/customui"">" _
      & "<mso:ribbon></mso:ribbon>" _
    & "</mso:customUI>"

    ActiveProject.SetCustomUI (customXml)
End Sub
```

It is the empty *mso:ribbon* tag that does the work.

> **i** If you click on SetCustomUI then press **F1** for HELP, Project 2010 HELP provides sample code as well.

The *imageMso* parameter controls the image displayed on the ribbon. You can use any of the built-in Office images. To see a list of all valid image names and what they look like:

1. Search Bing or Google for *2007 Office System Add-In: Icons Gallery*

2. The best result is a page on www.microsoft.com from which you can download the Office2007IconsGallery.EXE file.

3. Open the Office2007IconsGallery.exe file and follow prompts to unzip the Office2007IconsGallery.xlsm file.

4. Make sure you have macros enabled then open the file in Excel 2007 or Excel 2010.

5. Click the *Developer* tab and then any of the new *Gallery* icons to see all Office icons.

6. Click an icon you want and a form pops up with the name you use in the *imageMso* parameter.

There is an Office 2010 version of icons, but it is only available for Word 2010. To find it, search the Internet for *Office2010IconsGallery*.

Hands On Exercise

Exercise 5-1

Create a new menu or toolbar.

1. Record a macro to display the Gantt chart and then the *Tracking* table.

2. Use the code detailed earlier in this module to add the *Macros* menu and a menu item to run your recorded macro.

3. Use the code detailed earlier in this module to add the *MyMacros* toolbar and add a button to it to run your recorded macro.

Module 06

Managing Run-Time Errors

Learning Objectives

After completing this module, you will be able to:

- Understand why run-time errors happen

- Add error handling to your code

- Understand and choose between two main types of error handling

Inside Module 06

Managing Errors

All VBA code, when first written, works perfectly and continues to work perfectly. Yeah, right! In reality, we encounter three types of errors in our code:

- **Compile Errors** can be caused by a typing mistake or an *IF* statement without an *End If*.

- **Run-Time Errors** occur when code tries to do something illegal that the compiler did not detect, such as using an *Object* variable without initializing it with a *Set* statement.

- **Logical Errors** happen when logical errors occur such as creating a new toolbar called *MyToolbar* when a toolbar with that name already exists or by trying to open a file that does not exist. The compiler can never trap this type of error and will always create errors when the code runs.

Your code cannot run until Project has successfully compiled it (usually automatically in the background). Therefore, once you correctly enter your code and it compiles, only the second and third error types should concern you at run-time. There are three types of run-time error handling you can use, including:

1. *No* **error handling** – The system performs *No* error handling, so each error stops the code and displays a message describing the error. To catch the obvious problems, it can be useful to perform your early testing with *No* error handling. *No* error handling is great while you debug your code. It can be useful to allow errors to occur and to display error messages so that you can track down potential problems and write code error handlers for as many errors as possible.

2. *Resume Next* **error handling** – Using this method, errors do not stop the code, but you have to test for errors after every statement that might cause an error. Examples are opening a file or setting up an application object for another program. This method is the simplest and easiest to use, as all error checking happens immediately after the statement that might cause the error.

3. *Goto* **error handling** – Using this method, an error triggers the system to jump to a specified location in your routine. Obviously, the error handling code at this location needs to manage any error that might occur in the procedure. This method of error handling is more useful if you have a number of statements that might cause the same error.

To force *No* error handling (the default state at the beginning of every *Sub* and *Function*), use the following code:

```
On Error Goto 0
```

This is not an obvious statement but does the job! To initiate *Resume Next* error handling, use the following code:

```
On Error Resume Next
```

This statement says that when there is an error, resume executing with the next statement. To initiate *Goto* error handling, use the following code:

```
On Error Goto ErrorHandler
```

The *ErrorHandler* label is a label in your sub procedure. I present an example for using this method of error handling in the *Using Goto Error Handling* section of this module.

Finally, before you see errors generated in your code, I strongly recommend that you consider preventing errors **before they happen**. For example, before opening a file you should test for the file's existence, as in the following example:

```
Dim MyPath As String
    MyPath = "C:\MyProject.mpp"
    If Dir(MyPath) = "" Then
        MsgBox MyPath & " doesn't exist", vbCritical
        End
    End If
```

In the preceding code example, the *Dir* function is a VBA function that lists all files in a path. The *Dir("C:*.mpp")* command finds all .mpp files in C:\. Testing for a full name, as above, returns only one name if that file exists. If the file cannot be found, the *Dir* function returns an empty string (""). When you test for the file's existence before trying to open it, you write code that avoids an error rather than code that handles an error.

Warning: Project 2010 when first released has a bug that prevents errors for some methods from occurring. For example FileOpen does not create an error if the file does not exist. Check all code to confirm that errors are generated when they should be. The first Cumulative Update (CU) for Project 2010 fixes this problem so make sure you download and install all the latest Service Packs and CUs for Project.

Whenever possible, write code that tests for problems before they occur. For example use the Dir method to test for a file's existence before trying to open it. Do not rely on error handling in Project 2010 until you have installed at least the first CU.

Tip: Search HELP for Dir and learn what options it has. Dir is a very powerful file search tool for your VBA code.

Using Resume Next Error Handling

The *AddToolBar* sub from the previous module is a good example of using *Resume Next* error handling. The first part of the sub is duplicated here:

```
Sub AddToolbar()
Dim MyBar As CommandBar
Dim MyButton As CommandBarButton
    On Error Resume Next
    Set MyBar = CommandBars("My Bar")
    If MyBar Is Nothing Then
        Set MyBar = CommandBars.Add(Name:="My Bar", _
            Position:=msoBarFloating, Temporary:=True)
        MyBar.Visible = True
    End If
End Sub
```

The *Set MyBar = CommandBars("My Bar")* command fails if the *My Bar* variable does not exist and the system sets the *MyBar* variable to *Nothing*. To test for the existence of the *MyBar* variable, use `If MyBar is Nothing Then`. So the macro reaches the *IF* statement, use the *On Error Resume Next* command to force the macro to continue if the bar does not exist.

Using Goto Error Handling

To use *Goto* error handling, I rewrote the preceding code as follows:

```
Sub AddToolbar()
Dim MyBar As CommandBar
Dim MyButton As CommandBarButton
    On Error GoTo ErrorHandler
    Set MyBar = CommandBars("My Bar")
    'Remaining code for Sub
    Exit Sub

ErrorHandler:
    Set MyBar = CommandBars.Add(Name:="My Bar", _
        Position:=msoBarFloating, Temporary:=True)
    MyBar.Visible = True
    Resume Next
End Sub
```

The main part of the preceding code actually looks simpler, but it assumes there may be only one error (the *My Bar* command bar does not exist), when there might actually be a variety of errors or statements causing errors in the procedure. The error handler needs to be able to handle all possible errors in the procedure, or to run until a *Resume Next* statement executes. After executing an *On Error GoTo* statement, any error causes execution to start at the first line of code after the named label. The *Resume Next* command in the error handler code returns execution to the statement after the one that caused the error.

You can have a number of error handlers, each with their own label, but using the *On Error Resume Next* command quickly becomes simpler and easier to manage. Notice that you need an *Exit Sub* statement before the error handler code; otherwise the error code runs even when there is no error!

You can get information on handling errors programmatically using VBA's *Err* object, as described in the *Using the Err Object* section later in this module.

Selecting an Error Handling Method

If you want to set an *Object* variable to an object (such as a toolbar or application) whose existence is uncertain, use the *On Error Resume Next* option. If there are a number of similar statements that might create the same or similar errors, then use the *On Error Goto ErrorHandlerLabel* option. You can swap from one form of error handling to another as often as you like. Remember, to turn off error handling entirely, use the following code:

```
On Error Goto 0
```

Using the Err Object

When you use *Resume Next* error handling to test for an error, use the *Err* object with the following code:

```
If Err.Number<>0 Then
    'Error handling Code
End If
```

Use caution when applying the *Err* object, as it may still be set from a previous error. The system automatically resets the *Err* object's properties to *zero* or to *zero-length strings* ("") after an *Exit Sub, Exit Function*, or *Exit Property* statement.

To manually reset the *Err* object, use the following statement:

```
Err.Clear
```

Using an *If Err* statement is the same as using an *If Err.Number* statement since *Number* is the *Error* object's default property. The other useful property of the *Err* statement is the *Description* property. I prefer not to rely on defaults, so I test the *err.number* statement. A general error message using the *If Err* statement follows:

```
If Err.Number<>0 Then
    MsgBox "Error opening file:" & vbCrLf & Err.Description
End If
```

In the previous code example, I use the `&  vbCrLf  &` string to add a new line so the error message displays on two lines, as shown in Figure 6 - 1. The *vbCRLF* constant is a built-in VBA constant that adds a carriage return and line feed to the string.

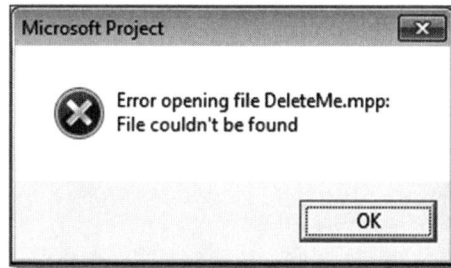

**Figure 6 - 1: Critical error message
using two lines**

Using the *Err* object makes your error messages more informative, providing you with insight into what code caused the error and information on why it occurred. Making sure that each error message is unique helps you here!

Hands On Exercise

Exercise 6-1

Test your VBA code for errors.

1. Using the code to create a toolbar in Module 06, test the error handling by editing the code from:

   Set MyBar = CommandBars("My Bar")

   To:

   Set MyBar = CommandBars("My Other Bar")

This creates an error as *My Other Bar* should not exist.

2. Single step through the code to see what happens.

3. Modify the code to use *On Error Goto*.

Module 07

Creating and Running UserForms

Learning Objectives

After completing this module, you will be able to:

- Understand UserForms
- Create a basic UserForm
- Add code to a UserForm
- Run a UserForm

Inside Module 07

Understanding UserForms

Occasionally, you want to display a form to gather information from the user, UserForms let you do this in VBA. Rather than delving into a comprehensive example, I present the basic concepts and show you how to use the most popular controls. Please note that UserForms in VBA are fairly primitive; you cannot do nearly as much with UserForms in Project as you can with forms in Microsoft Access or in programming languages such as Visual Basic. Because of their limited abilities, keep your use of UserForms to a minimum. Keep them simple and do not expect to achieve miracles with them!

If your application does require more sophistication than Project VBA provides, consider writing a Visual Studio Tools for Office (VSTO) add-in. I cover developing add-ins using Visual Studio in Section 3. I also demonstrate more complex UserForms in Modules 10 and 16.

Figure 7 - 1 shows a UserForm created with some basic, popular controls, including a *TextBox*, a *ComboBox* (pick list), and a *CommandButton*. Figure 7 - 1 shows the *Properties* window on the left (display it by pressing the F4 function key) with properties for the UserForm, and shows the toolbox with all available controls.

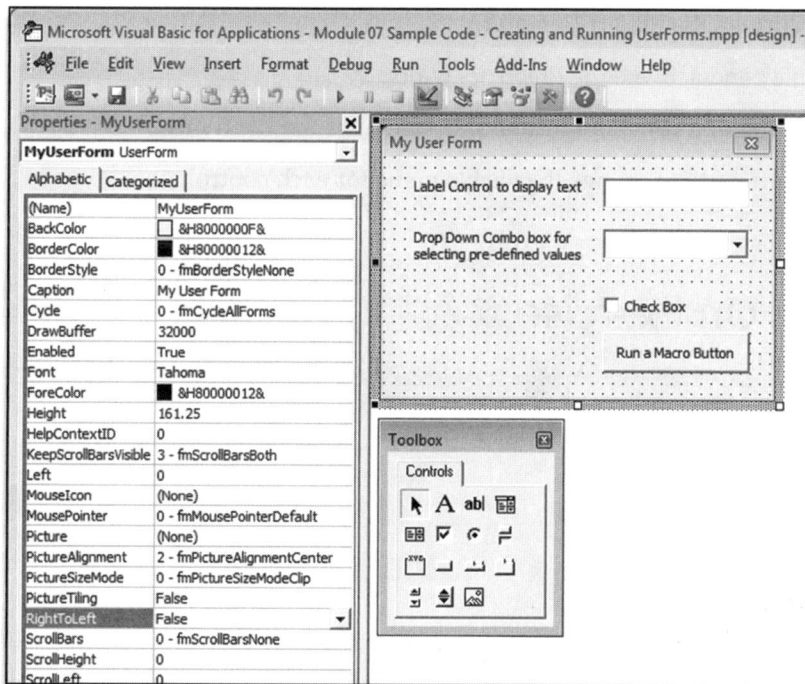

**Figure 7 - 1: VBE with sample
UserForm and Properties window**

> Hover your mouse over the different Toolbox icons to read what they are. You can then search Help to find out more.

Creating a UserForm

To create a new UserForm, complete the following steps in the VBE:

1. Click Insert ➤ UserForm.

The system displays the new UserForm, along with a floating *Toolbox* dialog. To add a control to a UserForm, continue with these steps:

2. Select the control you want in the *Toolbox* window.

3. Drag the control to the UserForm and drop it at the location where you want.

4. Use the resizing handles to change the size of the control.

5. Press **Ctrl+R** to activate the Project Explorer.

6. Select the UserForm in the Project Explorer.

7. Press **F4** to display and activate the *Properties* window.

8. In the *Name* field, enter a valid and meaningful name for the UserForm.

9. Edit the *Caption* property to change the visible name for each control.

Hands On Exercise

Exercise 7-1

Add sample controls to a UserForm.

1. Click Insert ➤ UserForm.

2. Click and drag the *TextBox* control from the *Toolbox* window to the UserForm and drop it in the desired location.

3. Use the resizing handles to change the size of the control.

4. Add a *ComboBox, CheckBox,* and a *CommandButton* to your UserForm, as shown previously in Figure 7 - 1.

5. Show *Properties* and add meaningful names for each control and captions to text boxes.

Adding Code to a UserForm

To add code to the UserForm shown in Figure 7 - 1, use the following steps:

1. Right-click the UserForm and select the *View Code* item. By default Project adds a *UserForm_Click* event as shown in Figure 7 - 2.

2. From the procedure dropdown menu select the *Initialize* option as shown in Figure 7 - 2.

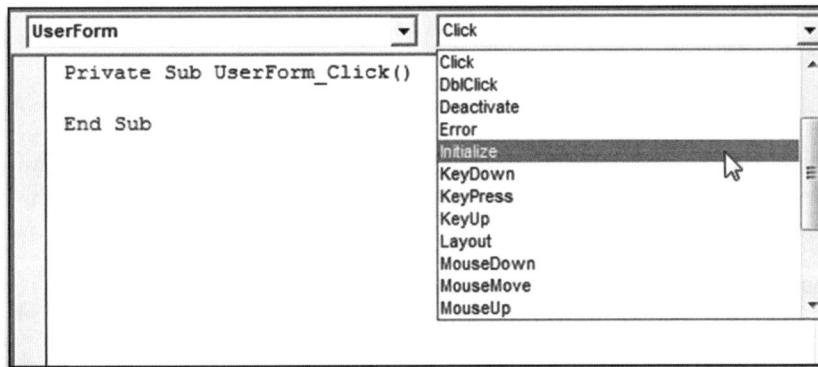

Figure 7 - 2: Adding the Initialize event to a UserForm's code.

3. You can delete the *UserForm_Click()* code as we do not need it.

4. Enter the following code to initialize the form and add options to the *ComboBox* control.

```
Option Explicit

Private Sub UserForm_Initialize()
'Macro that runs the first time the form opens
    MyComboBox.AddItem "My First Option"      'MyComboBox is the name of the
    MyComboBox.AddItem "My Second Option"     'Combobox added to the form
    MyComboBox.AddItem "My Third Option"
    MyComboBox = "My First Option"
    MyTextBox.Text = ActiveCell.Task.Name
    MyCheckBox = True
End Sub

Private Sub RunMyMacro_Click()
'Macro that runs when the Run a Macro button is clicked
    If MsgBox("Do you want to change the Task Name?", vbYesNo) = vbYes Then
        ActiveCell.Task.Name = MyTextBox
    End If
    MyForm.Hide
End Sub
```

The code shows two events. The *UserForm_Initialize* event runs when the system first displays the UserForm. The *RunMyMacro_Click* event runs when the user clicks the *RunMyMacro* CommandButton. All UserForms have a *UserForm_Initialize* procedure regardless of the name of the UserForm.

UserForm_Initialize and *RunMyMacro_Click* are both events. This means that when something happens, such as opening the form (the *Initialize* event) or clicking a command button, (the *Click* event) you can write code that the system executes when the event happens. I discuss more about events in Module 08.

The *UserForm_Initialize* sub adds three items to the *ComboBox* control and then sets defaults for each control. The *Textbox* control (named *MyTextBox*) gets the name of the current task. I use the *CommandButton* control to change the name of the task and to close the form.

To display the UserForm, execute the following code in the *Immediate* window:

```
MyUserForm.Show
```

Note that *MyUserForm* is the text entered in the *Name* property field in the *Properties* pane shown in Figure 7 - 1. You must select the UserForm itself and not any of the controls for the *Properties* pane to show the *Name* property for the UserForm.

You can create a simple procedure to show the form as follows:

```
Sub ShowMyUserForm
    MyUserForm.Show
End Sub
```

If you do not have code to close the UserForm, close it by clicking the *Close* button (**X**) in the top right corner of the form window.

This module provides only a basic introduction to UserForms. Experiment with the sample form to learn more about UserForms. To see more examples of using UserForms, refer to Module 16.

Hands On Exercise

Exercise 7-2

Create another UserForm.

1. In a new project, create a UserForm to display the form shown in Figure 7 - 1 (or load file Module 7 Sample Code.mpp).

2. Edit the code to change the values in the ComboBox and add some new items.

3. Explore some of the properties and methods of a UserForm by copying the name of a UserForm from the *Name* property into the *Immediate* window then typing a period character. Intellisense then displays a pick list for you, so that you can select properties or methods that look interesting, and then press the F1 function key for Help on it.

Module 08

Controlling Microsoft Project Using Events

Learning Objectives

After completing this module, you will be able to:

- Understand what constitutes an event
- Understand why events are useful
- Program your own events

Inside Module 08

What Are Events and How Can They Help You?

Events provide a powerful programming tool in VBA and in other programming languages such as dot net languages like VB, C#, and others. I discuss only *Project* and *Task* events in this module, but Microsoft Project 2010 also provides *Resources* and *Assignments* events that the system handles in exactly the same way as *Task* events.

Events allow code to run automatically when they occur in the application. For example, an event occurs whenever you open a project, close a project, or save a project. Another example of an event is new task creation.

Opening files, deleting or changing tasks and a number of other actions all raise events. You can add your own code to any of these events and customize how Project behaves. Some events happen after the action and some happen before. For example, the *File Open* event occurs after the file is open and the *File Close* event occurs immediately before the file closes. That way the file remains available for your code to perform actions against it after the event fires and before the file actually closes.

Events that occur before an action can actually prevent the action from completing. These events always have the word **Before** somewhere in their name. For example, if a task edit does not meet certain codified rules, then your code can cancel the task edit action.

Understanding Project Events

Project events relate to the whole project (or file). Typical events for a file are:

- File Open

- Before File Close

- Before File Save

- Calculate

To create code for one of these events, complete the following steps:

1. In the VBE, press the **Ctrl+R** key combination to display the *Project Explorer*.

2. Expand the Microsoft Project Objects folder for your file.

3. Double-click the *ThisProject (your file name)* file.

4. In the upper left corner of the code window, click the *Object* pick list button and select the *Project* item.

5. In the upper right corner of the code window, click the *Event* pick list button and select the event you wish to use.

Figure 8 - 1 shows the *Object* and *Procedure* pick lists.

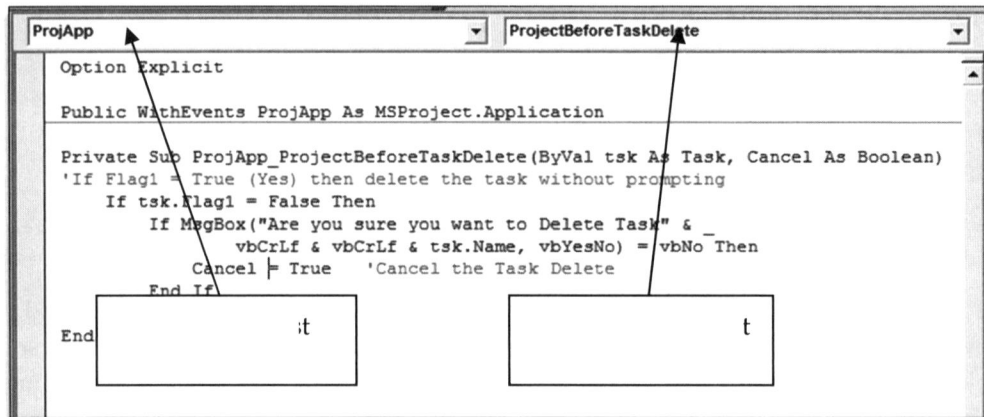

Figure 8 - 1: Object and Procedure pick lists called out

The following code runs every time the user opens a project and scrolls the timescale to a useful date. If the project starts in the future the code jumps to the project's start date. If the project finished in the past the code jumps to the project's finish date. Otherwise, it jumps to today's date. This is very useful for projects covering a long period. As described in the Author's Introduction, I also include code to select specific views depending on the name of the logged-in user. Create the named views and tables first for the code to work.

```
Private Sub Project_Open(ByVal pj As Project)

      'Jump to a logical date for this project
      If Date < pj.ProjectStart Then
          EditGoTo Date:=pj.ProjectStart
      ElseIf Date < pj.ProjectStart Then
          EditGoTo Date:=pj.ProjectFinish
      Else
          EditGoTo Date:=Date
      End If

      'Select a View based on the name of the logged in user
      Select Case UserName
          Case "User Name 1"
              ViewApply "Gantt Chart User Name 1"
              TableApply "Entry User Name 1"
          Case "User Name 2"
              ViewApply "Gantt Chart User Name 2"
              TableApply "Entry User Name 2"
          Case Else
              ViewApply "Gantt Chart"
              TableApply "Entry"
      End Select
End Sub
```

To get all projects to scroll to the current date copy the code above to the *ThisProject* object of the *ProjectGlobal (Global.mpt)* file. Note that your project file must contain at least one task for the event to trigger when you next open the project.

Understanding Task Events

Task events occur when task values change. Unfortunately, they are not as easy to code as *Project* events. To write code for *Task, Resource,* and *Assignment* events, you need code in three different places:

1. The *ThisProject* file as a *Project Open* event to call the *enable events* code.

2. A module to hold the *enable events* code that is, in turn, called from the *Project Open* event.

3. A *Class* module to hold the code for the event itself.

Unfortunately, *Task, Resource,* and *Assignment* events are rather complex to create but provided you follow the steps below they work well.

> Events such as task changes may not be triggered in all cases or they may trigger other events as well. Sometimes changing one task changes other tasks in the plan, ultimately causing task change events to trigger for a number of other tasks. You need to carefully and thoroughly test your code to make sure that events do what you want them to do; no more and no less!

The instructions below take you through the creation of a *Before Task Delete* event that displays a confirmation dialog before allowing the user to delete the task. In this code, if the *Flag1* field is set to *Yes* for the selected task, then the code does not display the confirmation dialog and the user can delete the task without prompting. To create this event, complete the following steps:

1. Go to the VBE (press the **Alt+F11** key combination) and open the *ThisProject* object.

2. Create a *Project Open* event and add this code:

```
Private Sub Project_Open(ByVal pj As Project)

    MsgBox "Hello, you have opened a project with an " & _
        "Open Project and a Before Delete event."

'The following code calls a routine in Module DeleteCode
'To enable the Before Task Delete Event
    EnableEvents
End Sub
```

3. Insert a new module and rename it from *Module1* to *DeleteCode*.

4. In the new module, enter the following code:

```
Public Del As New clsDelete
Sub EnableEvents()
    Set Del.ProjApp = MSProject.Application
End Sub
```

In the preceding code sample, the *Del* variable and the *clsDelete* variable refer to the *Class Module* name created next. They can both have other names, but make sure that you make the names the same for the other steps; otherwise, the events will not work.

5.   Click Insert ➢ Class Module.

6.   Press **F4** to display the *Properties* window and rename the *Class* to *clsDelete*

> If you start all class names with cls, they all appear together in IntelliSense lists. This is always useful if you cannot remember the exact name and have several Class modules.

The system calls the *EnableEvents* procedure from the *Project Open* event so that it automatically runs every time the user opens a project file. To add the *Delete* class code, complete these steps:

1.   In the *Class* module, enter:

```
Public WithEvents ProjApp As MSProject.Application
```

The *ProjApp* name is a variable name. You can use any valid name you wish, but remember it for step 6.

2.   Either you can type the procedure name and parameters, or you can select it from the class module window. To select the *ProjectBeforeTaskDelete* declaration from the *Procedure* pick list, do the following:

2.1.   Click the *Object* pick list button and select the *ProjApp* item.

2.2.   Click the *Procedure* pick list button and select the *ProjectBeforeTaskDelete* item. The list will hold all events available for tasks, resources, and assignments.

3.   Enter code for the whole *Delete Class* declaration as follows:

```
Private Sub ProjApp_ProjectBeforeTaskDelete( _
        ByVal tsk As Task, Cancel As Boolean)
'Only allow the task to be deleted if Flag1 is False
'Or the user says Yes to the MsgBox prompt
   If tsk.Flag1 = False Then
      If MsgBox("Are you sure you want to Delete Task" & _
            vbCrLf & """" & tsk.Name & """?", vbYesNo) = vbNo Then
         Cancel = True    'Cancel the Task Delete
      End If
   End If
End Sub
```

In the code above, every pair of double-quotes appears as a single double-quote in the final message, as shown in Figure 8 - 2. To test the code, save and close the project, then reopen it.

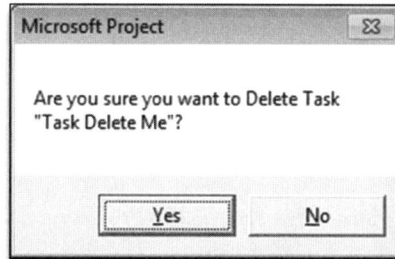

Figure 8 - 2: Message Displayed by ProjectBeforeTaskDelete Event

If your code did not run at all, your macro security may be set too high. Change it to *Medium* or *Low*.

In the *ByVal tsk As Task, Cancel As Boolean* event declaration, the *tsk* variable is a *Task* variable that you can use to get all task information for the task that triggered the event.

Cancel is only available for all *Before* events. Set *Cancel* to *True* to stop the action that triggered the event. In the example above, the system will cancel the *Task Delete* action.

Some events are duplicated in the *Procedure* drop down list, but have a 2 at the end of their name. In Project 2002, Microsoft needed to redo events, so they added the 2 versions for backwards compatibility. You will not need to worry about them, so ignore the event names ending with a 2.

Hands On Exercise

Exercise 8-1

Create a *Task* event.

1. In a new project file, or one of your own, add an event that occurs whenever the user creates a new assignment (assigns a resource to a task).

2. Add a message that the system displays only if the user assigns a resource at 100% units. The message should suggest making the assignment more realistic, since no one really works a full 100% of each working day on one task!

Module 09

Creating the Project Control Center Macro

Learning Objectives

After completing this module, you will be able to:

- Structure and design your macros before writing them
- Understand the functions of the Project Control Center macro, how to construct it, and how it helps you

Inside Module 09

Structuring Your Macros

Before I introduce you to the very useful *Project Control Center* macro, you first need to understand how to structure and design your macros. Doing a little bit of design early in the process can save you hours (if not days) later on.

Structuring your macros is about defining the task your macro must perform and then logically designing your macro in small chunks of code. You can split large macros into separate modules, each performing separate functions. For example, you might have one module for reporting in Excel, one for collecting the data, and another for small utility functions that you copy and reuse in many macros. You might have another module for all code communicating with a database. This technique helps break a big solution into small discreet chunks that are easier to manage, understand and debug.

Another productive technique for creating large macros is to split the development into several iterations. The first iteration might get all data needed, and export it to a .csv file that is ready for testing in Excel. A second iteration might get all data from Excel, and the final iteration performs all report formatting. A real world analogy is planning a long walk by splitting it into a number of one-day hikes. Planning each one-day hike is then easy and the entire long walk is then a matter of combining the daily hikes into one long walk.

Try not to reinvent the wheel every time you create a macro. Keep small utility functions together that you might use again. The more working code you can copy, the quicker you develop your new macro. Note what practices and techniques work for you and then learn from them by reusing what works and avoiding what does not work. Excel makes a great reporting tool, but for VBA beginners, automating another program can be a difficult challenge. To make the coding easier, try to reuse someone else's working code (such as the code in this workbook) and then adapt what works for you for future macros.

If you are developing a macro to create project reports in Excel, you have three choices where to put your VBA code:

1. Write all your code in Project VBA, sending data and formatting instructions to Excel.

2. Write all your code in Excel VBA, reading data from Project files.

3. Write code in Project VBA that reads the data and exports it to Excel, and then write code in Excel VBA that does all the report formatting. Excel templates are great tools for holding pre-formatted reports along with the code to run them.

Writing Project VBA code that works only with Project and writing Excel VBA code that works only with Excel is the easiest way to develop code, and incidentally produces the fastest running code. Every transfer of information and formatting instruction passed between programs is relatively slow. By putting all the formatting code into Excel, you bypass this overhead. However, either Project or Excel must incur the overhead to get the report's data transferred between them. Code that controls one application from another is more difficult to write, but not that hard. Module 13 contains some great code for working with Excel to provide you with the best start possible for your macros. Rather than talking theoretically about structuring macros, I show you how to use the *Project Control Center* macro to build a multi-project reporting tool.

Project Control Center Macro Overview

I designed the *Project Control Center* macro to create basic multi-project reports. You can easily add to it and each addition typically works on all projects linked to the *Project Control Center* project file. By the time you reach the end of this workbook, the Project Control Center example will include the following functionality:

- Read summary data for all projects, including resource hours per week for each project.

- Display the driving tasks that affect the selected task's *Start* date in any project.

- Create an *S-Curve* report in Excel showing cumulative cost and work against baseline cumulative cost and work over time.

- Create *Who Does What When* report in Excel.

- Update the *Standard* calendar for all projects in the *Project Control Center* project file.

- Create a snapshot of all projects in one consolidation.

By the time you complete this workbook and practice with your own macros, you will be able to customize the Project Control Center into a powerful and very productive tool. My intention is that the *Project Control Center* macros will pay for this book many times over in increased productivity.

The remaining topics in this module describe the basic code required to loop through all projects and read basic summary data into the Project Control Center to create a summary report. This code forms the first iteration towards the completed solution.

Designing the Project Control Center

For the design of this multi-project reporting tool, we set the following high-level goals:

- Can report across multiple Microsoft Project .mpp files.

- Easy and simple to use by project and program managers.

- Reports on project status, resource usage per week and percent complete. This set of reports should be easy to expand at a later date.

- The tool must be low cost, flexible, and work with many groups of projects where any one project may belong to any one group of projects (programs of projects).

- Must be robust so that renaming or moving a file will not corrupt any file or data.

You are likely to have additional high-level goals, but the preceding goals will suit our purposes for this example.

There are many available solutions on the market that meet or exceed these goals, including Microsoft Project Server. However, what these goals imply is something much simpler than a large commercial solution, and because there are no complicated reporting needs, they are much more basic as well. A tool that sits below the level of advanced tools such as Project Server meets the need nicely for teams and small departments looking for their first multi-project reporting tool. Creating your own small multi-project reporting tool is a very useful step towards implementing a full Enterprise Project Management (EPM) system. Think low tech, low cost, high value.

Because this book focuses on Project VBA, I base the design around a .mpp file that contains tasks representing each of the projects in a single program of projects. One of Microsoft Project's features is the ability to include a hyperlink for each task. We exploit the hyperlink feature by having tasks representing each project in the program, with each task's hyperlink pointing to the .mpp file for that project. To add a project, simply add a task with a hyperlink pointing to the new .mpp file and the macro does the rest. This program file serves as a directory holding the pointers to all the subprojects.

Hyperlinks are essentially text strings containing the path of a file, with the ability to click the hyperlink to open the file automatically. Therefore, the first benefit of our special .mpp file is a list of all projects in the program, with the ability to open any one of them just by clicking the hyperlink. Moreover, we gained this benefit without writing a single line of code!

The Project Control Center structure consists of one .mpp file holding a list of all projects in a program, and we use each task to report on one project. We use a Project VBA macro to open each project individually, using the file path in the hyperlink, and then read all the project level data.

As I mentioned previously, one productive way to develop new systems is to break a big solution into a number of small chunks and deliver them as a series of iterations. We already know enough to begin writing the first iteration. You will learn to add much more functionality in later modules.

Deliverables for Project Control Center

Now that you have the goals for the code, the next step is to create logical blocks for the code. We often call this pseudo code which describes the steps needed to achieve the desired result. I do this by writing a list of comments (including their leading single quotes) so I can copy and paste the list of steps directly into a module ready for coding. We can write the comments directly in the VBE, in Word, Notepad or any text editor. Following is a list of my comments, written in a Microsoft Word document, but written in the VBA code format:

```
Sub ReadAllProjectData
'Calculate the date for the start of the week
'This macro assumes Monday is the start of each week
'Calculate the date for this week's Monday
'Delete any current data such as resources
'For Each Task in the Project Control Center project
'Extract File path from the Hyperlink
'Test File exists (hasn't been renamed)
'Open the project file read only with no updates from resource pools or links.
'Make sure the project has its week start on Monday
'Read project level data from the Project Summary Task
'Close the project and don't save any changes
'End of Loop for project
'Tidy up
End Sub
```

After you copy and paste these comments to your module in the VBE, you now know **what** your code should do and you can focus on writing one chunk of VBA code at a time. By structuring your solutions like this, you gain the following benefits:

- A more logical design for your code.

- The ability to focus on and code small chunks of code at one time.

Understanding the Project Control Center Code

Below is the code required for the basics of the *Project Control Center* macro:

```
Option Explicit

Sub ReadAllProjectData()
Dim StartOfWeek As Date
Dim Tsk As Task
Dim prjPCC As Project
Dim prj As Project
Dim Path As String

'Calculate the date for the start of the week.
'    This macro assumes Monday is the start of each week
'    Calculate the date for this Monday
    StartOfWeek = Date - Weekday(Date) + vbMonday

'Delete any current data such as resources
    'Nothing to do here yet

'For Each task in the Project Control Center project
    Set prjPCC = ActiveProject
    prjPCC.StartWeekOn = pjMonday
    For Each Tsk In prjPCC.Tasks
        If Not Tsk Is Nothing Then 'test for empty tasks

'Extract File path from the Hyperlink
        Path = Tsk.HyperlinkAddress
'Convert from URL to file directory notation
        Path = Replace(Path, "/", "\")
'Convert ASCII character #20 to spaces
        Path = Replace(Path, "%20", " ")

'Test file exists (hasn't been renamed)
        If Dir(Path) = "" Then      'Only if file exists, open it
            Tsk.Name = "File not Found"
        Else

'Open the project file read only with no updates from resource pools or links.
            FileOpen Name:=Path, ReadOnly:=True, _
                noAuto:=True, openpool:=pjDoNotOpenPool
            Set prj = ActiveProject

    'Make sure the project has its week starts on Monday
            prj.StartWeekOn = pjMonday

    'Read project level data from the project Summary Task
            With prj.ProjectSummaryTask
                Tsk.Name = .Name
                Tsk.PercentComplete = 0    'Remove actuals
                Tsk.Start = .Start
                Tsk.Duration = .Duration
                Tsk.PercentComplete = .PercentComplete
```

```
                Tsk.PercentWorkComplete = .PercentWorkComplete
                Tsk.BaselineStart = .BaselineStart
                Tsk.BaselineFinish = .BaselineFinish
            End With

    'Close the project and don't save any changes
            prj.Activate    'Make correct project active
            FileClose pjDoNotSave
        End If
      End If
    'End of Loop for all projects
    Next Tsk

'Tidy up and format time scale on Gantt Chart
    prjPCC.Activate     'Make sure the main project is active
    ViewApply "Gantt Chart"

    TimescaleEdit MajorUnits:=pjTimescaleMonths, MinorUnits:=pjTimescaleDays, _
      MajorLabel:=pjMonthLabelMonth_mmm_yyy, MinorLabel:=pjDayOfMonth_dd, _
      MinorCount:=7, MinorTicks:=True, Separator:=True, MajorUseFY:=False, _
      MinorUseFY:=True, TierCount:=2

    EditGoTo Date:=Date

    Set prjPCC = Nothing
    Set prj = Nothing
End Sub
```

If you are overwhelmed at the sight of all this code, then relax and take slow deep breaths, as I explain everything! You are already familiar with the comments, but the code evolved enough so that I added one or two extra comments. As with the comments, I discuss the code one block at a time.

```
'Calculate the date for the start of the week.
'    This macro assumes Monday is the start of each week
'    Calculate the date for this Monday
    StartOfWeek = Date - Weekday(Date) + vbMonday
```

Before you can read weekly data, you need to make sure that every project starts its week on the same day. This code ensures consistency across all project files.

Date is a VBA function that returns today's date. *Weekday* is another VBA function that tests the date (in this case *StartOfWeek*) and returns the day of the week. The *vbMonday* constant is a VBA constant representing Monday as a number *(2 – Sunday is 1)*. The *Date – Weekday(Date)* constant returns the date of last Saturday. Adding the *vbMonday* constant, therefore, returns the date of last Monday.

```
'Delete any current data such as resources
    'Nothing to do here yet

'For Each task in the Project Control Center
    Set prjPCC = ActiveProject
    prjPCC.StartWeekOn = pjMonday
    For Each Tsk In prjPCC.Tasks
        If Not Tsk Is Nothing Then 'test for empty tasks
```

The *Set prjPCC = ActiveProject* statement sets the *prjPCC* project variable to the active project. By setting a project variable to the *Project Control Center* project, even when another project is open and active, you can still work with all the *Project Control Center's* tasks. There is no need to switch from one project to another to copy or read data.

```
'Extract File path from the Hyperlink
        Path = Tsk.HyperlinkAddress
        If Left$(Path, 1) = "." Then
            Path = ActiveProject.Path & "\" & Path
        End If
        Path = Replace(Path, "/", "\")
        Path = Replace(Path, "%20", " ")
```

Each task has a hyperlink and part of it is the hyperlink address, available via the *HyperLinkAddress* property. The system often stores hyperlinks as paths **relative to** the current project's path. The *FileOpen* command cannot always resolve relative paths successfully so you need to precede the relative path with the path to the current project.

All relative paths start with two period characters (..). If they exist, add the current project's path to the front so that the *FileOpen* operation can resolve the address. While this may not be completely clear now, if you look at the value in the path variable as you single step through the code, the results are obvious to you. Experiment with and without different statements in this block of code to see what works and what does not.

Hyperlinks use forward slashes while file paths require backward slashes. The *Replace* command is yet another VBA function you can use to swap one string for another within a nominated string. The first *Replace* function swaps "/" for "\". Another part of hyperlink addresses is that the software represents every space by %20. The second *Replace* function swaps %20 for *spaces*. After these statements, the path should hold a valid address that you can test with the *Dir* function and then use with the *FileOpen* command.

> You could use the *FollowHyperlink* method, belonging to the *Application* object, to open each project. This works, but if the file is already open or belongs to a Resource Pool, then the system displays various dialogs when opening the project. This is problematic because you want the macro to run without any manual user intervention. Getting the hyperlink address and then using it in a *FileOpen* statement gives you much more control over the process.

```
'Test file exists (hasn't been renamed)
      If Dir(Path) = "" Then       'Only if file exists, open it
         Tsk.Name = "File not Found"
      Else
```

Rather than trap an error, we will test that the file exists and that you have not moved, deleted or renamed it. The *Dir()* VBA function returns an empty string ("") if the file defined in the *Path* variable cannot be found. If you cannot find the file, then the project's task name is set to "File not Found" and the function skips the rest of the code in the loop for this project.

```
'Open the project file read only with no updates from
'resource pools or links.
   FileOpen Name:=Path, ReadOnly:=True, noAuto:=True, openpool:=pjDoNotOpenPool
   Set prj = ActiveProject
```

The *FileOpen* command has a variety of parameters you can learn about via Help. The goal with the *FileOpen* command is to open the file without any prompts requiring user input. The *ReadOnly* command is self-explanatory, but you do want to open each file in read-only mode in case someone already has the file open for editing. The *noAuto* command means that you do not want the system to run any macros set to run automatically on the *FileOpen* command. Again, we use this to prevent any possible interruptions or problems when opening the file. The *openpool* command forces the project to open while ignoring any shared resource pool to which it is connected, which again prevents any possible problems.

Setting the *prj = ActiveProject* variable is not really necessary, but it is neater to have a separate variable so there is no confusion about the project methods and properties with which you are working. Sometimes users can switch between projects while macros are running. Saving a variable that points to the newly-opened project guarantees that the code still runs with the correct project, even if the user changes the active project.

> Tip: Do not rely on users to do what you want or expect! Always make your code as tolerant as possible to any user actions.

```
'Make sure the project has its week start on Monday
      prj.StartWeekOn = pjMonday
```

Later on we add code to this macro to read timephased data. Forcing the project to have the expected *WeekStartingOn* value avoids problems where different projects start weeks on different days.

```
'Read project level data from the project Summary Task
        With prj.ProjectSummaryTask
            Tsk.Name = .Name
            Tsk.PercentComplete = 0     'Remove actuals
            Tsk.Start = .Start
            Tsk.Duration = .Duration
            Tsk.PercentComplete = .PercentComplete
            Tsk.PercentWorkComplete = .PercentWorkComplete
            Tsk.BaselineStart = .BaselineStart
            Tsk.BaselineFinish = .BaselineFinish
        End With
```

The preceding code is the "meat and potatoes" of the macro. It reads data directly from the opened project's project summary task and stores it in the task for the project in the *Project Control Center's* project file. The *With* statement makes the code cleaner and makes it run slightly faster.

```
'Close the project and don't save any changes
        prj.Activate    'Make correct project active
        FileClose pjDoNotSave
```

Just in case a user manually switches projects while the macro is running, this code first makes sure the expected project is active before closing it with the *pjDoNotSave* constant. This is a quicker way to close a project than waiting for it to save and makes sure that the macro does not make erroneous changes.

```
'End of Loop for all projects
            End If
        End If
    Next

'Tidy up and format time scale on Gantt Chart
    prjPCC.Activate     'Make sure its active
    ViewApply "Tracking Gantt Chart"
    TimescaleEdit majorunits:=pjTimescaleMonths, _
        Majorlabel:=pjMonth_mmm_yyy, _
        Minorunits:=pjTimescaleWeeks, _
        Minorlabel:=pjWeek_mmm_dd
    EditGoTo Date:=Date

    Set prjPCC = Nothing
    Set prj = Nothing
```

The first block of code ends the *If* and *Loop* statements. The second block displays the *Tracking Gantt* view, with the timescale zoomed to months and weeks before moving the timescale to today's date. We display the *Tracking Gantt* view so that baseline dates also appear.

Finally, we release the main *Object* variables by setting them to **Nothing**.

Rod Gill recommends that you set all *Object* variables to **Nothing** at the end of each routine. While this is not strictly necessary, failing to do so can cause occasional problems.

Without doing difficult coding yourself, you now have a useful piece of code you can use with your own macros. The next stage is to add more and more functionality to the Project Control Center until you have a productive set of tools to enhance your project reporting and file management productivity. Adding to the Project Control Center is what the rest of this workbook is all about; teaching you new techniques and much more about the "ins and outs" of Project VBA programming.

As far as predicting how long it takes to develop a macro, once you have some practice in developing macros, it should not be too difficult to estimate times for each of the commented chunks in the design step. Then add the required percentages for system testing and a margin for extra features and your estimate should be reasonably accurate. Note that no accuracy is possible without design or without measuring how long each macro actually takes you to develop!

Rod Gill recommends you add to your best estimate of time to code your macro, 20% to fix all final problems during the first month the macro is used and another 20% to allow for modifications and minor additions that will inevitably occur once your users get to "play" with the macro.

When running the *ReadAllProjectData* procedure in Project 2003, if one of the linked projects has VBA code in it, then the system prompts you to enable macros. Because the file is one to which you created a hyperlink, it should be safe, making this level of security annoying. The only way around it is to set your macro security level to *Low* before running the macro, and then resetting it to at least *Medium* afterwards. For security reasons, you cannot reset security levels via VBA. To prevent the prompt you can apply a security certificate. If the projects are all yours, you can use the *SelfCert* utility to create a certificate.

Hands On Exercise

Exercise 9-1

Explore the Project Control Center macro code.

1. Open a copy of Module 9 Sample Code.mpp or enter the code above into a blank project.

2. In row 1 of the project, press **Ctrl+K** to insert a hyperlink. Browse to any of your Project files and select it.

3. In row 2 add a hyperlink to another of your Project files.

4. Press **Alt+F8** to open the *Macros* dialog.

5. Double-click the *ReadAllProjectData* macro to run it.

The code runs and fills in all project details. If not, check your code and single step through it to see what does and does not happen. A first check is in the VBE where you can click Compile ➢ Compile VBAProject. If you see any errors, resolve them and then try to run the macro again.

6. Add your own VBA code to read the *Cost* data and *Baseline Cost* data as well.

Module 10

Displaying Driving Tasks

Learning Objectives

After completing this module, you will be able to:

- Understand and use a macro to display tasks driving the Start date of a selected task
- Add a toolbar to the application to run the file's macros

Inside Module 10

Designing the Driving Task Macro

A common frustration among many Microsoft Project users is, "Why is my task starting when it is?" The answer is not always easy to determine, without the help of a macro that displays the answer for you.

> Microsoft Project 2007 introduced a new *Task Driver* feature to display what is driving the active task as one of its built-in features. With Projecvt 2010, Microsoft enhanced this feature and now calls it the Task Inspector. Therefore, this macro is not so useful for you if you are a Project 2007 user, or later. However, this code lists **all** predecessors and their dates and lags which is important when analyzing the Critical Path, while the task driver/task inspector feature does not.
>
> It is useful for you to understand how the macro works and how to design it. Information like the predecessor finish dates are not provided by Project's built-in *Task Driver* feature.

I designed the macro so that it works by selecting a task and then clicking a button on a toolbar to start the macro. The macro determines what predecessor tasks and other factors drive the selected task *Start* date, and then it displays the answer in a UserForm. So what conditions can control the *Start* date of a task? The following situations can drive the *Start* date of any task:

- A task constraint (usually because the user typed a *Start* date or *Finish* date, or dragged and dropped the task's Gantt bar in the Gantt chart)

- Predecessors you created by linking tasks

- Predecessors to the task's summary task

- An *Actual Start* date for the task

- Linked fields from another application

- Levelling delay

A task's *Start* date may also have an unexpected value if Microsoft Project's calculation mode is set to *Manual* (set under *Options*) or if in Project 2010 a task is *Manually* rather than *Automatically* scheduled. This provides us with enough information to build the basic *Sub* procedure that determines what is driving the *Start* date of any task.

Remembering that I recommend building macros iteratively, for this macro, I use the following iterations:

1. Build the basic task-driving macro and display results to the *Immediate* window.

2. Add information for all task dependencies and display results in the *Immediate* window.

3. Add a UserForm to display the results to users.

4. Add a toolbar to enable the user to run the macro by clicking a button.

Designing the Main Procedure

The main comments for this routine are as follow:

```
Sub WhatsDrivingMyTask()
'Declare Variables
Read start date of selected task
'Test Calculation mode and
'prompt user to allow automatic mode. 'Cancel Macro if permission denied
'Test Task Constraint
'Test Predecessors
'Test Predecessors on Summary task
'Test Actual Start Date
'Test for any Linked Fields
'Tidy Up
End Sub
```

The code to determine task predecessors is the most complex and I suggest putting this code into a separate procedure. A separate procedure is especially useful because it looks like we need to call it once for the selected task's predecessors and once for the predecessors of the selected task's summary tasks. Comments for the *Check Predecessors* code might be:

```
Function CheckPredecessors(tskCheck as Task)
'Note that predecessors and successors are both dependency
'  Objects, so test From or To property to determine if a
'  Dependency is a Predecessor or Successor.
'Declare Variables
'For each predecessor in tskCheck's predecessors
'If the dependency is a predecessor get link type and Lag
'If FF or FS then get dependency finish date
'Else If SF or SS then get start date
'Return result
End Function
```

Please do not let my example limit the comments you add to code as you go. The more comments you have and the more meaningful they are, the better your code.

The comments now provide enough structure to code the macro and to predict how long it might take you to develop. Knowing that the *CheckPredecessors* code will work best as a separate function is something that will come after a little experience. Without that experience, the steps you might follow are:

1. Write all code as one procedure.

2. Realize that the code is the same to get the active task's predecessors and the active task's summary task's predecessors.

3. Move predecessor code to a separate procedure.

4. Realize that making the *CheckPredecessors* procedure a function rather than using a global variable would work more simply.

> Any block of code that needs to be run a number of times or could be re-used elsewhere most productively lives in a seperate *Sub* procedure. If that block of code needs to return a value to the calling procedure make it a *Function*.

With only a small amount of code to create for each comment, this macro is fairly straight forward when you understand how dependencies work in Project VBA.

Understanding Task Dependencies

When you link two tasks in Microsoft Project, the system creates a link record. In Project VBA, we call the link a *Task Dependency* and it is an object. The *TaskDependency* object has a number of useful properties, including:

- **From** is a *Task* object representing the task driving the link.

- **To** is a *Task* object representing the task driven by the dependency. Using the **From** and **To** *Task* objects, you can recover the selected and predecessor tasks details.

- **Type** returns a number that represents the link type (such as Finish to Start, Start to Start, etc.). Use project constants in your code (for example, *pjFinishToStart*) rather than using any number returned.

- **Lag** is the lag for the link that you specify either as a string, such as *"2w"*, or as a number representing the number of working minutes (8*60 for 8 hours).

Understanding the Task Driver Code

The first iteration of this code sends all information to the *Immediate* window. I add the UserForm as a separate step. Following is the basic code:

```
Option Explicit

Sub WhatsDrivingMyTask()
'Declare Variables
Dim Tsk As Task
Dim Str As String
Dim StartDate As Date

'Get selected Task and read start date
   Set Tsk = ActiveCell.Task
   If not Tsk is nothing then
      Msgbox "Please select a valid task before running the macro.", _
         Vbcritical + vbokonly
      End
   End If
   StartDate = Tsk.Start

   Debug.Print Tsk.Name     'Display selected Task's name

'Test Calculation mode and prompt user to allow automatic mode.
   If Application.Calculation = pjManual Then
      'Cancel Macro if permission denied
      If MsgBox("Calculation Mode is set to manual, " _
            & "is it okay to set to Automatic?", _
               vbYesNo + vbCritical) = vbNo Then
         MsgBox "Macro cancelled by user." _
            & "Calculation mode needs to be on automatic.", vbInformation
         End
      Else
         Application.Calculation = pjAutomatic
      End If
   End If

'Placeholder for Project 2010 manual mode code

'Test Task Constraint
   If Tsk.ConstraintType <> pjASAP Then
      Debug.Print "Constraint is " & _
         Choose(Tsk.ConstraintType, _
         "ALAP", "MSO", "MFO", "SNET", "SNLT", "FNET", _
         "FNLT") & ", Date: " _
         & Format(Tsk.ConstraintDate, "Medium Date")
   Else
      Debug.Print "Constraint is ASAP"
   End If

'Placeholder for Test Predecessors function

'Placeholder for Test Predecessors on Summary task

'Test Actual Start Date
   If Tsk.ActualStart = "NA" Then
      Debug.Print "No Actual Start date"
   Else
      Debug.Print "Actual Start Date: " & Tsk.ActualStart & vbCrLf
```

```
    End If

'Test for Linked Fields
    If Tsk.LinkedFields Then
        Debug.Print "There are linked fields."
    Else
        Debug.Print "No linked fields"
    End If

'Test for leveling delay
    If Tsk.LevelingDelay > 0 Then
        Debug.Print "Leveling delay: " & Tsk.LevelingDelay / 60 / 24 & "ed"
    Else
        Debug.Print "No leveling delay"
    End If

'Tidy Up
End Sub
```

The above code is the main routine. I explain this before explaining the *CheckPredecessors* code. The first section with variable declarations should now seem straightforward to you. If not, please revisit earlier modules in this workbook to reinforce your knowledge.

```
'Test Calculation mode and prompt user to allow automatic mode.
    If Application.Calculation = pjManual Then
        'Cancel Macro if permission denied
        If MsgBox("Calculation Mode is set to manual, " _
            & "is it okay to set to Automatic?", _
            vbYesNo + vbCritical) = vbNo Then
            MsgBox "Macro cancelled by user. Calculation mode needs to be on " _
                & "automatic.", vbInformation
            End
        Else
            Application.Calculation = pjAutomatic
        End If
    End If
```

Calculation is a property of the *Application* object and returns the current state as two numbers, again represented by constants. If the returned value is equal to the *pjManual* project constant, then the macro needs to ask the user's permission to force automatic calculation. With calculation set to *Manual*, trying to determine what causes the task to start when it does is meaningless. Therefore, the first *MsgBox* call requests permission and displays a *Yes* and *No* button version with the critical icon. Figure 10 - 1 shows the dialog.

117

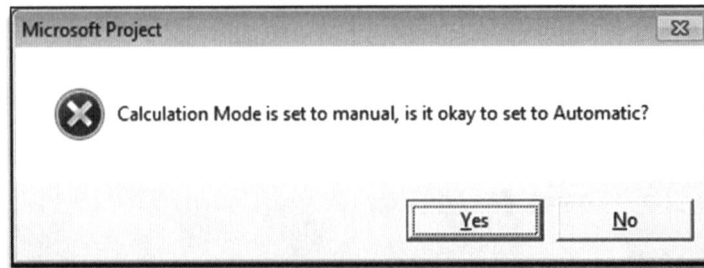

Figure 10 - 1: First Msgbox

If the user clicks the *No* button, the macro displays a warning message using the *MsgBox* call and then the *End* statement ends all code. If the user clicks the *Yes* button, then the system forces calculation to *Automatic* status and the macro continues.

```
'Test Task Constraint
   If Tsk.ConstraintType <> pjASAP Then
      Debug.Print "Constraint is " & Choose(Tsk.ConstraintType, _
         "ALAP", "MSO", "MFO", "SNET", "SNLT", "FNET", _"FNLT") & ", Date: " _
         & Format(Tsk.ConstraintDate, "Medium Date")
   Else
      Debug.Print "Constraint is ASAP"
   End If
```

Once you remember that all code starting with **pj** is a built-in Project constant, this code becomes easy to understand, with the exception of the *Choose* statement. *Choose* is another VBA function that is available to all VBA implementations. The *Tsk.ConstraintType* command returns a number and the *Choose* function returns the value of the relevant parameter. For example, if your task has a *Start No Earlier Than* constraint, the *Tsk.ConstraintType* command returns the value 4. The fourth parameter in the *Choose* statement after the *Tsk.ConstraintType* command is "SNET" so the system returns "SNET" as the result or value of the *Choose* function.

If there is no task constraint, then the default constraint value is *pjASAP* (As Soon As Possible) so the *Debug.Print "Constraint is ASAP"* code is executed by the *Else* part of the *IF .ConstraintType <> pjASAP Then* statement.

```
'Test Predecessors
   Debug.Print "Predecessors: " & CheckPredecessors(Tsk)

'Test Predecessors on Summary task
   If Tsk.OutlineLevel > 1 Then
      Debug.Print "Summary Task Predecessors: " & _
         CheckPredecessors(Tsk.OutlineParent)
   Else
      Debug.Print "No Summary Task Predecessors"
   End If
```

For Project 2010 users, add the following code where the 'Project 2010 Placeholder code comment is above:

```
'Test Project 2010 Scheduling mode
    If Tsk.Manual = True Then
        Debug.Print "Task is Manually Scheduled"
        Exit sub
    End If
```

This code simply tests for manual scheduling mode. If *true*, then manual scheduling is the sole driver of the task. I include placeholders only for task dependency code as it is more complex and lives in the second iteration.

```
'Test Actual Start Date
    If Tsk.ActualStart = "NA" Then
        Debug.Print "No Actual Start date"
    Else
        Debug.Print "Actual Start Date: " & Tsk.ActualStart & vbCrLf
    End If

'Test for Linked Fields
    If Tsk.LinkedFields Then
        Debug.Print "There are linked fields."
    Else
        Debug.Print "No linked fields"
    End If

'Test for leveling delay
    If Tsk.LevelingDelay > 0 Then
        Debug.Print "Leveling delay: " & Tsk.LevelingDelay / 60 / 24 & "ed"
    Else
        Debug.Print "No leveling delay"
    End If

'Tidy Up
End Sub
```

Apart from knowing which properties to use, this is simple to code. For linked tasks, I simply pressed "L" while the system displayed an IntelliSense list for a *TaskObject* command. The *LinkedFields* command looked suitable, so I selected it and then pressed **F1** for Help (which confirmed its suitability). I am not aware of a property that details to which field the system links a task. In Microsoft Project, look for the small green triangle in the top right corner of a cell that indicates a linked cell.

Many schedulers do not use leveling at all, so you may choose to edit the code to only add a leveling message if a leveling delay exists.

Iteration 2 adds the *CheckPredecessors* code and replaces the *Test Predecessors* placeholders with:

```
'Test Predecessors
    Debug.Print "Predecessors: " & CheckPredecessors(Tsk)

'Test Predecessors on Summary task
    If Tsk.OutlineLevel > 1 Then
        Debug.Print "Summary Task Predecessors: " & _
        CheckPredecessors(Tsk.OutlineParent)
    Else
        Debug.Print "No Summary Task Predecessors"
    End If
```

The *CheckPredecessors* code is as follows:

```
Function CheckPredecessors(Tsk As Task) As String
'This routine looks at all predecessors of Task T
'Note that predecessors and successors are both dependency Objects.
'So test From or To property to determine if a Predecessor or Successor.
'Declare Variables
Dim Dep As TaskDependency
Dim Str As String

'For each predecessor in tsk's predecessors
'If the dependency is a predecessor get link type and Lag
    For Each Dep In Tsk.TaskDependencies
        If Dep.To.ID = Tsk.ID Then
            If Dep.Lag = 0 Then
                Str = Str & Dep.From.ID & ", " & _
                    Choose(Dep.Type + 1, "FF", "FS", _
                        "SF", "SS") & ", "
            Else
                Str = Str & Dep.From.ID & ", " & _
                Choose(Dep.Type + 1, "FF", "FS", _
                "SF", "SS") & Dep.Lag / 60 / 8 & "d, "
            End If

            'If FF or FS then get dependency finish date
            'Else If SF or SS then get start date
            If Dep.Type = pjFinishToFinish Or _
                    Dep.Type = pjFinishToStart Then
                Str = Str & Format(Dep.From.Finish, _
                    "Short Date") & ", " & Dep.From.Name & "; "
            Else
                Str = Str & Format(Dep.From.Start, _
                    "Short Date") & ", " & Dep.From.Name & "; "
            End If
        End If
    Next Dep

'Return result
    If Str = "" Then
```

```
        Str = "No Dependencies"
    Else
        CheckPredecessors = Left(Str, Len(Str) - 2) 'Remove trailing ;
    End If
End Function
```

The first line deserves some explanation.

```
Function CheckPredecessors(Tsk As Task) As String
```

The *Tsk as Task* function describes the parameter that the system must pass to the *CheckPredecessors* code. For this function, you can now use the *Tsk* variable to reference the current task. The *String* code states that the *CheckPredecessors* function returns a string and forces any code that uses the *CheckPredecessors* function to treat the returned value as a string. This avoids run time errors when the system forces a string into a date or number variable because the compiler flags a problem before you run the code.

```
    If Dep.To.ID = Tsk.ID Then
        Str = Dep.From.ID & ", " & _
            Choose(Dep.Type + 1, "FF", "FS", "SF", "SS")
        If Dep.Lag = 0 Then
            Str = Str & ", "
        Else
            Str = Str & Dep.Lag / 60 / 8 & "d, "
        End If
```

The loop statement should be familiar to you by now so the next interesting bit of code is:

```
If Dep.To.ID = Tsk.Id
```

The *Dep* function represents the dependency the macro is currently reading. The *To* command is the *Task* object for the task driven by the link. This test says that if the ID of the driven task is the same as the task passed to the function, then we have a predecessor rather than a successor.

The *Dep.Type* function returns a number from 0 to 3 representing the dependency type so we use the *Choose* function to return a string describing the *Task* type. If the lag is greater than zero, then append the lag to the string. In either case append *", "* as a spacer before you append the preceding task's name.

```
'If FF or FS then get dependency finish date
    'Else If SF or SS then get start date
        If Dep.Type = pjFinishToFinish Or Dep.Type = pjFinishToStart Then
            Str = Str & Format(Dep.From.Finish, _
                "Short Date") & ", " & Dep.From.Name
```

```
        Else
            Str = Str & Format(Dep.From.Start, _
                "Short Date") & ", " & Dep.From.Name
        End If
    End If
Next Dep
```

The above code finishes the loop and appends the *Finish* date of the preceding task and its name to the string. Depending on the type of link, the *Start* or *Finish* date is required. The macro retrieves the task name by getting the *From* task object and reading its *Name* property.

```
'Return result
    If Str = "" Then
        Str = "No Dependencies"
    Else
        CheckPredecessors = Left(Str, Len(Str) - 2) 'Remove trailing ;
    End If
End Function
```

Finally, if the *Str* string is empty *(="")*, then set it to the *No Dependencies* string. The *CheckPredecessors = Left(Str, Len(Str) - 2)* string sets the value returned by the *CheckPredecessors* function to the calling code. Because the function was defined as returning a string, *Str* has to be a string as well, otherwise a compile error occur.

Hands On Exercise

Exercise 10-1

Test the Iteration 1 and 2 code.

1. Either download Module 10 Sample Code.mpp or enter the code into a module.

2. Test the code to make sure it works and edit the code, if necessary. Iteration 2 code is in the *TaskDriversCode2* module.

3. Make sure you understand the code. Do not proceed to Iteration 3 until you confirm that all the code works with no known bugs. Adding another layer of code and editing code with errors in it creates a very confusing situation.

4. For an advanced test, add code to test for links to any summary task above the selected task. For example, the selected task could have been indented 4 times and either of the top two *Summary*

tasks could have a link which is driving the selected task. You will need to add a loop until you reach a *Summary* task with an outline level of 1.

5. For completeness, add code to handle the selected task being a summary task. In this case the code drives the selected summary task's start date by its sub tasks. You will need to loop through all sub tasks: the *Tsk.OutlineChildren* property provides a collection of all sub tasks.

Adding a UserForm to Display the Results

The first iteration of this macro outputs a string to the *Immediate* window to report its findings. In this iteration we add a UserForm to improve the user experience for your macro. There are three steps to adding a UserForm to this macro:

1. Create the UserForm.

2. Write code to open and close the UserForm.

3. Write code to enable the *Command* buttons.

Figure 10 - 2 shows the completed UserForm with sample data.

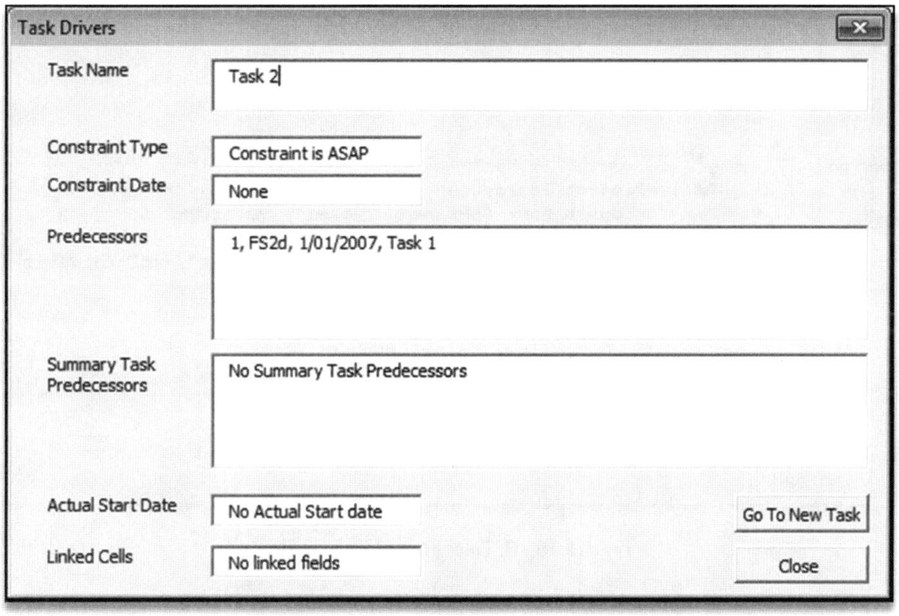

Figure 10 - 2: Activated UserForm with sample data

A good naming convention to use for all *Text* boxes in a UserForm is to use the two most important words in the text description label. For example *TaskName* makes an obvious name for the first field. For the *Summary Task Predecessors* box I used *SummaryPredecessors*. You can make names more specific by preceding them with *lbl* if the control being named is a label, or *btn* if a button and so on.

```
Sub TaskDrivers()
    TaskDriveResults.Show
End Sub
```

The preceding code is all I need to display the UserForm. It is better to code Initializing the fields in the *UserForm* class itself. Double-click the UserForm's background or in the Project Explorer right-click the UserForm in your project and click the *View Code* option.

Figure 10 - 3 shows all of the *Class* code for the UserForm. The *GotoNewTask* and *Quit* commands are the names of the two command buttons. Either type their code manually or select their names in the VBE from the *Object* pick list (in the upper left corner of *Code* window). UserForm is active in the *Object* list in Figure 10 - 3. The *WhatsDrivingMyTask2* procedure is the same as the *WhatsDrivingMyTask* procedure but contains all code for iteration 2. You do not need different procedures for each iteration; I have numbered them because I want to show you the code for each stage.

```
UserForm                                    ▼    Activate

    Option Explicit

    Private Sub UserForm_Activate()
        WhatsDrivingMyTask2
    End Sub

    Private Sub GotoNewTask_Click()
    Dim str As String
    Dim ID As Long

        str = InputBox("Enter Task ID to Go to")
        ID = Val(str)
        If ID = 0 Then
            MsgBox "Macro cancelled by user or " _
                & "invalid number entered", vbInformation
            Exit Sub
        End If

        If ID > ActiveProject.Tasks.Count Then
            MsgBox "You don't have that many Tasks!", vbInformation
        ElseIf ActiveProject.Tasks(ID) Is Nothing Then
            MsgBox "Task Id you entered is for an empty Task", vbInformation
        Else
            EditGoTo ID:=ID
            WhatsDrivingMyTask2
        End If
    End Sub

    Private Sub Quit_Click()
        TaskDriveResults.Hide
    End Sub
```

Figure 10 - 3: UserForm Class code

The *GotoNewTask_Click* command is worth explaining. I first wrote the procedure for it as follows:

```
EditGoTo ID:= CLng(InputBox("Enter Task ID to Go to"))
WhatsDrivingMyTask3
```

The *CLng* code converts what is passed to it into a *Long* variable (an Integer handles numbers between -32768 and +32768; a *Long* variable handles plus or minus 2 billion) as the *EditGoto* method expects a *Long* value.

This works fine provided you enter a valid ID; the Task ID number must exist. Any of the following conditions make this code fail:

- The user pressed the *Cancel* button in the *InputBox* dialog, so *InputBox* returned an empty string ("").

- The user selected the ID of a blank row in the schedule.

- The user selected the ID of a row below the last task.

- The user enters characters that cannot convert to a number.

Sometimes it takes a simple version of code plus extensive testing to devise a final, working solution. Never be afraid of using this process as it can often be quick and produces the best quality code. Create a prototype or basic working solution then test, test, and test again!

The code I finally developed is:

```
Private Sub GotoNewTask_Click()
Dim str As String
Dim ID As Long

    str = InputBox("Enter Task ID to Go to")
    ID = Val(str)
    If str = "" Then
        MsgBox "Macro cancelled by user ", vbInformation
        Exit Sub
    ElseIF ID = 0 Then
        MsgBox "Invalid number entered", vbInformation
        Exit Sub
    End If

    If ID > ActiveProject.Tasks.Count Then
        MsgBox "You don't have that many Tasks!", vbInformation
    ElseIf ActiveProject.Tasks(ID) Is Nothing Then
        MsgBox "Task Id you entered is for an empty Task", vbInformation
    Else
        EditGoTo ID:=ID
        WhatsDrivingMyTask3
    End If
End Sub
```

The *InputBox* code always returns a string, and returns an empty string if the user clicks the *Cancel* button. The *CIng* code raises a type error if asked to convert an *empty* or *none* numeric string to a number, so the *str* variable is converted by using the *Val* function. The code converts an *empty* or *none* numeric string by the VBA *Val* function as *zero*. VBA automatically converts the numeric value returned by the *Val* function to the *Long* type required by ID. You now have a valid ID number, so test for blank tasks or an ID greater than the number of tasks in the project.

Next, to open the UserForm which in turn triggers the *UserForm_Activate* code, add a *TaskDrivers* sub procedure shown earlier in this topic. Finally, you need to edit the code in the *WhatsDrivingMyTask* procedure to display the results in the UserForm rather than the *Immediate* window.

Consider commenting out the *Debug.Print* statements rather than deleting them. You know the *Debug* code works so if you have difficulties with the UserForm, the *Debug* code remains available for testing. Once you have the *UserForm* code working, make a backup and then delete the commented *Debug* code. The following code shows only the old code commented out with the new code to display results. In the sample project, there is a new procedure for this called *WhatsDrivingMyTask3* in the *TaskDriversCode3* module.

```
    If Tsk.ConstraintType <> pjASAP Then
'       Debug.Print "Constraint is " & _
'           Choose(Tsk.ConstraintType, _
'               "ALAP", "MSO", "MFO", "SNET", "SNLT", "FNET","FNLT") _
'               & ", Date: "& Format(Tsk.ConstraintDate, "Medium Date")
        TaskDriveResults.ConstraintType = _
            Choose(Tsk.ConstraintType, "ALAP", "MSO", _
                "MFO","SNET", "SNLT", "FNET", "FNLT")
        TaskDriveResults.ConstraintDate = _
            Format(Tsk.ConstraintDate, "Medium Date")
    Else
'       Debug.Print "Constraint is ASAP"
        TaskDriveResults.ConstraintType = "Constraint is ASAP"
        TaskDriveResults.ConstraintDate = ""
    End If
    TaskDriveResults.TaskName = Tsk.Name
```

The *TaskDriveResults* procedure is the name of the form (entered into properties while the UserForm is selected). *ConstraintType* and *ConstraintDate* are both names for textboxes. The default property for textboxes is *Text*. The following all work:

- TaskName = "New Name"

- TaskDriveResults.TaskName = "New Name"

- TaskDriveResults.TaskName.Text = "New Name"

The last version is most accurate and easier to copy and use in Visual Studio and Visual Studio Tools for Office (VSTO). See Section 3 for help in creating VSTO applications. The first version however is more readable and I leave it up to you to decide on which format. If you ever encounter any problems using one format, try one of the others to see if it helps. In the following code I use the *With* statement to make the code less verbose.

```
  With TaskDriveResults
'     Debug.Print "Predecessors: " & CheckPredecessors(Tsk)
      .Predecessors = CheckPredecessors(Tsk)

'     Debug.Print "Summary Task Predecessors: " _
'         & CheckPredecessors(Tsk.OutlineParent)
      .SummaryPredecessors = CheckPredecessors(Tsk.OutlineParent)

'     Debug.Print "No Summary Task Predecessors"
      .SummaryPredecessors = "No Summary Task Predecessors"

'     Debug.Print "No Actual Start date"
      .ActualStart = "No Actual Start date"

'     Debug.Print "Actual Start Date: " & Tsk.ActualStart & vbCrLf
      .ActualStart = Tsk.ActualStart & vbCrLf

'     Debug.Print "There are linked fields, check that" _
```

```
         & " the Start and Finish fields are not one of them."
         .LinkedCells = "There are linked fields"

'        Debug.Print "No linked fields"
         .LinkedCells = "No linked fields"

'        Debug.Print "No leveling delay"
         .LevelingDelay = "No leveling delay"
```

You should find this code relatively simple to understand, especially if you remember that the *CheckPredecessors* function is a function created earlier in the module in iteration 2.

Iteration 4 adds a button on a toolbar to run the *TaskDrivers* procedure which in turn opens the UserForm. The *UserForm_Initialize* code runs the *WhatsDrivingMyTask3* procedure and the *Quit* command button, when clicked, closes the UserForm by running the *GotoNewTask_Click* event.

Hands On Exercise

Exercise 10-2

Testing the UserForm

1. Set up the UserForm and add the code into the *WhatsDrivingMyTask2* procedure.

2. Make sure everything works as you expect.

Adding a Toolbar to Run the Macro

To make it easy for your users to run the code, add a toolbar to the application. You already learned about events in Module 09, so it should be simple enough to display a toolbar when you open a macro project, and then hide it when the project is closed. You can do this using the *Open* and *Close* project events.

Module 05 introduced you to creating toolbars. Below is the code to automatically create and remove a *My Macros* toolbar. Add the following code to the module with all the other code:

```
Sub AddToolbar()
Dim MyBar As CommandBar
Dim MyButton As CommandBarButton
    On Error Resume Next
    Set MyBar = CommandBars("My Macros")
    If MyBar Is Nothing Then
        Set MyBar = CommandBars.Add(Name:= "My Macros", _
            Position:=msoBarFloating, Temporary:=True)
```

```
        MyBar.Visible = True
    End If

    Set MyButton = MyBar.Controls("MyButton")
    If MyButton Is Nothing Then
        Set MyButton = MyBar.Controls.Add(Type:=msoControlButton)
        With MyButton
            .Style = msoButtonCaption
            .Caption = "Task Driver"
            .OnAction = "Macro ""TaskDrivers"""
        End With
    End If
End Sub

Sub DeleteBar()
    On Error Resume Next
    CommandBars("My Macros").Delete
End Sub
```

Add the following to the *ThisProject* file in the Project Explorer window in the VBE:

```
Private Sub Project_Open(ByVal pj As Project)
    AddToolbar
End Sub

Private Sub Project_BeforeClose(ByVal pj As Project)
    DeleteBar
End Sub
```

There should be nothing new to you in this code; it is simply a variation on code you already worked with in earlier modules. From this point forward, the code examples show you code you have seen before and you can use them as building blocks to help you code new macros.

Hands On Exercise

Exercise 10-3

Complete the last Iteration by adding a button to a toolbar.

1. Try adding the *Event* code to display the *My Macros* toolbar.

2. Test the whole macro again.

Save your final macro as a project so that you can use it again as a starting point for a future macro.

Module 11

Sharing and Distributing Your Macros

Learning Objectives

After completing this module, you will be able to:

- Run a macro from any project
- Distribute your macros to other Microsoft Project users

Inside Module 11

Sharing and Distributing your Macros

In Module 10 you created a useful macro to show what factors drive a selected task. A little bit of testing quickly shows you that the macro only works for the project in which the macro resides. To make the macro work in any project you have open, you need to make it available to them.

Once your macro is accessible to all other projects, the macro can run on any project you currently have open. This module shows you how to make a macro accessible to other project files and then shows you how to share your macros with other users.

Running Your Macros from All Projects

By default, when you declare a *Sub* or *Function* procedure, it is visible only to other *Sub* and *Function* procedures in the same module. To make them visible to all your modules and procedures, precede the *Sub* and *Function* declarations with the word *Public*, as shown in the following examples:

```
Public Sub TaskDriversMain()
Public Function CheckPredecessors(Tsk As Task) As String
```

Using the *Public* declaration you make the procedures visible to all modules and open projects, but the project containing the macros still needs to be open. You also need to add *Public* to all procedures called by higher level procedures. You can now call your macros from any open project, but you still must open the project containing the macro. If you need four or five macros, this could mean that you need to open four or five project files, cluttering up your workspace. How can you make this easier?

Using the Global.mpt File

The Global.mpt file contains the default copies of all objects, including *Views, Tables, Filters, Modules, Forms, Reports, Maps, Calendars, Fields, Maps,* and *Groups.* In Microsoft Project, if you want to make a new view available to all your projects, you use the Organizer (in Project 2010, click Tools ➤ Organizer – File tab) to copy it to the Global.mpt file. The same holds true for *Modules* and *Forms*; copy them to the Global.mpt file and they become visible to all projects.

By default anything in the Global.mpt file is visible to all of your projects, so you do not need the *Public* declarations. However, *Public* declarations do not harm your code and in the interests of moving code to and from the original projects, it is better to leave them in place.

> Only move to the Global.mpt file macros that you want to run on any project. Macros that should only be run on specific projects should reside in those projects. All macros should be tested outside the Global.mpt file to prevent cluttering it up with unfinished and maybe faulty macros .

Automatically Move Macros into the Global.mpt

Before moving macros, you first need a design. In moving macros, your goals are to:

- Move all required *Modules* and *Forms* to the Global.mpt file.

- Automate the *Module* and *Forms* transfer.

- Have a toolbar that is permanently visible for Global.mpt macros.

- Maintain the temporary toolbar for the macro project.

- Make it easy to update Global.mpt code from modified macros in the original project.

Remember that if the goals (deliverables) for your code are not clear, your code gets messy and development frequently takes significantly longer to finish. To achieve these technical goals you need to do the following:

- Write code to move the *Modules* and *Forms*.

- Add a button to the macro project's toolbar to run the *Copy to Global* code.

- Ensure you have two sets of toolbars, one for all macros in the Global.mpt file and one for each project file with a macro. Once in the Global.mpt file, the code needs to work with a different *Global* toolbar. When you close the macro project you delete the *My Macros* toolbar.

- Move all *Toolbar* procedures into a separate module so that you can update the main module easily without needing to edit *Global Toolbar* code each time. This is one example where having multiple modules saves you time and helps simplify your code.

- Create a module in the Global.mpt file for all *Global Toolbar* code. You add to this every time you add another macro as you do in the following modules.

Before doing any of these tasks, you need to tidy up your existing code. You can delete the old lines for *Debug.Print* code that you commented out and you need to move the *Toolbar* creation code into a separate module. Module 11 Sample Code.mpp has this work completed for you. For example, I renamed the *WhatsDrivingMyTask2* procedure to *WhatsDrivingMyTask,* and the updated *TaskDrivers Form* code accordingly.

Because you are creating multiple modules, it is important to give them meaningful names. A project file with modules named Module1, Module2, and Module3 provides no clue what code may be contained in them or how the code is structured. You can rename a module in the VBE by selecting it in Project Explorer then pressing the **F4** function key and editing the *Name* property.

Finally re-test everything to make sure your changes did not introduce any bugs.

Copying Modules and Forms to the Global.mpt

The easiest way to create code for this is to record a macro of the steps you need to manually move a module to the Global.mpt file using the Organizer. The results of a recorded macro should look something like this (I added line continuation characters):

```
OrganizerMoveItem Type:=3, FileName:="My Macro Project.mpp", _
    ToFileName:="Global.MPT", Name:="MyModule"
OrganizerMoveItem Type:=3, FileName:="My Macro Project.mpp", _
    ToFileName:="Global.MPT", Name:="MyUserForm"
```

Type defines the type of object you copy. To improve the readability of the code, replace the number 3 with the *pjModules* project constant.

> **i** Notice in the preceding code that the system considers the UserForm as a module. This is because the *Forms* page in the Organizer refers to *Microsoft Project Custom* forms and not to VBA UserForms.

The final code should look like:

```
Public Sub CopyToGlobal()
    Application.DisplayAlerts = False
    OrganizerMoveItem Type:=pjModules, FileName:="Module 18 Sample Code.mpp", _
        ToFileName:="Global.MPT", Name:="TaskTaskDriversCode"
    OrganizerMoveItem Type:=pjModules, FileName:="Module 18 Sample Code.mpp", _
        ToFileName:="Global.MPT", Name:="TaskDriveResults"
    Application.DisplayAlerts = True
End Sub
```

I use the *DisplayAlerts* command to stop warning message displays in Project. If the module already exists in the Global.mpt file, then Microsoft Project displays a warning dialog. If I set the *DisplayAlerts* command to *False*, then these warning dialogs do not appear.

> **X** **Warning:** You must reset *DisplayAlerts* to *True* at the end of the macro so that the user continues to get normal warnings while working in Microsoft Project.

> **X** **Warning:** You cannot copy code automatically to the *ThisProject* file in the Global.mpt file or any other project. This is a recent security feature. You must manually copy your event code into the *ThisProject* file.

Keep the *CopyToGlobal* code in the main module or even a separate module because we do not need this code in the Global.mpt. In Module 11 Sample Code.mpp, the above code is in the *CopyGlobalCode* module.

Adding the CopyToGlobal Toolbar Button

To make it easy for your users to access your macro, add a button to the *My Macros* toolbar to give them something to click to perform the copying. I added the following code to the *AddToolbar* procedure in the *ToolbarCode* module in the Module 11 Sample Code.mpp file:

```
Set MyButton = Nothing
   Set MyButton = MyBar.Controls("Copy To Global")
   If MyButton Is Nothing Then
      Set MyButton = MyBar.Controls.Add( _
         Type:=msoControlButton)
      With MyButton
         .Style = msoButtonCaption
         .Caption = "Copy To Global"
         .OnAction = "Macro ""CopyToGlobal"""
      End With
   End If
```

This code must be in the macro file as only the macro project and not the Global.mpt file needs it. The *Set MyButton = Nothing* statement is the first statement so that if the *Set MyButton = MyBar.Controls("Copy To Global")* statement fails because the button does not exist, then *MyButton* equals *Nothing*. Otherwise it continues to point to the first button which the system does not detect and creates the missing button. The toolbar for the macro project should look like Figure 11 - 1 in Project 2010 and Project 2007 and earlier. You now have an easy way to distribute macros in a project file to other Microsoft Project Users.

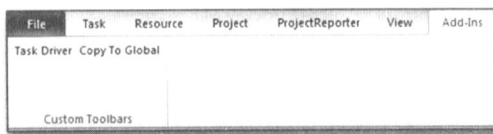

Figure 11 - 1: My Macros Toolbar in Project 2010 and Project 2007 or earlier.

Adding a Macro Command to the Ribbon

Project 2010 replaces menus with a ribbon. Using VBA you can programmatically add a new tab with buttons to run your macros. However, because Project 2010 has a binary file format (unlike the new text-based formats for Office 2007 onwards) you have to use the *SetCustomUI* method instead of the methods used by Excel and Word 2007 onwards. Follow these steps to add a new tab and button to run the *TaskDriverMain* macro:

1. The *SetCustomUI* method requires a .xml string. If you are not familiar with xml, then get hold of an XML editor to ensure your structure is correct. Here is a sample xml file to call the *TaskDriverMain* macros.

```
<mso:customUI xmlns:
   mso="http:="//schemas.microsoft.com/office/2009/07/customui">
   <mso:ribbon>
      <mso:qat/>
      <mso:tabs>
         <mso:tab id="TaskDriver" label="Task Driver="
            insertBeforeQ="mso:TabFormat">
            <mso:button id="TaskDriver"
               label="Show what is driving the selected Task"
               onAction="TaskDriverMain="/>
         </mso:tab>
      </mso:tabs>
   </mso:ribbon>
</mso:customUI>
```

2. To make the custom ribbon tab appear in all projects, open the VBE and in Project Explorer (press **Ctrl+R** to show it) and double-click the *ThisProject* file in the Global.mpt folder.

3. Add the following code:

```
Private Sub Project_BeforeClose(ByVal pj As Project)
    DeleteCustomTab
End Sub

Private Sub Project_Open(ByVal pj As Project)
    CreateCustomTab
End Sub
```

4. Add the following code to a new module:

```
Sub CreateCustomTab()
Dim strXML As String
  strXML = "<mso:customUI xmlns:mso=""http://schemas.microsoft.com" _
            & "/office/2009/07/customui"">"
  strXML = strXML & "<mso:ribbon>"
  strXML = strXML & "<mso:tabs>"
  strXML = strXML & "    <mso:tab id=""TaskDriverTab"" label=" _
            & """Task Driver"" insertBeforeQ=""mso:TabFormat"">"
  strXML = strXML & "    <mso:group id=""VBAGroup"" label=" _
            & """VBA Macros"" autoScale=""true"">"
  strXML = strXML & "    <mso:button id=""TaskDriver"" label=" _
            & """Show what is driving the selected Task"" " _
            & "onAction=""TaskDriverMain""/>"
  strXML = strXML & "    </mso:group>"
  strXML = strXML & "    </mso:tab>"
  strXML = strXML & "</mso:tabs>"
  strXML = strXML & "</mso:ribbon>"
  strXML = strXML & "</mso:customUI>"
  ActiveProject.SetCustomUI (strXML)
End Sub
```

```
Sub DeleteCustomTab()
Dim strXML As String
  strXML = "<mso:customUI xmlns:mso=""http://schemas.microsoft.com" _
           & "/office/2009/07/customui"">"
  strXML = strXML & "<mso:ribbon></mso:ribbon></mso:customUI>"
  ActiveProject.SetCustomUI (strXML)
End Sub
```

First, I explain the pure XML code. You can copy the sample code and edit it to fit your needs. There are also an increasing number of articles on XML for Office ribbons, so please search for the latest information on the Internet. The XML header defines the reference for the structure of the XML code. After that there is a hierarchy made up of the ribbon, tab, and one or more groups with one or more buttons in a group.

To use the XML code in your macro, you must convert it to a single string so you can pass it to the *SetCustomUI* method. The *CreateCustomTab* sub does just that. I have split lines to fit the narrow width of this page. Notice that in the XML code there are a number of double-quotes ("). A double-quote denotes the beginning or end of a string, so to enter a double-quote within a string you need to have two double-quotes. So, wherever you see two double-quotes together in the code above, the end result is one double-quote in the final string. I have also tried to maintain the XML code indenting for readability and debugging purposes.

The *ActiveProject.SetCustomUI (strXML)* code takes the XML string and adds your custom buttons to the active project. Passing an XML string with an empty ribbon code will remove all custom tabs. The *Custom* tab looks something like Figure 11 - 2.

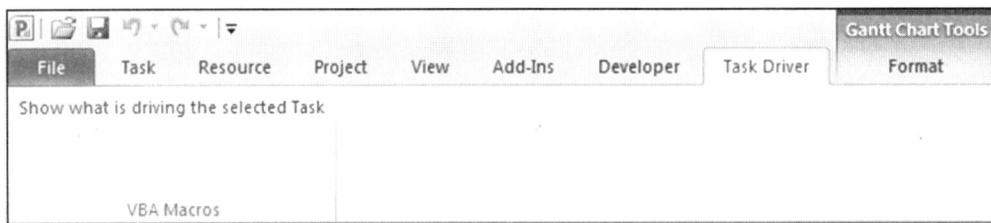

Figure 11 - 2: A Custom tab in Project 2010

Editing the Global.mpt Code to Create a Global Macros Toolbar

The final step is to transfer the *Task Drivers* macro to the Global.mpt file, edit the *Toolbar* code in the Global.mpt file, and edit the *Project Open* event. This edit creates a new *Global Macros* toolbar. I created a *GlobalToolbarCode* module with this code in the following code sample:

```
Sub AddToolbar()
Dim MyBar As CommandBar
Dim MyButton As CommandBarButton
    On Error Resume Next
    Set MyBar = CommandBars("Global Macros")
    If MyBar Is Nothing Then
       Set MyBar = CommandBars.Add( _
            Name:="Global Macros", Position:=msoBarFloating, Temporary:=True)
       MyBar.Visible = True
    End If
```

```
      Set MyButton = MyBar.Controls("Task Driver")
      If MyButton Is Nothing Then
         Set MyButton = MyBar.Controls.Add(Type:=msoControlButton)
         With MyButton
            .Style = msoButtonCaption
            .Caption = "Task Driver"
            .OnAction = "Macro ""TaskDriversMain"""
         End With
      End If
   End Sub


   Sub DeleteBar()
      On Error Resume Next
      CommandBars("Global Macros").Delete
   End Sub
```

The only difference is the name of the toolbar. The *DeleteBar* command is not needed anymore (the toolbar displays permanently), but I left it just in case I need it in the future. The *Project Open* event in the *ThisProject* statement in the Global.mpt file is as follows:

```
Private Sub Project_Open(ByVal pj As Project)
   ViewApply "Gantt Chart"
   EditGoTo Date:=Date
   AddToolbar
End Sub
```

The *EditGoto* statement automatically moves the timescale to today's date. Adding more macros requires extra code in the *GlobalToolBar* module.

Hands On Exercise

Exercise 11-1

Automate the transfer of macros to the Global.mpt file.

1. Get the *Copy* code to work on your system.

2. If you have a macro of your own in a separate .mpp file, add code to automate its copying to the Global.mpt file and get it to work.

Module 12

Working with Time Phased Data

Learning Objectives

After completing this module, you will be able to:

- Understand how the system handles time phased data
- Read and write time phased data
- Create a macro to read time phased data for an S-Curve graph and write it to a .csv file

Inside Module 12

Understanding Time Phased Data

Time phased data is the information you see in Microsoft Project on the right side of the *Task* and *Resource Usage* views. Rather than just a single value for the task, the system accounts for the hours or costs by time period so you can look at a particular week, day or hour and find out the amount of work for that period. Using Project VBA, you can read and write time phased data in exactly the same way you can do it manually in either of these *Usage* views. Once you can handle time phased data programmatically, you can update projects with data from timesheet systems and create all sorts of time-based reports.

Project VBA handles time phased data using the *TimeScaleValue* object. A *TimeScaleValue* object holds data for a particular time slice in your schedule, which is the same as a particular cell in a *Usage* view. A *TimeScaleValues* collection is a collection of *TimeScaleValue* objects; and, therefore, holds time phased data for a specified date and time range. You fill *TimeScaleValues* collections using the *TimeScaleData* method.

> In Project 98, the *TimeScaleData* method was called *TimeScaledData*. This can still be used for backwards compatibility, but for future compatibility, you should only use the *TimeScaleData* syntax.

The *TimeScaleData* method is available for:

- Tasks

- Resources

- Assignments

- Any time scaled data (such as Work, Cost etc. available in a usage view)

- Any date and time range

- Any time units available in Project (hours, days, weeks etc.).

When providing dates for the *TimeScaleData* method, Project VBA rounds them up to a whole time unit. For example, if you specify a weekly time interval, but provide a start date halfway through a week, the system returns the value for the whole week.

Therefore, if you want only the last 3 days of a week to start your date range, you either need to use daily intervals and subtotal daily values into weeks or create two separate *TimeScaleData* calls, one for the first three days and the other for the rest of the time frame in weeks.

Reading Time Phased Data

The sample code below reads data for a particular task and resource for every day of the project by day:

```
Sub TimePhasedDataTest()
Dim tsv As TimeScaleValue
Dim tsvs As TimeScaleValues
    'Time Phased for Task data for whole project 1
    Set tsvs = ActiveProject ProjectSummaryTask.TimeScaleData( _
        StartDate:=ActiveProject.ProjectStart, _
        EndDate:=ActiveProject.ProjectFinish, Type:=pjTaskTimescaledWork, _
        TimeScaleUnit:=pjTimescaleDays, Count:=1)
    For Each tsv In tsvs
        Debug.Print "Start: " & Format(tsv.StartDate, _
            "Long Date"), "Work: " & Val(tsv.Value) / 60 & "h"
    Next tsv
    Debug.Print   'Blank line

    'Time Phased for Resource "Res"
    Set tsvs = ActiveProject.Resources("Res").TimeScaleData( _
        StartDate:=ActiveProject.ProjectStart, _
        EndDate:=ActiveProject.ProjectFinish, Type:=pjResourceTimescaledWork, _
        TimeScaleUnit:=pjTimescaleDays, Count:=1)
    For Each tsv In tsvs
        Debug.Print "Start: " & Format(tsv.StartDate, "Long Date"), _
            "Work: " & Val(tsv.Value) / 60 & "h"
    Next tsv
End Sub
```

The line continuations make the preceding code 8 lines longer than it needs to be, so this sample code is actually quite compact. I wrote the code in two blocks, one to read *Task* data the other to read *Resource* data. I defined two variables named *tsv* and *tsvs*. As a good naming convention always name collections of variables with a plural name such as *tsvs*. The *tsv* object is, therefore, a single object, not a collection of objects.

The *Set tsvs = ActiveProject.ProjectSummaryTask.TimeScaleData* collection creates the time scale collection of time scale objects based on the project summary task. As parameters for the method, I use the *Start* and *Finish* dates of the project. With two tasks in a test project, each with a duration of *5d*, linked with a *Finish to Start* dependency, and with the same resource assigned on each task at *50%* units, the schedule looks like Figure 12 - 1.

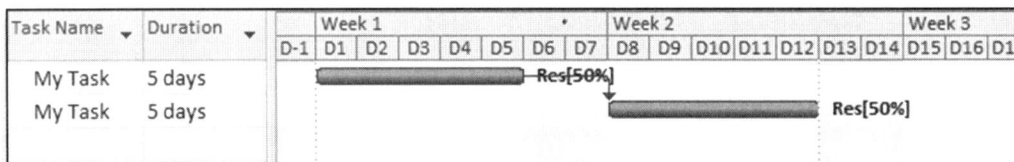

Figure 12 - 1: Test schedule

The *Resource* and *Task Usage* views both show a total of 4 hours per day for the entire 2 weeks of the project. The *TimePhasedDataTest* procedure prints first the *Task* data, then the *Resource* data to the *Immediate* window with the following results (assuming a start date of 1-Mar-2010):

```
Start: Monday, 1 March 2010        Work: 4h
Start: Tuesday, 2 March 2010       Work: 4h
Start: Wednesday, 3 March 2010     Work: 4h
Start: Thursday, 4 March 2010      Work: 4h
Start: Friday, 5 March 2010        Work: 4h
Start: Saturday, 6 March 2010      Work: 0h
Start: Sunday, 7 March 2010        Work: 0h
Start: Monday, 8 March 2010        Work: 4h
Start: Tuesday, 9 March 2010       Work: 4h
Start: Wednesday, 10 March 2010    Work: 4h
Start: Thursday, 11 March 2010     Work: 4h
Start: Friday, 12 March 2010       Work: 4h

Start: Monday, 1 March 2010        Work: 4h
Start: Tuesday, 2 March 2010       Work: 4h
Start: Wednesday, 3 March 2010     Work: 4h
Start: Thursday, 4 March 2010      Work: 4h
Start: Friday, 5 March 2010        Work: 4h
Start: Saturday, 6 March 2010      Work: 0h
Start: Sunday, 7 March 2010        Work: 0h
Start: Monday, 8 March 2010        Work: 4h
Start: Tuesday, 9 March 2010       Work: 4h
Start: Wednesday, 10 March 2010    Work: 4h
Start: Thursday, 11 March 2010     Work: 4h
Start: Friday, 12 March 2010       Work: 4h
```

In the preceding result, notice the 0h for Saturday and Sunday. Note that I use the *ActiveProject.ProjectSummaryTask* collection which is the same as using row zero in the schedule. I could have used the *ActiveProject.Tasks(0)* collection and got the same result.

When entering the *Type* and *TimeScaleUnit* parameters, IntelliSense displays a complete list of all options; so it is easy to select the one you want and get it right the first time. Note that the type for the *Task* block is *pj**Task**TimescaledWork* while the type for the *Resource* block is *pj**Resource**TimescaledWork*.

A common issue with using time scaled values is that if a time scale range is greater than the relevant date range for the source *Task, Resource,* or *Assignment* object, then the *tsv.Value* statement returns an empty string (""). The *Val(tsv.Value)* statement converts the empty string to a zero which is much more useful. Timescale value properties always return work in *minutes*, so dividing by 60 gives you *hours* of work. Further dividing by the *ActiveProject.HoursPerDay* statement gives the result in *days* if wanted.

Exporting Time Phased Data into a .csv file

In this module, you learn how to export Time Phased Data to a .csv file. In Module 14 you export it to Excel and produce the data for an S-Curve graph. Figure 12 - 2 shows a sample S-Curve.

In Figure 12 - 2, if today is week 18 then the project is clearly behind schedule. In fact, it looks like there was no work done for 2 weeks (flat line on the *Work* graph around week 17). The schedule also shows greatly increased hours per week (the line is steeper) from week 19 onwards and that progress should catch up with the baseline around week 21. The project schedule is finishing 2 weeks late and with more work than predicted.

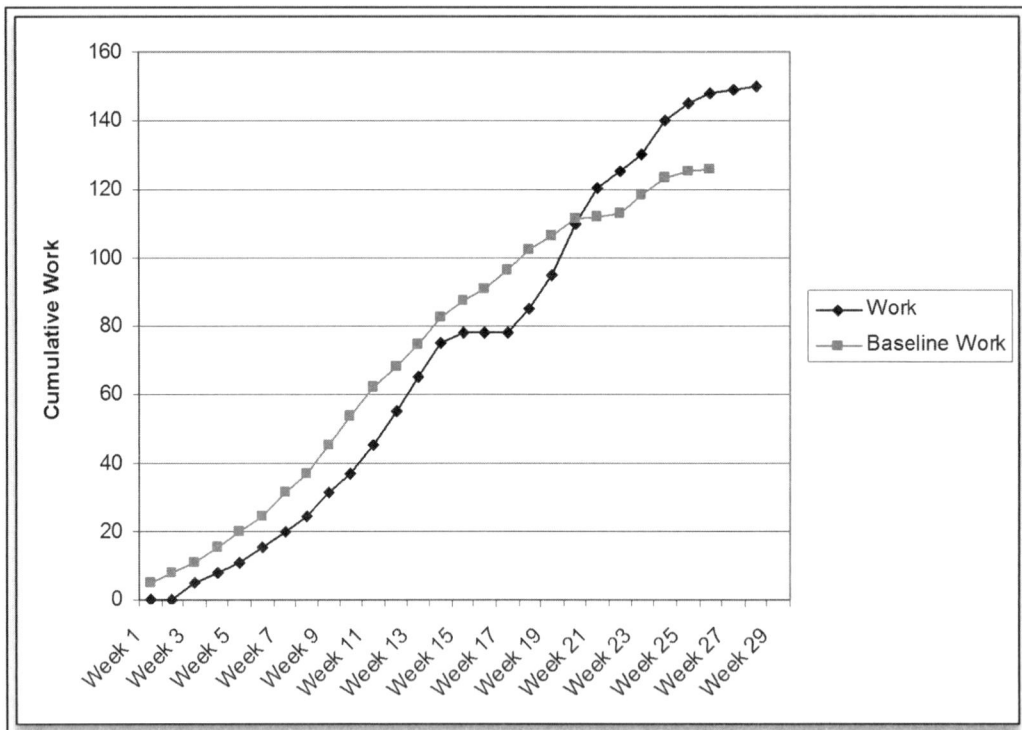

Figure 12 - 2: A sample S-Curve report

An S-Curve graph is a graph of the cumulative *Work* or *Cost* compared against the cumulative *Baseline Work* or *Baseline Cost*. You can graph various *Earned Value* variables as well, but we traditionally use cumulative *Cost* and *Work*. The result is a graph that clearly shows progress against the baseline, with the steepness of the curve indicating hours per week usage (the steeper the curve the more hours per week).

This macro exports the basic data and relies on Excel to calculate and plot cumulative hours. Microsoft Project can provide cumulative *Work* and cumulative *Cost* data, but not cumulative *Baseline Work* or cumulative *Baseline Cost*.

The code for this macro appears in two parts with the first part adding two methods to the *Text* class created in Module 05 of the Basic VBA module available for download from www.projectvbabook.com. The two methods are *FileOpenWrite* and *WriteLine*. The code follows:

```
Sub FileOpenWrite()
    Open prvPath For Output As #1
End Sub

Sub WriteLine(strLine As String)
    Write #1, strLine
End Sub
```

Enter this code into the VBE in the *clsTextFile* class module (see the Project VBA Module 12.mpp file). By clicking on the *Open* and *Write* words then pressing **F1** for Help, you can quickly find out what these VBA commands do.

By reusing and adding to the *Text* class and using the preceding code for time phased data, the macro to export time phased data for a whole project is as follows:

```
Sub SCurveCsvFile()
Dim tsv As TimeScaleValue
Dim tsvs As TimeScaleValues
Dim txt As New clsTextFile
    txt.FilePath = "C:\TimeScaleData Work.csv"
    txt.FileOpenWrite

    Set tsvs = ActiveProject.ProjectSummaryTask. TimeScaleData(StartDate:= _
        ActiveProject.ProjectSummaryTask.Start, _
        EndDate:=ActiveProject.ProjectSummaryTask.Finish, _
        Type:=pjTaskTimescaledWork, TimeScaleUnit:=pjTimescaleWeeks, Count:=1)
    For Each tsv In tsvs
        txt.WriteLine Format(tsv.StartDate, _
            "Medium Date") & ", " & Val(tsv.Value) / 60
    Next tsv

    'Tidy Up
    txt.FileClose
End Sub
```

The preceding code sample includes seven lines of code plus variable declarations and the *Text* class! You can edit the file part of the .csv file to be whatever you want. The *ProjectSummaryTask* property is a *Task* object and can, therefore, return a *TimescaleValues* collection. The code above is for *Work* by week from the project's start to finish. The *txt.WriteLine* statement takes a string as a parameter so your code needs to build the string for the entire row to be saved to the .csv file.

Hands On Exercise

Exercise 12-1

Work with TimeScaleData code.

1. Get the *SCurveCsvFile* code to work by entering the code or using the Module 12 Sample Code.mpp file.

2. Add code to export Baseline Work to *C:\TimeScaleData Baseline Work.csv*.

3. Add code to export Cost and Baseline Cost to two more .csv files.

Writing Time Phased Data

Writing time phased data is slightly more complicated than reading it. If you want to update the timescale values for an assignment that lasts for five days, for example, and you get a *TimeScaleValues* statement for the five days, then you can easily update those five *TimeScale* objects. However, if you have actual data for six days, then a *TimeScaleData* object for day 6 does not exist (the assignment is only 5 days long) and you need to add one day using the *tsvs.Add* method.

That is the extra complication. Provided you make sure you do not try to refer to a *TimeScaleValue* time slice that does not exist, writing time phased data is as easy as reading it. The following code updates every day of *Task1* with 1h for day 1, 2h for day 2 and so on.

```
Sub TimePhasedDataWritetest()
Dim tsv As TimeScaleValue
Dim tsvs As TimeScaleValues
    'Update Task 1 with Actual Data
    With ActiveProject.Tasks(1)
        Set tsvs = .TimeScaleData(StartDate:=.Start, EndDate:=.Finish, _
            Type:=pjTaskTimescaledActualWork, _
            TimeScaleUnit:=pjTimescaleDays, Count:=1)
    End With
    For Each tsv In tsvs
        tsv.Value = 60 * tsv.Index
    Next tsv
End Sub
```

The *With ActiveProject.Tasks(1)* statement avoids specifying *ActiveProject.Tasks(1)* for every parameter, and so makes simpler, easier-to-read code. This code happily assigns *Actual Work* to Saturday and Sunday, but this is only a test, after all. Day 1 will get one hour, day 2 gets two hours and so on.

If you need to extend the task with two extra days of work, then add the following code at the very end of the procedure:

```
tsvs.Add Value:=(tsvs.Count + 1) * 60
tsvs.Add Value:=(tsvs.Count + 1) * 60
```

Remember that the *Work* value must always be in *minutes*.

Hands On Exercise

Exercise 12-2

Write TimeScaleData code.

1. Get the *TimePhasedDataWriteTest* code to work by entering the code or using the Module 19 Sample Code.mpp file. Make sure you have a Task 1 before running the code.

2. Try creating a .csv file with actual values, and then read it into your project and update a task with it. You will need Unique ID's to identify the correct task and match dates in the .csv file with *tsv.Start* dates.

Updating the Project Control Center with Resource Data

In this section, we combine the Project Control Center's Update code created in Module 09 with code to read time phased data for all resources with work in all projects. We do this to get an overall picture of resource usage across all projects. The quality of this information is directly proportional to the accuracy with which you assigned resources to tasks in all projects. If you assigned no resources, no data exists to copy. If you assigned all resources at *100%* units, then you only get an idea of what resources are working on what projects. If you assign resources accurately and realistically on all projects, then you get an accurate picture of total hours of work assigned to all resources across all projects in the Project Control Center.

Before adding functionality to your code, you first need to finish adding the *Task Drivers* code to the Global.mpt file. To do this you need to copy all relevant modules to the Global.mpt file.

Counting the modules created so far, my Project Explorer looks like Figure 12 - 3.

Figure 12 - 3: Current Project Explorer window

Remember that there are no macros shipped with Project 2010 which is why the built-in macros shipped with Project 2007 or earlier are not visible in Figure 12 - 3. If you need to use the 2007 macros, you can copy them from the old Project 2007 Global.mpt to a .mpp file in Project 2007 using the Organizer, then copy from the .mpp file to Project 2010 Global.mpt file using Project 2010.

The *Global Toolbar* code should now contain the following:

```
Sub AddToolbar()
Dim MyBar As CommandBar
Dim MyButton As CommandBarButton
    On Error Resume Next
    Set MyBar = CommandBars("Global Macros")
    If MyBar Is Nothing Then
        Set MyBar = CommandBars.Add(Name:="Global Macros", _
          Position:=msoBarFloating, Temporary:=True)
        MyBar.Visible = True
    End If

    Set MyButton = Nothing
    Set MyButton = MyBar.Controls("Task Driver")
    If MyButton Is Nothing Then
        Set MyButton = MyBar.Controls.Add(Type:=msoControlButton)
        With MyButton
            .Style = msoButtonCaption
            .Caption = "Task Driver"
            .OnAction = "Macro ""TaskDriversMain"""
        End With
    End If
End Sub
```

I explained this code previously in Module 04. You only need to copy macros to the Global.mpt file that you want available to any single project file. The Project Control Center (PCC) macros live in the Project Control Center.mpp file, as they need to work only with the list of projects in that file. Therefore, you can keep PCC macros out of the Global.mpt file to help keep it simpler.

Designing the Get Resource Procedure

To read all resource data from each project you need to do the following:

- Delete any existing resource data from the Project Control Center first.

- Call the procedure to get data after setting the Project Control Center task's duration to the same overall duration as the linked project.

- Loop through all resources in the linked project.

- For each resource, do the following:

    - Confirm that it is not a blank *Resource* row and that it has work (it is assigned to at least one task).

    - Test to see if a resource with the same name already exists in the Project Control Center.

    - If the resource does not exist, add it to the Project Control Center project.

    - Assign the resource to the task in the Project Control Center.

    - Create a timescale collection for the assignment in the linked project for the entire duration of the linked project.

    - For each time slice, add the value for the linked project's resource to the *Project Control Center* assignment.

The complex part of this macro is understanding that you need the timescale data for each resource in each linked project. You copy the weekly value for the total work for the resource into the same time slice for a new assignment in the Project Control Center project. Essentially the task in the Project Control Center will end up with the same total hours per week for each resource as the project summary task of the project it represents.

To understand this code you need to get it working and then look at the results. You can single step through the code to see what happens during each step. Remember that you are not copying every assignment from the linked project, but just the total work for each resource for each week.

The comments for this macro could be as follows:

```
Sub GetResourceUsageData
'Loop through all resources in the Linked Project
'Only copy data if resource is not blank and has Work
'Point to the same resource in the PCC or if it doesn't exist,
    'add it
'Add an assignment for the resource to the task in the PCC
'Create a timescale collection for the assignment and the
    'Resource in the linked project for the whole duration of
    'the linked project
'For each time slice, add the value for the linked project
    'resource to the same time slice in the PCC assignment
End Sub
```

The code for the procedure is:

```
Sub GetResourceUsageData(prjPCC As Project, Tsk As Task, prjLinked As Project)
'This procedure reads all Resource Usage data from the
'linked project to the PCC project.
Dim tsvsPCC As TimeScaleValues
Dim tsvsLinked As TimeScaleValues
Dim tsvLinked As TimeScaleValue
Dim Res As Resource
Dim ResPCC As Resource
Dim A As Assignment
    On Error Resume Next

'Loop through all resources in the Linked Project
    For Each Res In prjLinked.Resources
        'Point to the same Resource in the PCC or
            'if it doesn't exist, add it
        If Not Res Is Nothing Then
            If Res.Work > 0 Then
                'See if Resource exists in PCC already
                Set ResPCC = Nothing
                Set ResPCC = prjPCC.Resources(Res.Name)
                If ResPCC Is Nothing Then
                    Set ResPCC = prjPCC.Resources.Add(Res.Name)
                End If

                'Add an Assignment for the Resource to the Task for
                'the Linked Project in the Project Control Center
                    Set A = Tsk.Assignments.Add(Tsk.ID, ResPCC.ID, 1)

                'Create a timescale collection for the Assignment and the Resource
                'in the linked project for the whole duration of the Linked Project
                    Set tsvsLinked = Res.TimeScaleData(prjLinked.ProjectStart, _
                        prjLinked.ProjectFinish, pjResourceTimescaledWork, _
                        pjTimescaleWeeks)
                    Set tsvsPCC = A.TimeScaleData(Tsk.Start, Tsk.Finish, _
                        pjAssignmentTimescaledWork, pjTimescaleWeeks)

                'For each time slice, add the value for the linked project Resource
                'to the same time slice in the Project Control Center Assignment
                    For Each tsvLinked In tsvsLinked
                        'Add work for current time slot
                        'to the same time slot in the PCC
                        tsvsPCC(tsvLinked.Index).Value = _
                            Val(tsvsPCC(tsvLinked.Index).Value) + Val(tsvLinked.Value)
                    Next tsvLinked
            End If
        End If
    Next Res
End Sub
```

The good news is that explaining this code is about as complex as it gets! There are two *TimeScaleValues* collections, one for each project. The *Project Control Center* collection is for the new assignment of the resource to the task with the linked project's hyperlink. The other collection is for the linked project and will be for the total weekly work for each resource in turn. Both collections must be for the same date range and time units, which in this case is the duration of the project in weeks.

You need to use the *On Error Resume Next* command because you want to trap attempts to point to a resource in the Project Control Center. If the attempt fails, then you know that the resource does not exist, so you can create it with the same name as in the linked project.

```
For Each Res In prjLinked.Resources
    If Not Res Is Nothing Then
        If Res.Work > 0 Then
            'See if Resource exists in PCC already
            Set ResPCC = Nothing
            Set ResPCC = prjPCC.Resources(Res.Name)
            If ResPCC Is Nothing Then
                Set ResPCC = prjPCC.Resources.Add(Res.Name)
            End If
```

The preceding block of code is simple: loop through each resource, testing for blank rows in using exactly the same steps you learned for tasks. You are only interested in copying data for resources that are assigned to a task (Work>0). To test if a resource with the same name already exists in the Project Control Center, first set the *ResPCC Resource Object* variable to *Nothing*. Now assign it to a resource with the same name as the linked project (Res.Name). If the resource already exists, you now have an *Object* variable (ResPCC) pointing to it. If the resource does not already exist, the *ResPCC* variable will still be *Nothing*, so add the resource to the Project Control Center using the *Set ResPCC = prjPCC.Resources.Add(Res.Name)* method. The *Add* method returns the *Resource* object of the newly added resource.

```
Set A = Tsk.Assignments.Add(Tsk.ID, ResPCC.ID, 1)
```

In the preceding code, the *Tsk* variable points to the current task in the Project Control Center for the open linked project. This code adds an assignment of the current resource to it and is ready to add all the time slice values from the resource in the linked project. *A* is an *Assignment Object* variable that points to the new assignment.

```
Set tsvsLinked = Res.TimeScaleData(prjLinked.ProjectStart, _
    prjLinked.ProjectFinish, pjResourceTimescaledWork, pjTimescaleWeeks)
Set tsvsPCC = A.TimeScaleData(Tsk.Start, Tsk.Finish, _
    pjAssignmentTimescaledWork, pjTimescaleWeeks)
```

These two statements create the *TimeScaleValues* collections, one for the new assignment in the Project Control Center and one for the resource in the linked project. Both collections need to be for weekly work and cover the same time period. The *Project Control Center* task updates to the same duration as the linked project earlier in the update code.

```
For Each tsvLinked In tsvsLinked
    If tsvsPCC(tsvLinked.Index).Value <> "" Then
        tsvsPCC(tsvLinked.Index).Value = Val(tsvLinked.Value)
    End If
Next tsvLinked
```

The previous code is the key to the entire procedure. I removed the comments and outdented the code a little to help make it easier to read. For every week, copy the week's value for the **Resource** in the linked project into the same week for the **Assignment** in the Project Control Center.

The result is that all the *Project Control Center* tasks now have an assignment for each resource in the linked project for that task. The *Resource Usage* view in the Project Control Center now shows the total work for all resources across all the projects. This is truly a useful report!

Following is the code I added to the *ReadAllProjectData* procedure:

```
Dim Res As Resource
'Delete any current data such as resources
    For Each Res In ActiveProject.Resources
        Res.Delete
    Next Res
```

We need this code to delete all resources to make room for fresh data. I added the following code as well, just before the *FileClose* statement. The code calls the *Get Data* procedure and passes the current *Project* objects and the current *Task* object (Tsk), so the *ReadAllProjectData* procedure knows what project and task to work with.

```
'Get Resource Usage data
GetResourceUsageData prjPCC, Tsk, prj
```

Hands On Exercise

Exercise 12-3

Work with timescaled Resource data.

1. Get the sample code to work. You will need to add several hyperlinks to tasks so the macro has some projects (with Resource Assignments) to open.

2. Look at the results and single step through the code until you understand the function of the code.

Advanced Challenge: Add code to copy Baseline Work for every week as well.

Module 13

Controlling Excel with Project VBA

Learning Objectives

After completing this module, you will be able to:

- Export data to Excel
- Open Excel templates from Microsoft Project and run a macro in the template
- Control Microsoft Excel from Microsoft Project
- Control Microsoft Project from Microsoft Excel

Inside Module 13

Using Excel for Project Reporting

Microsoft Excel is a fantastic reporting tool for project data. By creating reports in Excel, you provide a medium in which most people can happily edit, e-mail, or print your reports. Excel, like Microsoft Project, features a full implementation of VBA. However, most people are not aware of how easy it is to control everything in Excel from Project, and how easy it is to control everything in Project from Excel!

VBA automation is the process used to control one program from another. The first section in this module explains automation. The rest of this module, as you should expect by now, creates a number of useful macros and code snippets that you can use in many of your Project and Excel macros.

Understanding VBA Automation

An automation client (any of the Microsoft Office applications) initiates automation by binding an object to an automation server (most Office applications including Project and Excel). There are two techniques to bind to another application; **Early** binding and **Late** binding. *Late* binding occurs when you declare a variable with a type object. The *Object* variable is very flexible (a bit like the *Variant* variable); it can point to any object, including other applications. However, you must be careful to track what an *Object* variable is pointing to, otherwise errors occur. There is no IntelliSense when *Late* binding is used.

Early binding requires you to create a reference to the *Object* library used by the other application, and then use variable types relevant to the other application. For example, in Excel you could use *Range* objects, *Workbooks*, etc. For creating a reference, you get full IntelliSense and the compiler can detect when you try to assign objects like *Workbooks* to Excel ranges. *Early* binding is the better option to use because it prevents a wide range of errors that the compiler catches for you, and makes creating code quicker and easier because of IntelliSense. I show you an example of *Late* binding; but otherwise, all code in this module uses *Early* binding only.

The only disadvantage with *Early* binding is that you need to reset references if you copy your macro to a PC with a different version of Excel or Project.

> **i** When searching Help for information on application automation, use the search text "controlling one application from another".

Using Late Binding

Late binding refers to the idea that you bind your object to the other application as late as possible with no compilation checks. For example, with the *xlApp* variable shown in the following code sample, there is nothing to stop you from assigning the *xlApp* variable to an Excel range, to a Word range, or to any other object. While this might sound useful, it inevitably leads to confusing code and code problems that are difficult to find and fix.

The following code starts a new copy of Excel, displays a message in cell A1 and then leaves Excel open and active when the macro ends.

```
Sub StartExcelLateBinding()
Dim xlApp As Object
    Set xlApp = CreateObject("Excel.Application")
    xlApp.Visible = True
    xlApp.WorkBooks.Add
    xlApp.Range("A1") = "Hello World"
    Set xlApp = Nothing
End Sub
```

With *Late* binding, all variables are the *Object* type. The *CreateObject* type creates an object for the specified application. The *Application* object is the most useful object to bind to as it gives you access to everything (in this example) in Excel.

Applications that you launch with the *CreateObject* function always start hidden (their *Visible* property is set to *False*). To make the application visible to your user, set the *Visible* property to *True*. To add a new workbook and enter a text string into A1, the Excel VBA code would be as follows:

```
Workbooks.Add
Range("A1") = "Hello World"
```

If you try to run the same code in Project, the Project VBA compiler attempts to find a *Workbooks* collection in Project. Obviously, it does not exist so the compilation fails. To make the code work in Project, change it to the following:

```
xlApp.WorkBooks.Add
xlApp.Range("A1") = "Hello World"
```

This makes the compiler happy. When the code runs, it reads the *xlApp* variable and then communicates with the Excel Automation Server (part of Excel). It gets details of the *Workbooks* collection so it can run the *Add* method. You need to use the leading *xlApp* variable with *Early* binding as well.

The *xlApp = Nothing* setting releases the *xlApp* object and the connection between Project and Excel ends. The main advantage of *Late* binding is that it is Excel version independent.

Using Early Binding

Early binding requires you to create a reference to the other application's object library. To create a reference, complete the following steps:

1. In the VBE, click Tools ➢ References.

2. For a reference to Microsoft Excel, select the *Microsoft Excel Object Library XX.0* reference in the list of libraries. Figure 13 - 1 shows that I selected the Excel Library for Excel 2010 (version 14). When you reopen the *References* dialog, all checked references appear at the top of the list.

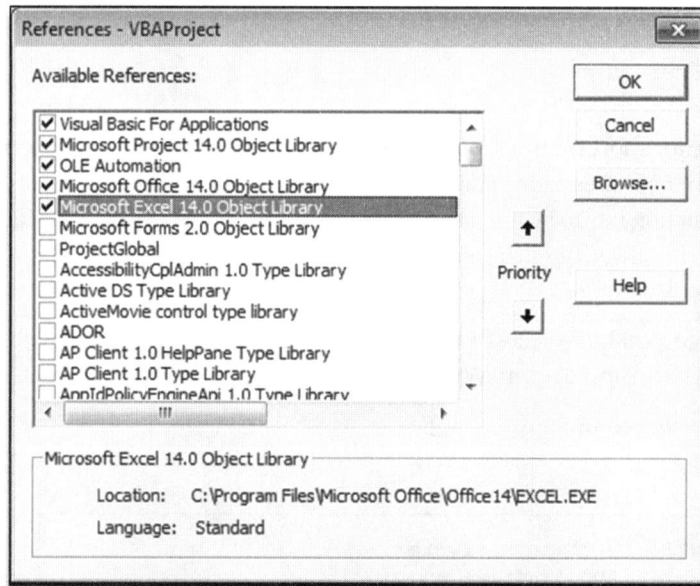

Figure 13 - 1: References dialog with Excel 2010 Library selected

Following is the same example used for *Late* binding, but converted to *Early* binding:

```
Sub StartExcelEarlyBinding()
Dim xlApp As Excel.Application
    Set xlApp = CreateObject("Excel.Application")
    xlApp.Visible = True
    xlApp.WorkBooks.Add
    xlApp.Range("A1") = "Hello World"
    Set xlApp = Nothing
End Sub
```

Project 2000 and later supports a different way of creating a new object:

```
Sub StartExcelEarlyBinding2()
Dim xlApp As Excel.Application
    Set xlApp = New Excel.Application
    xlApp.Visible = True
    xlApp.WorkBooks.Add
    xlApp.Range("A1") = "Hello World"
    Set xlApp = Nothing
End Sub
```

157

The *New* keyword creates a new instance, just as the *CreateObject* function does. In fact, I can further simplify the first two lines of code to:

```
Dim xlApp As New Excel.Application
```

This final simplification is fine for short routines, but for more major development, the intermediate version runs faster as there is an overhead with the last version. The *New* keyword does not work with *Late* binding as an object can be anything; so a *CreateObject* function has to be used to accept the program in an Excel.Application so VBA knows what type of object to create. There are three big differences between the *Late* binding and *Early* binding code samples:

1. By creating a reference, you have access to all of Excel's variable object types. The *Excel.Application* variable type is effectively the Excel application. With it, you can access all of Excel's objects, methods, and properties.

2. IntelliSense works, as shown in Figure 13 - 2.

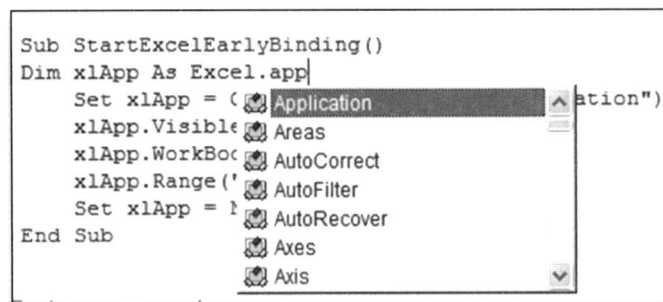

Figure 13 - 2: IntelliSense works with early binding

3. You can click on any Excel object, method, or property and then press **F1** for Help, taking you directly to the relevant Excel VBA Help.

Having both IntelliSense and Excel VBA Help available makes it much easier for you to develop your macros, especially when you are learning. With *Object* variables there is no IntelliSense; you have to know in advance the correct object, method, or property name and spelling. In addition, with *Early* binding, since the *xlApp* variable is an *Excel.Application* type, you cannot use the *xlApp* variable for anything other than pointing to Excel applications. If you do, the compiler flags a warning. This prevents many type-conversion errors when you run your code aiding faster development.

A disadvantage of *Early* binding is that the reference is dependent on a specific version of the referenced application. As explained in Module 06 (in Learning VBA ebook), references will automatically update when you upgrade to new versions, but if you send a macro to someone with an earlier version of the application than the one you referenced, the references will not update and compilation fails with an error.

If you do use *Late* binding because of version problems, it is often quicker to write your code with *Early* binding and then convert to *Late* binding with *Object* variables once the code is working.

All of the following code samples assume you have a reference set to the Excel Object Library. Any version of Excel will work starting with Excel 95.

Changing Security to enable Office Automation

Microsoft has added extra security to stop one program controlling another by default. In the application to be controlled (in the case below Project VBA controls Excel, so in Excel):

1. Click the Microsoft Office button, and then click *Options*.

2. Click the *Trust Center* tab, and then click *Trust Center Settings*.

3. Click the *Macro Settings* tab, click to select the *Trust access to the VBA project object model* check box, and then click the *OK* button.

4. Click the *OK* button.

If you want Excel to control Project, carry out the instructions above in Project as well. There is a Microsoft support article about this, see: http://msproj.com/1001

Using VBA to add a Reference to Excel

Each reference has a GUID (a unique 36 character string), a major and a minor version number. To add a reference using code, you need to know these values. To determine these values for Excel:

1. Open the VBE (remember **Alt+F11** is the shortcut).

2. Open the *Immediate* window by pressing **Ctrl+G**.

3. In the *Immediate* window enter *?activeproject.VBProject.References("Excel").Guid* then press **Enter** on your computer keyboard. The software then displays the GUID for you.

4. Enter *?ActiveProject.VBProject.References("Excel").Major* and press **Enter** on your computer keyboard to get the major version number.

5. Enter *? ActiveProject.VBProject.References("Excel").Minor* and press **Enter** on your computer keyboard to get the minor version number.

The *Immediate* window should then look like Figure 13 - 3.

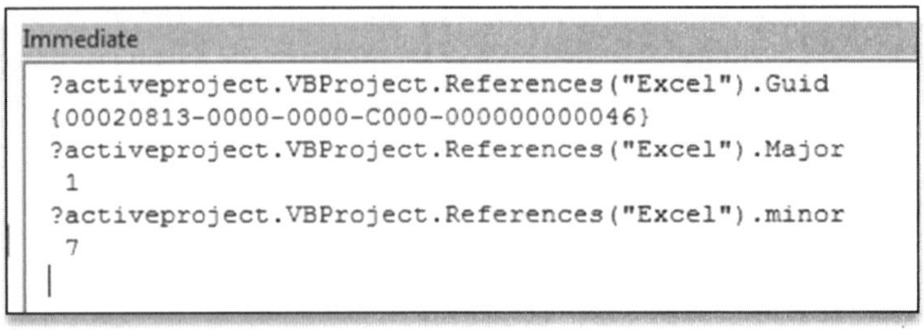

Figure 13 - 3: The Immediate window showing version values for Excel 2010

Once you confirm these values, then you are ready to write some code. First though, I need to explain how to handle the possibility that any version of Excel might be installed, and possibly more than one. Ideally the reference should be to the newest version, so your code should start by trying to create a reference to Excel 2010 then work down to 2003 or even earlier. If you have not installed Excel 2010, the *Add* method generates an error and the code loops to try the next earlier version.

```
Sub AddReferenceToExcel()
Dim Major As Long
Dim Minor As Long
    On Error Resume Next
    Major = 1
    With ActiveProject.VBProject.References
        .Remove .Item("Excel")
        Major = 1
        For Minor = 7 To 5 Step -1
            Err.Clear
            .AddFromGuid "{00020813-0000-0000-C000-000000000046}", Major, Minor
            If Err.Number = 0 Then
                Exit For        'No error, so reference set
            End If
        Next Minor
    End With
End Sub
```

Note that if there is no error, the code exits the *For* loop with a reference set for the newest version. You can do the same exercise for Microsoft Word: use Word instead of Excel and for Project when writing code in Excel VBA but use MSProject.

Taking Advantage of Early and Late Binding

There is a way to benefit from both worlds by using *Early* binding when developing and testing to benefit from Intellisense, syntax checking and named constants and using *Late* binding when you release code to users so it is version independent. To do this I take advantage of a VBA language feature called *conditional compiling*. This next code sample shows how *conditional compiling* works:

```
#Const Coding = True

Sub ConditionalCompilingExample()
#If Coding Then
    Dim xlApp As Excel.Application
#Else
    Dim xlApp As Object
#End If
    Set xlApp = CreateObject("Excel.Application")
    xlApp.Visible = True
    xlApp.WorkBooks.Add
    xlApp.Range("A1") = "Hello World"
    Set xlApp = Nothing
End Sub
```

If the *Coding* constant is *True*, then we use *Early* binding, otherwise we use *Late* binding. We now have the best of both worlds, just by setting the value of one constant.

If you use an Excel constant in Project VBA, then once we turn on *Late* binding, those *xl* constants will no longer compile. Instead you need to create new constants in Project VBA. For example, the code to left align the active cell in Excel is:

```
ActiveCell.HorizontalAlignment = xlHAlignLeft
```

This needs re-coding as:

```
#If Coding Then
    xlApp.ActiveCell.HorizontalAlignment = xlHAlignLeft
#Else
    Const xlHAlignLeft = -4131
    xlApp.ActiveCell.HorizontalAlignment = xlHAlignLeft
#End If
```

By typing *? xlHAlignLeft* then pressing **Enter** on your computer keyboard in the Excel *Immediate* window, I learned that the *xlHAlignLeft* code has the value *-4131*. With *Late* binding we have to manually create the *xl* constants.

Connecting to an Already Open Copy of Excel

If the program supports it, your code runs more reliably if you start a new copy of the application to which you wish to bind. However, not all applications support multiple copies running at the same time. Excel happily runs multiple versions of itself, but Microsoft Project does not. If Excel is already open with information your macro needs, opening a fresh copy of Excel is unnecessary. To connect to an already active copy of Excel use the following VBA code:

```
Sub ConnectToExistingExcelApplication()
Dim xlApp As Excel.Application
   On Error Resume Next
   Set xlApp = GetObject(, "Excel.Application")
   If xlApp Is Nothing Then
       MsgBox "Failed to connect to Excel, macro ended"
   Else
       MsgBox "Connected to existing Excel Application"
   End If
   xlApp.Visible = True

'Tidy up
   xlApp.UserControl = True
   Set xlApp = Nothing
End Sub
```

If you attempt to connect to Excel and a copy of Excel is not running, then a run time error occurs. That is why you need the *On Error Resume Next* statement, so you can test for a successful binding after attempting to connect using the *GetObject* function. Note also that the *GetObject* function has two parameters. Typically you do not need the first parameter, hence the leading comma.

If the *xlApp* value *is Nothing* the test returns *True*, then no copy of Excel is running. If you still need Excel, then go ahead and create one with the *CreateObject* function or the *New* keyword.

The other new code worth noting is the *xlApp.UserControl = True* code. Without it, if nothing was done with Excel, setting the *xlApp* value to *Nothing* also closes Excel. By using the *xlApp.UserControl = True* code Excel assumes it is under user control and does not close Excel when your Project macro sets the *xlApp* value to *Nothing*.

I use all the lines in the code above in all my macros controlling Excel and have had no problem using versions of Project 98 or later, and using Excel 95 or later. Call me lucky, but my experience is that each new version of Project and Excel has been backwards compatible. In fact, I still have a number of old Project 98 macros that currently run unchanged in Project 2003. As noted elsewhere, Project 2010 VBA has introduced some errors, but the first Cumulative Update (CU) has fixed them. Overall, VBA has proved to be robust and supports all versions of Project and Excel, so good job Microsoft!

> If you try to use a feature in an older version of Project or Excel introduced in a later version, then it will not work. Any feature that exists in all versions almost always works unchanged in VBA for any version.

Exporting a List of Resources to Excel

The macro on which you are about to work exports a list of all resources in the active Project to Excel. This is a precursor to the *WhoDoesWhatWhen* macro, which exports to Excel all tasks and all resources in all projects in the Project Control Center.

The goal is simple: export a list of resources to Excel. Following is a set of comments to describe the macro deliverables:

```
Sub ExportResourceNames()
'Start Excel and create a new Workbook
'Create Column Titles
'Export Resource Names and the Project Title
'Tidy up
Exit Sub
```

Below is the code to complete this macro. Much of it involves formatting Excel cells. Because this is not a book on Excel VBA, I recommend that you study the Excel VBA Help articles for information about Excel objects, methods, and properties. I also recommend that you single step through the code to see what happens with each statement. Developing Excel VBA code is easier when you know Excel well; just as developing Project VBA is easier when you know Project well.

```
Sub ExportResourceNames()
Dim xlApp As Excel.Application
Dim xlRange As Excel.Range
Dim Res As Resource

'Start Excel and create a new Workbook
    Set xlApp = CreateObject("Excel.Application")
    xlApp.Visible = True
    xlApp.WorkBooks.Add

'Create Column Titles
    Set xlRange = xlApp.Range("A1")
    With xlRange
        .Formula = "Who Does What When Report"
        .Font.Bold = True
        .Font.Size = 14
        .EntireColumn.ColumnWidth = 30
    End With
    With xlRange.Range("A2")
        .Formula = "As of: " & Format(Date, "mmm d yyyy")
        .Font.Bold = True
        .Font.Italic = True
        .Font.Size = 12
        .Select
    End With

    xlRange.Range("A4") = "Resource Name"
    xlRange.Range("B4") = "Project Title"
    With xlRange.Range("A4:B4")
        .Font.Bold = True
        .HorizontalAlignment = xlHAlignCenter
        .VerticalAlignment = xlVAlignCenter
    End With
```

```
'Export Resource Names and the Project Title
   Set xlRange = xlRange.Range("A5")
   For Each Res In ActiveProject.Resources
       If Not Res Is Nothing Then
          With xlRange
              .Range("A1") = Res.Name
              .Range("B1") = ActiveProject.Name
          End With
       End If
       Set xlRange = xlRange.Offset(1, 0)      'Point to next row
   Next Res

'Tidy up
   xlRange.Range("B1").EntireColumn.AutoFit
   Set xlApp = Nothing
End Sub
```

Although I call the preceding macro *WhoDoesWhatWhen*, this is only the first code writing iteration, so I export only resource information to Excel. The key to understanding Excel VBA is to learn how to use the Excel *Range* object. Search through Excel VBA Help for information about the *Range* object and then experiment with using it in Excel VBA. Excel VBA code is easy to move to Project; you simply need an Excel *Application* object preceding the code or an Excel variable (like the *xlRange* variable in the code above) that you specify using an Excel *Application* object, as in *Excel.Range*.

Running Excel VBA Code Using Project VBA

One way of organizing a larger macro is to use Project VBA to open an Excel template or a copy of an existing Excel workbook, to export data to Excel, and then run a macro in the Excel file to do all the report formatting. One advantage of this method is that your worksheets can already include formatting and any needed formulas, reducing the amount of code you need to write in your macro.

To open a copy of an Excel template and run a macro in the template (assuming the *xlApp* function already points to an open copy of Excel), use the following code:

```
xlApp.Workbooks.Add "MyTemplate.xlt"
xlapp.Run "MacroNameInTemplate", OptionalArgument
```

The template name can include a full path and you can specify up to 30 arguments or parameters for the macro. The system returns control to your Project VBA macro after the Excel VBA macro completes.

Controlling Microsoft Project from Excel

Suppose you have VBA code in an Excel file with which you want to open a Microsoft Project file and then read and write some data. Although you can use *Late* binding in Excel to control Microsoft Project you should use *Early* binding instead. *Early* binding provides a quicker development environment and through Intellisense makes all Project's objects, methods and properties visible in Excel. To set up a reference to Microsoft Project from Excel, use the following code:

1. In Excel's VBE, click Tools ➢ References

2. Select the *Microsoft Project Object Library* option from the list of libraries as shown in Figure 13 - 4.

3. Click the *OK* button.

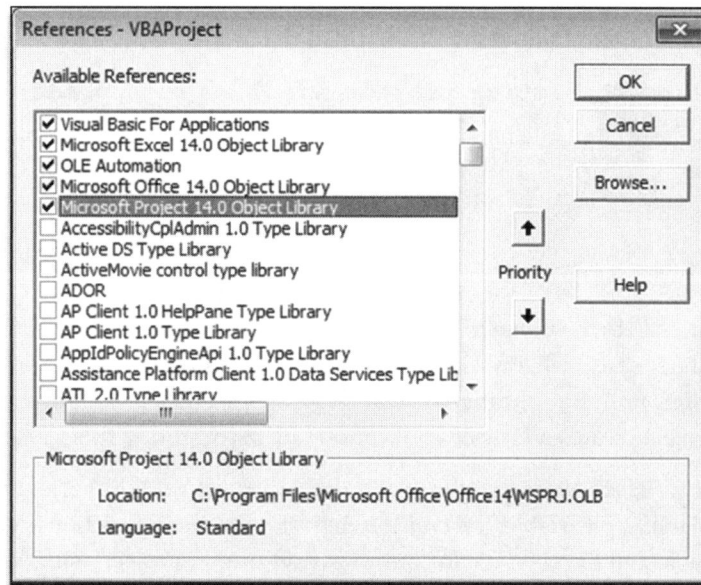

Figure 13 - 4: References dialog in Excel

The code to add a reference to Project from Excel is:

```
Sub AddReferenceToProject()
Dim Major As Long
Dim Minor As Long
    On Error Resume Next
    Major = 1
    For Minor = 7 To 5 Step -1
        Err.Clear
        ActiveWorkbook.VBProject.References.AddFromGuid _
            "{A7107640-94DF-1068-855E-00DD01075445}", Major, Minor
        If Err.Number = 0 Then
            Exit For         'No error, so reference set
        End If
    Next Minor
End Sub
```

Note that the only difference to the code that creates a reference to Excel is the GUID.

Microsoft Project allows only a single running version of itself, so you must test for an already running version of the software with the *GetObject* function before launching a new copy. The code to do this follows:

```
Sub AutomateProjectFromExcel()
Dim projApp As MSProject.Application
    On Error Resume Next
    Set projApp = GetObject(, "MSProject.Application")
    If projApp Is Nothing Then
        Set projApp = New MSProject.Application
    End If

    MsgBox "The name of the active project is: " & projApp.ActiveProject.Name
    projApp.Visible = True

    'Tidy Up
    Set projApp = Nothing
End Sub
```

Do you recognize the similarities with the *ConnectToExistingExcelApplication* macro? MSProject is the key name to remember, as it appears in IntelliSense as well. Project is not a valid object type (in Excel), however, so remember to use MSProject. For example, the *Dim projApp* application in Excel VBA will set the variable to the Excel application. Predefining application with MSProject creates a Project application object (provided there is a reference set to Project).

In the preceding code, the *ActiveProject.Name* function is not valid in Excel VBA, but after creating a reference to Project and defining and setting a *projApp* variable, the *projApp.ActiveProject.Name* function now compiles. Now that you have the Project application object in Excel, you can control everything in Project using VBA from Excel.

Creating the S-Curves Macro in Excel

In Module 12 you learned how to export time phased data to .csv files. I finish the *S-Curve* macro here, but I use Excel rather than .csv files to export the data to. Again, this is not the place to teach Excel VBA, so you need to read Excel VBA Help and single step through the code to understand Excel VBA code better.

The design of this macro is to use graphs, and a data table already existing in an Excel template, to receive the exported Project data, and then run an Excel macro to adjust the graph's data. Use the following code to create the *S-Curve* graph for the active project only. The deliverable comments for this code are as follows:

```
Sub CreateSCurveGraph
'Setup Excel
'Open copy of Template
'Set up Range variable and delete any old data
'Export time phased data based on Project Summary Task
'Call Excel Template Macro
'Tidy up
End Sub
```

The Excel template should include formulas to create the cumulative totals. Although Microsoft Project calculates **cumulative Work** automatically, it does not calculate **cumulative Baseline Work**. Because you need to create cumulative totals for both *Work* values and *Baseline Work* values, it is easy to use formulas to calculate both values. Following is the complete code for the *S-Curve* macro:

```
Sub CreateSCurveGraph()
Dim xlApp As Excel.Application
Dim xlRange As Excel.Range
Dim tsvs As TimeScaleValues
Dim tsv As TimeScaleValue
   On Error Resume Next
   'Setup Excel
   Set xlApp = GetObject(, "Excel.Application")
   If xlApp Is Nothing Then
      Set xlApp = CreateObject("Excel.Application")
   End If
   xlApp.Visible = True

   'Open copy of Template
   xlApp.Workbooks.Add CurDir & "\Module 13 Excel Code S-Curve.xlt"

   'Set up Range variable ready to export
   Set xlRange = xlApp.Range("Start")
   xlRange.CurrentRegion.Offset(3, 0).ClearContents
   xlRange.Range("A2:B3").ClearContents

'Export timed data based on Project Summary Task
   Set tsvs = ActiveProject.ProjectSummaryTask. TimeScaleData( _
         ActiveProject.ProjectStart, ActiveProject.ProjectFinish, _
         pjTaskTimescaledWork, pjTimescaleWeeks)
   For Each tsv In tsvs
      xlRange.Offset(tsv.Index, 0) = tsv.StartDate
      xlRange.Offset(tsv.Index, 1) = Val(tsv.Value) / 60
   Next tsv

   Set tsvs = Nothing
   Set tsvs = ActiveProject.ProjectSummaryTask. TimeScaleData( _
         ActiveProject.ProjectStart, ActiveProject.ProjectFinish, _
         pjTaskTimescaledBaselineWork, pjTimescaleWeeks)
   For Each tsv In tsvs
      xlRange.Offset(tsv.Index, 2) = Val(tsv.Value) / 60
   Next tsv

   'Call Excel Template Macro
   xlApp.Run "SetupGraph"

   'Tidy up
   Set xlApp = Nothing
End Sub
```

Nothing in this code is new to you until you get to the following section:

```
'Set up Range variable ready to export
Set xlRange = xlApp.Range("Start")
xlRange.CurrentRegion.Offset(3, 0).ClearContents
xlRange.Range("A2:B3").ClearContents
```

Excel provides the ability to name cells (refer to Excel Help for complete instructions on how to name cells and ranges). In the sample template, I named cell A4 as *Start*, which provides a known starting cell. Even if I insert two extra rows as headers or titles, the named cell *Start* will move with the data titles row and the code continues to work, because it is all relative to the named cell *Start*. Setting the *xlRange = xlApp.Range("Start")* code sets the *xlRange* variable to point to the named cell *Start* (cell address A4).

The *xlRange.CurrentRegion.Offset(3, 0).ClearContents* code deletes the contents of all cells as if you had pressed **Ctrl+*** in Excel. The *Offset(3,0)* code means that the selected (by CurrentRegion) area is moved down 3 rows so that the deletion does not touch the formulas in cells D5:E6. Therefore, delete cell range A2:B3 separately. Single step through the code to see what happens during each step after you run the macro once to get data into Excel, and there is something for the macro to delete.

All remaining code (except for *xlRange.Offset(tsv.Index, 2) = Val(tsv.Value) / 60)* should be familiar to you by now. If the *xlRange* variable points to cell A4, then for the first time slice *(tsv.Index is 1) xlRange.Offset(tsv.Index,0)*, therefore, points to A5. Offsets always go by row, then column; so the *Offset(1,0)* code is one row down and zero columns to the right. Negative row numbers are rows up and negative columns are columns to the left.

This is a simple piece of code that allows the correct data to go into the correct cell using the *For Each* loop. The first *For Each* loop copies the start date of each week as well as the data. The *xlApp.Run "SetupGraph"* code runs the *SetupGraph* macro in the Excel template.

What about the Excel VBA code? Since this is useful code, following are the *SetupGraph* macro comments for the code.

```
Sub SetUpGraph()
'Get row number of last week and copy formulas down
'Delete all zeroes from bottom for accuracy
'Adjust source data ranges for chart
End Sub
```

In the above comments, the reason we need to delete the zeroes is because S-Curve lines normally stop on the last data point rather than continue in a flat line to the end of the timescale. This code starts from the last row and deletes all zeroes until the first non-zero entry. The effect on the graph is that it shows the date the project finishes and the baseline finish date. Following is the actual Excel VBA code:

```
Sub SetUpGraph()
Dim Row As Long
Dim rStart As Range
Dim R As Range
    Set rStart = Range("Start")

    'Get row of last week and copy formulas down
    Row = rStart.End(xlDown).Row
```

```
      rStart.Range("D3:E" & Row + 1 - rStart.Row).FillDown

      'Delete all zeroes from bottom for accuracy
      Set R = rStart.End(xlDown).Offset(0, 1)
      Do Until R <> 0 Or R.Row <= rStart.Row
          If R = 0 Then
              R.Range("A1,C1").ClearContents
          End If
          Set R = R.Offset(-1, 0)
      Loop
      Set R = rStart.End(xlDown).Offset(0, 2)
      Do Until R <> 0 Or R.Row <= rStart.Row
          If R = 0 Then
              R.Range("A1,C1").ClearContents
          End If
          Set R = R.Offset(-1, 0)
      Loop

      'Adjust source data ranges for chart
      ActiveSheet.ChartObjects(1).Activate
      ActiveChart.SetSourceData Source:=Sheets("SCurve") _
            .Range("A3:A" & Row & ",D3:E" & Row)
      rStart.Select
End Sub
```

All of this code is in the Module 13 Sample Code.xls file. The two macros combine to form the simplest and most efficient solution to creating an S-Curve graph in Excel. For these two macros to work correctly, you need an active project that contains tasks with resources assigned to them so there are *Work* values, and you must save a baseline so there are *Baseline Work* values.

If *Work* and *Cost* values are the same as the *Baseline Work* and *Baseline Cost* values, then you will see only one line. After saving a baseline, edit the schedule so that the *Current* data is different from *Baseline* data. Then the two lines on the graph separate the next time you run the macro.

Hands On Exercise

Exercise 13-1

Automate using Microsoft Excel with Microsoft Project.

1.   In a copy of one of your own project files insert a new module.

2.   In Excel's VBE, click Tools ➤ References.

3.   Select the *Microsoft Excel Object Library* option from the list of libraries shown in Figure 13 – 3.

4.   Click the *OK* button.

5. Edit the *ExportResourceNames* code described earlier to be an *ExportTaskNames* procedure.

6. In Excel add a reference to the Microsoft Project Object Library.

7. Modify the *AutomateProjectFromExcel* procedure described earlier to read all task names with their *Start* and *Finish* dates.

8. Add to the code to format all summary task names in Excel with the **Bold** font style.

Completing the Who Does What When Macro

The goal of the *Who Does What When* macro is to produce a report in Excel to show the tasks assigned to every resource for all projects in the Project Control Center. Up to this point, our macro only exports a simple list of resources to Excel. The three remaining things we must accomplish are:

1. Add a timescale from today forward for 3 months. To keep the report simple, we will limit the timescale from the current week to 13 weeks.

2. Add task assignments for each resource.

3. Make sure your code works for every project in the Project Control Center.

The third item is something you already know how to do. The first two items are more difficult, but simple enough if we break the tasks into logical steps. The comments for these steps are as follows:

```
Sub WhoDoesWhatWhen()
'Setup Excel
'Create Column Titles
'For every Project
'For every Resource
'For every Assignment
'Get weekly work for Assignment from this week for 13 weeks
'Point to top left of report
'Loop through all time slices entering the date
'  along the top of the report for each week
'Copy Resource Name, Project Name, Task ID, and Task Name
'For every time slice where Value<>"" copy hours
'End Assignment, Resource, Project
'Sort by Resource Name, Project, Task ID
'Create Pivot Table: Resource and Task by Project
End Sub
```

Merge these comments with the existing *ReadAllProjectData* macro started earlier in this module. You can use some of the code from the *ReadAllProjectData* procedure, and the finished macro is as follows:

```
Option Explicit

Public Sub WhoDoesWhatWhen()
Dim StartOfWeek As Date
Dim EndOfPeriod As Date
```

```
Dim Tsk As Task
Dim prjPCC As Project
Dim prj As Project
Dim Path As String
Dim Res As Resource
Dim A As Assignment
Dim tsvs As TimeScaleValues
Dim tsv As TimeScaleValue
Dim xlApp As Excel.Application
Dim xlRange As Excel.Range
Dim Off As Long

'Calculate the date for the start of the week.
'    This macro assumes Monday is the start of each week
'    Calculate the date for this Monday
    StartOfWeek = Date - Weekday(Date) + vbMonday
    EndOfPeriod = StartOfWeek + (13 * 7)

'Start Excel
    On Error Resume Next
    'Setup Excel
    Set xlApp = GetObject(, "Excel.Application")
    If xlApp Is Nothing Then
        Set xlApp = CreateObject("Excel.Application")
    End If
    xlApp.Visible = True

'Create Column Titles
    Workbooks.Add
    Set xlRange = xlApp.Range("A1")
    CreateColumnTitles xlRange

'Point to top left of report
    Set xlRange = xlApp.Range("A4")

'Enter the date along the top of the report for each week
    For Off = 0 To 13
        xlRange.Offset(0, 4 + Off) = StartOfWeek + Off * 7
    Next Off
    Set xlRange = xlRange.Offset(1, 0)

'For Each task in the Project Control Center
    Set prjPCC = ActiveProject
    prjPCC.StartWeekOn = pjMonday
    For Each Tsk In prjPCC.Tasks
        If Not Tsk Is Nothing Then 'test for empty tasks

'Extract File path from the Hyperlink
        Path = Tsk.HyperlinkAddress
        Path = Replace(Path, "/", "\")
        Path = Replace(Path, "%20", " ")

'For every Project, open the project file read only with
'no updates from resource pools or external links.
        FileOpen Name:=Path, ReadOnly:=True, _
            noAuto:=True, openpool:=pjDoNotOpenPool
        Set prj = ActiveProject
```

```
'Make sure the project has its week starts on Monday
        prj.StartWeekOn = pjMonday

'For each Resource with work
        For Each Res In prj.Resources
            If Not Res Is Nothing Then

'For every Assignment, if it is in report date range
            For Each A In Res.Assignments
                If A.Start <= EndOfPeriod And A.Finish >= StartOfWeek Then
                    xlRange.Range("A1") = Res.Name
                    xlRange.Range("B1") = prj.Name
                    xlRange.Range("C1") = A.TaskID
                    xlRange.Range("D1") = A.TaskName

'Get weekly work for Assignment from this week for 13 weeks
                    Set tsvs = A.TimeScaleData(StartOfWeek, _
                        StartOfWeek + 13 * 7, pjAssignmentTimescaledWork, _
                        pjTimescaleWeeks)

'Copy Resource Name, Project Name, Task ID, Task Name
'For every time slice where Value<>"" copy hours
                    For Each tsv In tsvs
                        If tsv.Value <> "" Then
                            xlRange.Offset(0, 3 + tsv.Index) = tsv.Value / 60
                        End If
                    Next tsv
                    Set xlRange = xlRange.Offset(1, 0)
                End If

'End Assignment, Resource, Project
            Next A
          End If
        Next Res

   'Close the project and don't save any changes
        prj.Activate   'Make sure project is active
        FileClose pjDoNotSave
      End If  'IF Not Tsk is Nothing

'End of Loop for all projects
   Next Tsk

'Format Report
'Sort by Resource Name, Project, Task ID
   FormatReport xlApp.Range("A4")

'Tidy up
   prjPCC.Activate    'Make sure its active
   Set prjPCC = Nothing
   Set prj = Nothing
   xlApp.Visible = True
End Sub
```

The preceding comments evolved from the first set I described before I wrote the code. This is often what happens, so I left them as is. This code is not difficult to create when tackled in small blocks. If you break your macros into small blocks with meaningful comments describing what the blocks should do, then all you need to do is code each block in turn. Focus your testing and debugging on getting the individual blocks to work, and only then on getting the blocks to work together.

Let me describe what is happening with this code. You have already seen the first part, so the first new code is probably the following:

```
For Off = 0 To 13
    xlRange.Offset(0, 4 + Off) = StartOfWeek + Off * 7
Next Off
Set xlRange = xlRange.Offset(1, 0)
```

The *xlRange* variable is an Excel *Range* variable currently pointing to *A4*. The *Offset* property returns a range offset from the range to its left. So the *xlRange.Offset(0,4)* statement is A4 plus zero rows down plus 4 columns to the right which is E4. *Off* is a *Long* variable. The *For Off= 0 to 13* statement runs the *xlRange.Offset* statement 14 times, and writes 14 values into the 14 cells. The value written is the *Date StartOfWeek* plus 7 times the *Off* variable value. This enters weekly dates for the current week plus 13 more weeks - just what our deliverable describes! Alternatively, you could calculate the number of weeks to the end of the project and use that number instead of 13 weeks (three months).

The *Set xlRange = xlRange.Offset(1, 0)* statement points to the *xlRange* range to the cell one row down, same column. If the *A.Start <= EndOfPeriod And A.Finish >= StartOfWeek Then* statement tests whether the current assignment is at least partly within the report period as defined by the *StartOfWeek* and *EndOfPeriod* variables. This test means that the macro includes only tasks assigned to resources with *Work* in the report's date range which also makes the report more relevant and speeds up execution because it does not create rows with no data.

That is it! You should be familiar with the rest of the code. Note that because the procedure got too long, I broke out the code to create the *Report Titles* into the *CreateColumnTitles* and *FormatReport* procedures. I passed the *Range* object for *A4* to both procedures so they do not need to see or use the *xlApp* object. This avoids making a number of variables global avoiding errors that are hard to find. The code and explanations for the *CreateColumnTitles* procedure is as follows:

```
Sub CreateColumnTitles(xlRange As Excel.Range)
'Create Column Titles
    With xlRange
        .Formula = "Who Does What When Report"
        .Font.Bold = True
        .Font.Size = 14
        .EntireColumn.ColumnWidth = 30
    End With
    With xlRange.Range("A2")
        .Formula = "As of: " & Format(Date, "mmm d yyyy")
        .Font.Bold = True
        .Font.Italic = True
        .Font.Size = 12
        .Select
    End With

    xlRange.Range("A4") = "Resource Name"
    xlRange.Range("B4") = "Project Title"
```

```
      xlRange.Range("C4") = "Task ID"
      xlRange.Range("D4") = "Task Name"
      With xlRange.Range("A4").EntireRow
          .Font.Bold = True
          .HorizontalAlignment = xlHAlignCenter
          .VerticalAlignment = xlVAlignCenter
          .NumberFormat = "mmm d yy"
          .WrapText = True
      End With
      xlRange.Columns("B").ColumnWidth = 20
      xlRange.Columns("D").ColumnWidth = 30
  End Sub
```

When you know Excel VBA, none of the preceding code is difficult to write or understand. You could create most of it by recording a macro in Excel to do the necessary formatting, copying the code to Project, and then adding the *xlRange* or *xlApp* objects in front of any Excel object.

> Why did I export the resource and project names for every assignment? The answer is so that I can use Excel *Pivot* tables on the data to create additional reports. One line for each week and task combination better supports the creation of *Pivot* tables, but the current format is more useful.

Following is the code and explanations for the *FormatReport* procedure:

```
  Sub FormatReport(xlRange As Excel.Range)
  'Does all report formatting including sorting
     xlRange.Columns("D").WrapText = True
     With Range(xlRange.Range("E1"), _
            xlRange.End(xlToRight).Address)
         .Orientation = 45
         .EntireRow.RowHeight = 48
         .EntireColumn.AutoFit
     End With
     xlRange.CurrentRegion.Offset(1, 4).NumberFormat = "#,##0\h"
     xlRange.Sort Key1:=xlRange, Order1:=xlAscending, _
        Key2:=xlRange.Range("B1"), Order2:=xlAscending, _
        Key3:=xlRange.Range("C1"), Order3:=xlAscending, _
        Header:=xlYes
  End Sub
```

The *WrapText* method wraps a long line of text into as many rows as needed within a single cell. With the *xlApp.Range(xlRange.Range("E1"), xlRange.End(xlToRight).Address)* statement it is more difficult to understand. This statement creates a range by specifying a start and end address using the *xlRange* address for flexibility so it changes automatically in the future when needed, so that the software formats all week *Start* dates at the same time.

The next few statements are self-explanatory, but the *Sort* method can be confusing. Think about how you sort in Excel using Tools ➤ Sort, in which you specify the columns, the sort order, and whether you want a header. That is exactly what the *Sort* code does. Note how the named parameters help you to understand the code.

Hands On Exercise

Exercise 13-2

Work with the *Who Does What When* report.

1. Launch the *WhoDoesWhatWhen* report. Provide a project in which each task has a hyperlink to a project with current assignments.

2. Copy the code to your Global.mpt file and add a button on the *Global Macros* toolbar.

3. Close Microsoft Project and then reopen it to confirm that the system adds a new button, and then test your code again. Module 13 Sample Code.mpp contains the complete code solution.

4. Add a fifth column before the time phased data for the total *Work* for the assignment.

5. Replace the number 13 (the number of weeks) with a constant that has a meaningful name.

6. Replace all other numbers with constants.

7. Edit the macro to export data for the next 6 months instead of 13 weeks.

Module 14

Create a Cost Margin Report

Learning Objectives

After completing this module, you will be able to:

- Create a macro to produce a Cost Margin report in Microsoft Project

- Create a custom field formula with VBA

- Specify the Cost Rate table used with each assignment

Inside Module 14

Understanding the Cost Margin Report

A *Cost Margin* report calculates the difference between your customer billing rate and your internal cost for each project. This report is a great example of a solution using VBA and formulae together. Before you create this macro, you must do the following:

1. Reserve two custom task *Cost* fields (for example Cost1 and Cost2).

2. Set your customer billing rate in the *Standard Rate* and set your internal cost using *Cost Rate Table B* for each resource in each project.

> To set the rate for Cost Rate Table B, double-click a resource, select the *Costs* tab, and then select the tab for Cost Rate Table B.

The comments for this macro are as follows:

```
Sub CostMarginReport
'This procedure requires exclusive use of Cost1 and Cost2.
'All data in these fields will be over-written.
'Standard Rate is assumed to be Customer rate.
'Rate B for each Resource is assumed to be Internal Rate.

'Create Cost Margin Table for report
'Assign new Table
'Set Rate B for every Assignment
'Copy new Cost to Cost1
'Reset Rate A as rate for every Assignment
'Set Formula for Cost2 to calculate margin
End Sub
```

The code for this macro is as follows:

```
Sub CostMarginReport()
'This procedure requires exclusive use of Cost1 and Cost2.
'All data in these fields will be over-written.
'Standard Rate is Customer rate.
'Rate B for each Resource is Internal Rate.
Dim Tsk As Task
```

```
Dim Res As Resource
Dim Assgn As Assignment
Const RateA = 0
Const RateB = 1

   On Error Resume Next

'Create and Apply copy of Task Sheet View
   ViewEditSingle Name:="Cost Margin Report", Create:=True, _
      Screen:=pjTaskSheet, ShowInMenu:=False, HighlightFilter:=False, _
      Table:="Cost", Filter:="All Tasks", Group:="No Group"
   ViewApply "Cost Margin Report"

'Create and Apply Cost Margin Table for report
   TableEdit Name:="Cost Margin Report", TaskTable:=True, Create:=True, _
      OverwriteExisting:=True, FieldName:="ID", Title:="", Width:=6, _
      Align:=2, ShowInMenu:=True, LockFirstColumn:=True, RowHeight:=1, _
      AlignTitle:=1
   TableEdit Name:="Cost Margin Report", TaskTable:=True, _
      NewFieldName:="Indicators", Title:="", Width:=6, Align:=2, _
      LockFirstColumn:=True, RowHeight:=1, AlignTitle:=1
   TableEdit Name:="Cost Margin Report", TaskTable:=True, _
      NewFieldName:="Name", _
      Title:="Task Name", Width:=40, Align:=pjLeft, _
      LockFirstColumn:=True, RowHeight:=1, AlignTitle:=1
   TableEdit Name:="Cost Margin Report", TaskTable:=True, NewFieldName:="Cost", _
      Title:="Customer Cost", Width:=12, Align:=2, _
      LockFirstColumn:=True, RowHeight:=1, AlignTitle:=1
   TableEdit Name:="Cost Margin Report", TaskTable:=True, _
      NewFieldName:="Cost1", Title:="Internal Cost", Width:=12, Align:=2, _
      LockFirstColumn:=True, RowHeight:=1, AlignTitle:=1
   TableEdit Name:="Cost Margin Report", TaskTable:=True, _
      NewFieldName:="Cost2", Title:="Cost Margin", Width:=12, Align:=2, _
      LockFirstColumn:=True, RowHeight:=1, AlignTitle:=1

'Create a new View for this report (including new Table) and apply
   ViewApply "Gantt Chart"
   OrganizerDeleteItem pjViews, ActiveProject.Name, "Cost margin"
   ViewEditSingle Name:="Cost margin", Create:=True, _
      Screen:=pjTaskSheet, Table:="Cost Margin Report", _
      Filter:="All Tasks", Group:="No Group"
   ViewApply "Cost margin"
   SetTitleRowHeight 6

'Set Rate B for every Assignment
   For Each Tsk In ActiveProject.Tasks
      If Not Tsk Is Nothing Then
         For Each Assgn In Tsk.Assignments
            Assgn.CostRateTable = RateB
         Next Assgn

      'Copy new Cost to Cost1
         Tsk.Cost1 = Tsk.Cost
      End If
   Next Tsk
```

```
'Reset Rate A as rate for every Assignment
   For Each Tsk In ActiveProject.Tasks
      If Not Tsk Is Nothing Then
         For Each Assgn In Tsk.Assignments
            Assgn.CostRateTable = RateA
         Next Assgn
      End If
   Next Tsk

'Set Formula for Cost2 to calculate margin
   CustomFieldSetFormula FieldID:=pjCustomTaskCost2, Formula:="[Cost]-[Cost1]"
   CustomFieldProperties FieldID:=pjCustomTaskCost1, _
      Attribute:=pjFieldAttributeNone, SummaryCalc:=pjCalcRollupSum, _
      GraphicalIndicators:=False, Required:=False
   CustomFieldProperties FieldID:=pjCustomTaskCost2, _
      Attribute:=pjFieldAttributeFormula, SummaryCalc:=pjCalcRollupSum, _
      GraphicalIndicators:=False, Required:=False
End Sub
```

After working with time phased data, this macro seems simple! The long first block of code is a recorded macro to create a new table, complete with column titles and widths, then a new view. To save space I removed the recorded date format because it is optional.

```
'Set Rate B for every Assignment
   For Each Tsk In ActiveProject.Tasks
      If Not Tsk Is Nothing Then
         For Each Assgn In Tsk.Assignments
            Assgn.CostRateTable = RateB
         Next Assgn

         'Copy new Cost to Cost1
            Tsk.Cost1 = Tsk.Cost
      End If
   Next Tsk
```

The preceding code loops through all tasks, and then loops through each task's assignments. If the task has any assignments, the code sets the *Cost Rate* table to *B*. Rate B is a constant set equal to 1, which is the value required to set the cost rate table to rate B. After a task gets the cost rate for all of its assignments, the code copies the newly calculated cost to the *Cost1* field reserved for the internal cost for each task. Now the internal cost is calculated, the cost rate table is reset to rate A, the customer rate so that the *Cost2* field can calculate the margin.

```
'Set Formula for Cost2 to calculate margin
   CustomFieldSetFormula FieldID:=pjCustomTaskCost2, Formula:="[Cost]-[Cost1]"
   CustomFieldProperties FieldID:=pjCustomTaskCost2, _
      Attribute:=pjFieldAttributeFormula, SummaryCalc:=pjCalcRollupSum, _
      GraphicalIndicators:=False, Required:=False
```

181

The preceding code adds the custom formula to calculate the margin and to force each summary task to sum the total margin for each of its subtasks. The code edits the *Cost2* field to add a rollup sum to summary tasks so you see a summary of customer costs as well as margin costs. We rename the *Cost* field *Customer Cost*. Figure 14 - 1 shows the result in Module 14 Sample Code.mpp.

		Task Name	Customer Cost	Internal Cost	Cost Margin	Week 1	Week 2
0		⊟ Module 14 Sample Code - Cost Margin Report	$6,000.00	$3,200.00	$2,800.00		
1		Task 1	$3,000.00	$1,600.00	$1,400.00		Res[50%]
2		Task 2	$3,000.00	$1,600.00	$1,400.00		Res[50%]

Figure 14 - 1: Cost Margin Report

This is a great example of combining the power of VBA and Project formulas.

Figure 14 - 2 shows the *Global* toolbar after you copy the *CostMarginCode* module to the Global.mpt file and add the following code to add the *CostMargin* button to the toolbar:

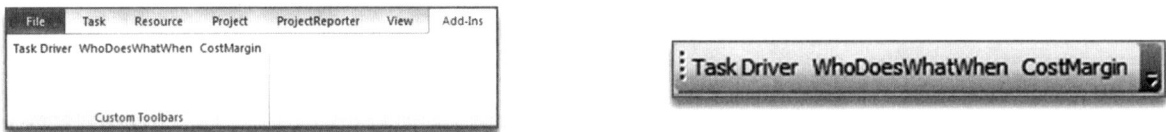

Figure 14 - 2: Global toolbar for Project 2010 and Project 2007 and earlier

```
Set MyButton = Nothing
Set MyButton = MyBar.Controls("CostMargin")
If MyButton Is Nothing Then
    Set MyButton = MyBar.Controls.Add(Type:=msoControlButton)
    With MyButton
        .Style = msoButtonCaption
        .Caption = "CostMargin"
        .OnAction = "Macro ""CostMargin"""
    End With
End If
```

This code is the same I used before, except for a different macro name for the *Caption* and *OnAction* properties.

Hands On Exercise

Exercise 14-1

Work with the Cost Margin Report.

1. Add code to handle an internal fixed cost. Use the task *Cost3* field to hold the new cost and edit the *Margin* formula to include it.

2. Name the module *CostMarginCode* then copy it to the Global.mpt file.

3. Add a button using the code supplied previously to the *Global Macros* button.

4. Test the code on different files.

5. Create a version that exports the report to Excel. You can do the *Margin* calculation with a formula in Excel.

Module 15

Consolidating Multiple Projects

Learning Objectives

After completing this module, you will be able to:

- Write a macro to create a snapshot report from multiple projects
- Understand options for consolidating projects

Inside Module 15

Creating Consolidated Project Reports

You create consolidated project reports by inserting any number of projects into a master project. To create a master project, open a new blank project in Microsoft Project and then click Insert ➤ Project. When you insert one project into another, you have two options:

1. The default option links each individual project into the master project. If you make changes to the master project, the subproject reflects the changes, and vice versa.

2. The other option allows you to insert individual projects into the master project **without** linking them. Using this option, the system **copies** everything from each subproject into the master project. The system does not reflect changes in either the master project or a subproject in the other.

> To create a master project using the second option, deselect the *Link to project* option in the *Insert Project* dialog.

Table 15 - 1 details the advantages and disadvantages associated with using both linked and unlinked master projects.

ADVANTAGES	
Linked Version	**Unlinked Version**
1. The system reflects changes to either the master project or a subproject in the other immediately. 2. You do not need a macro. 3. The report is always current.	1. Because the master project is a copy of all files, this makes a great snapshot for audit purposes. 2. The master project consolidates all resource information across all inserted projects without needing a shared resource pool file. 3. There are no links between files, so there is no risk of file corruption.
DISADVANTAGES	
Linked Version	**Unlinked Version**
1. Linked files are very prone to corruption if you move, overwrite, or rename any of them. 2. There is no snapshot or copy of schedules for an audit trail. 3. You need to use a separate resource pool file to consolidate the resource data. This increases the risk of corruption by creating even more links.	1. The report does not stay current. 2. The report needs a macro to create a new master project reliably. Since I typically update projects only once a week, having to run a macro is rarely a problem.

Table 15 - 1: Advantages and Disadvantages
of Consolidated project reports

I believe that the advantages of a consolidated resource report make consolidated projects without links the preferred solution. To easily create the consolidated project, you need a macro to use a list of projects and automatically create the consolidated project. The Project Control Center with its existing list of all current projects makes a great start for a consolidated report.

You do not want the consolidated report to mess up your Project Control Center, so the macro must create each report in a new file. Following are the comments for this macro:

```
Sub ConsolidateProjects
'Set project variable to Project Control Center
'Create new project
'Set project variable to new project
'For each project in the Project Control Center
'Insert into the consolidated report
'Move timescale to today's date and Format in Weeks
'Open Save dialog for user to save the report
End Sub
```

The code to insert each project into a master project is the only code in this example that you have not seen before. The quickest and easiest way to do it is to record a macro while you insert one project into another. Make sure you deselect the *Link to project* option in the *Insert Project* dialog before you select the file name. The short but very useful macro code is as follows:

```
Sub ConsolidateProjectsReport()
Dim prjPCC As Project
Dim Tsk As Task
Dim Path As String

'Set project variable to Project Control Center
    Set prjPCC = ActiveProject

'Create new project
    FileNew

'For each project in the Project Control Center
'Insert into the consolidated report
    Application.DisplayAlerts = False
    For Each Tsk In prjPCC.Tasks
        If Not Tsk Is Nothing Then 'test for empty tasks

'Extract File path from the Hyperlink
        Path = Tsk.HyperlinkAddress
        If Left(Path, 1) = "." Then
            Path = prjPCC.Path & "\" & Path
        End If
        Path = Replace(Path, "/", "\")
        Path = Replace(Path, "%20", " ")
        Application.ConsolidateProjects Filenames:=Path, _
```

```
            AttachToSources:=False, HideSubTasks:=True
        End If
    Next Tsk
    Application.DisplayAlerts = True

'Move timescale to today's date and format in weeks
    EditGoTo Date:=Date
    Application.TimescaleEdit _
        MajorUnits:=pjTimescaleMonths, _
        MajorLabel:=pjMonth_mmm_yyy, _
        MinorUnits:=pjTimescaleDays, _
        MinorLabel:=pjDayOfMonth_dd, MinorCount:=7

'Open Save dialog for user to save the report
    FileSaveAs
End Sub
```

As I previously mentioned, the only new code is the *ConsolidateProjects Method*. The first thing to note is that it belongs to the *Application* object, and therefore only works on the active project. The *AttachToSources* parameter matches the *Link to project* option in the *Insert Project* dialog. If you set the *HideSubTasks* statement to *True*, the system collapses all subtasks automatically and displays only the project summary tasks for each subproject.

The preceding code provides a useful example for using a *Project* object. In the *For Each Tsk In prjPCC.Tasks* statement, using the *ActiveProject* statement does not work because the active project is the new consolidated project, and not the *Project Control Center* project. To access the tasks for each project in the Project Control Center, you need a project variable such as *prjPCC*.

Because this macro needs to work with the list of projects in the Project Control Center, it is best to keep it in the Project Control Center.mpp file rather than moving to the Global.mpt file.

Hands On Exercise

Exercise 15-1

Work with the *Consolidated Report* macro.

1. Test the code in the *Consolidated Project Report* macro and make sure it works.

2. Copy the code to your *Project Control Center* project.

3. Add a button for this macro to the *My Macros* toolbar in the *Project Control Center* project.

4. In the report project created by running the macro, apply the *Resource Usage* view to see the consolidated resource usage across all projects. You may want to rename the resources in some projects so that they all use exactly the same names.

Module 16

Changing Working Time

Learning Objectives

After completing this module, you will be able to:

- Write code to work with calendars
- Use a tool to set non-working days to calendars in multiple projects

Inside Module 16

Working with Calendars

In Microsoft Project, calendars are useful tools, but we frequently ignore them. I lost count long ago of the number of projects that do not even have a Christmas or New Year's Day break included! This means that most project administrators (anyone responsible for administrating and reporting across multiple projects) have the tedious job of updating many schedules to include all organizational days off plus any other days that are not going to have any project work done.

While calendars do not affect the calculation of task durations, they do affect the calculation of *Finish* dates, so it is important to get them right. Know that there is a point of diminishing returns for the level of detail required in maintaining calendars. Generally, setting individual days to working or non-working is the threshold for diminishing returns and marking the calendar to exclude 2 hours when a resource visits the dentist goes beyond the call of duty. To change days use *Default, Nonworking* or *Working* times:

Step	Project 2010	Project 2007 and earlier
Open *Change Working Time* dialog	Click Project Tab ➤ click *Change Working Time* icon	Click Tools ➤ Change Working Time

Table 16 - 1: Showing the Change Working Time dialog

Designing the Update Calendars Macro

To make updating the *Standard* calendar in multiple projects easy, you can write a VBA macro (*UpdateCalendars* macro) to do it for you. The *UpdateCalendars* macro needs to work with two sets of data: the list of projects in the Project Control Center and the list of calendar changes you want to make to all projects. As you already have macros in the Project Control Center, it makes sense for this macro to live there as well. Now you must find a home for the list of calendar changes. For this macro, we will reuse the *Class* text file to save the calendar changes in a text file. The text file can have a fixed name and live in the same folder as the Project Control Center for simplicity.

The goals of the *UpdateCalendars* macro are to:

- Update the *Standard* calendar of all projects in the Project Control Center.

- Allow user entry and retention of dates (minimum 1 day) for calendar edits.

- Allow *Default, Nonworking*, or *Nondefault* working settings.

- Delete dates in the past from the calendar changes list.

- Provide an easy-to-use data entry form for calendar exceptions (changes).

This is a complex macro so to make it simpler; it will be easier for you to build it in four iterations:

1. Create a UserForm to accept data entry for all calendar exceptions.

2. Add the *clsTextFile* class to save all calendar exceptions to a text file when the form closes. Load the exceptions into the UserForm from the text file when the UserForm opens.

3. Add a macro to loop through all projects in the Project Control Center and execute the changes to the *Standard* calendar.

4. Add the macro to the *My Macros* toolbar in the Project Control Center.

By creating four iterations, you break one complex macro into four simpler macros. The following subtopics divide your iterations into simpler goals.

Create the Calendar Exceptions UserForm

This is undoubtedly the most challenging iteration and the riskiest in terms of being able to complete the macro, so it is the best one to tackle first. The form should show a list of all calendar exceptions entered by the user. Each record needs a *Start* and *Finish* date plus the working/non-working/default setting, with all records sorted by *Start* date for readability. In all likelihood, you will not have many rows to sort, so a simple **compare each record and swap if necessary** sort (also known as a bubble sort) algorithm works well. Figure 16 - 1 shows the UserForm in design mode.

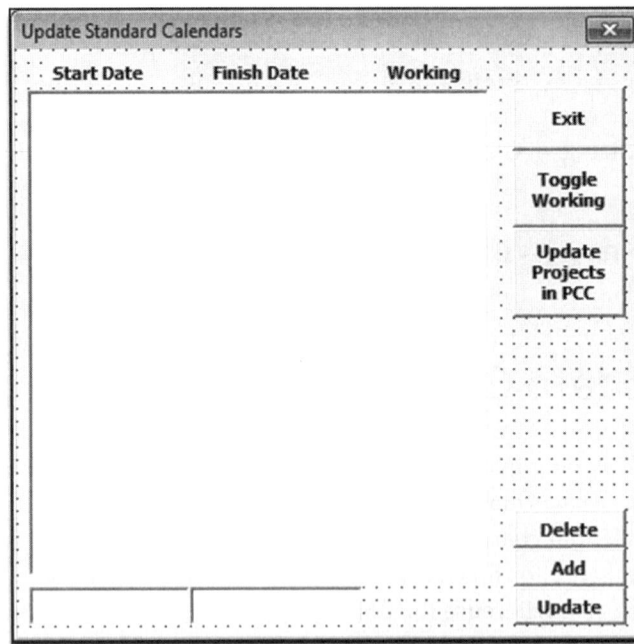

Figure 16 - 1: UpdateCalendars UserForm

The two controls in the lower left corner of the form are for entering a new *Start* and *Finish* date, and to edit any record the user selects. A limitation of VBA UserForms is that you cannot edit data in a list, so the two fields do this for you. To help make data entry easier and more accurate the following features are included:

- There are only 3 valid entries for the *Working* column (*Yes, No*, and *Default*), so there is a *Toggle Working* button that cycles between the three values with *No* as the default value.

- When you enter a *Start* date into the *Start* field (bottom left control) and press the **Enter** key or click in the *Finish Date* control, the *Start* date is populated to the *Finish Date* box. This makes for quick entry of single day date ranges.

- Whenever the user clicks on an existing record, the selected record's *Start* and *Finish* dates populate the entry fields at the bottom of the UserForm. Clicking the *Update* button then updates the selected record with any new values.

Figure 16 - 2 shows the same form as in Figure 16 – 1 but active with a single calendar exception added.

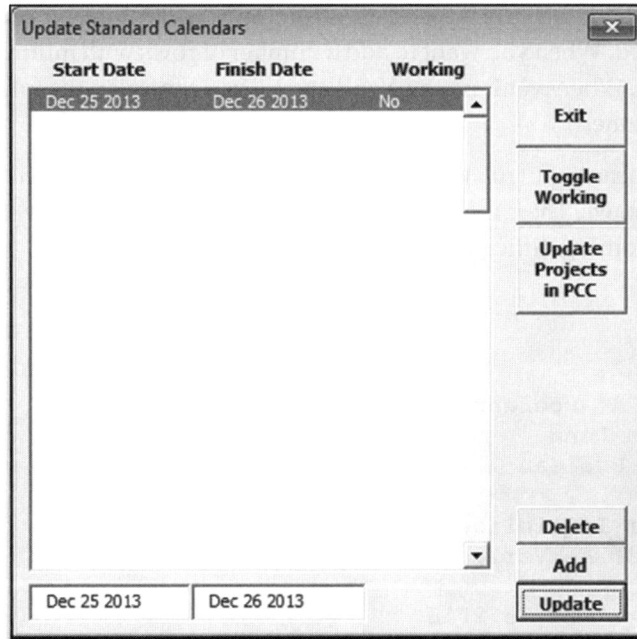

Figure 16 - 2: UserForm in Action

Table 16 - 2 details all the controls, their type and the name given them in the sample code.

Control Type	Control Name	Use
ListBox	NonWorkingDays	Lists all calendar exceptions
TextBox	StartDate	Editing box to hold Start date for new or edited row
TextBox	FinishDate	Editing box to hold Finish date for new or edited row
CommandButton	Quit	Closes the Form
CommandButton	ToggleWorking	Toggles through all Working values
CommandButton	UpdateProjects	Calls the UpdatePCCCalendars routine to update all projects in the Project Control Center with exceptions
CommandButton	DeleteException	Deletes the select row from the ListBox
CommandButton	AddException	Adds a row to the ListBox
CommandButton	Update	Updates values for selected row using values in the editing boxes

Table 16 - 2: Calendar Exceptions UserForm Controls

The most important control in this UserForm is the *NonWorkingDays ListBox* control. You can add rows to *ListBox* controls using their *AddItem* method. When you want to add a number of rows with multiple column lists, using the *List* property and an array is easier. Whenever I use the *NonWorkingDays* control in the following code, I am referring to the *ListBox* control with that name.

Give all controls and buttons meaningful names as suggested by their captions or function. Table 16 - 2 provides the names used in the code that follows. There is a lot of code to make all these features work, but by taking the code one small block at a time there is nothing difficult. Following is the code:

```
Option Explicit

Private DataChanged As Boolean
Private ListCount As Long
Private Updating As Boolean

Private Sub UserForm_Initialize()
Dim DataArray(100, 2) As Variant
Dim Row As Long
    DataArray(0, 0) = "Dec 25 2013"
    DataArray(0, 1) = "Dec 26 2013"
    DataArray(0, 2) = "No"
    ListCount = 1
    NonWorkingDays.ColumnHeads = False
    NonWorkingDays.List() = DataArray
    NonWorkingDays.ColumnCount = 3
    SortList
End Sub

Private Sub NonWorkingDays_Click()
    If Not Updating Then
        StartDate = NonWorkingDays.List(NonWorkingDays.ListIndex, 0)
        FinishDate = NonWorkingDays.List(NonWorkingDays.ListIndex, 1)
    End If
End Sub

Private Sub Quit_Click()
    frmNonWorkingDays.Hide
End Sub

Private Sub StartDate_AfterUpdate()
    If IsDate(StartDate) Then
        FinishDate = StartDate
    End If
End Sub

Private Sub ToggleWorking_Click()
    If NonWorkingDays.ListIndex >= 0 Then
        Select Case NonWorkingDays.List(NonWorkingDays.ListIndex, 2)
            Case "No"
                NonWorkingDays.List(NonWorkingDays.ListIndex, 2) = "Yes"
            Case "Yes"
                NonWorkingDays.List(NonWorkingDays.ListIndex, 2) = "Default"
            Case "Default"
                NonWorkingDays.List(NonWorkingDays.ListIndex, 2) = "No"
        End Select
```

```
            DataChanged = True
      End If
End Sub

Private Sub Update_Click()
      Updating = True
      NonWorkingDays.List(NonWorkingDays.ListIndex, 0) = _
            Format(CDate(StartDate), "mmm d yyyy")
      NonWorkingDays.List(NonWorkingDays.ListIndex, 1) = _
            Format(CDate(FinishDate), "mmm d yyyy")
      DataChanged = True
      SortList
      Updating = False
End Sub

Private Sub UpdateProjects_Click()
      'UpdatePCCCalendars
End Sub

Private Sub AddException_Click()
      Updating = True
      NonWorkingDays.List(ListCount, 0) = Format(CDate(StartDate), "mmm d yyyy")
      NonWorkingDays.List(ListCount, 1) = Format(CDate(FinishDate), "mmm d yyyy")
      NonWorkingDays.List(ListCount, 2) = "No"
      ListCount = ListCount + 1
      DataChanged = True
      SortList
      Updating = False
End Sub

Private Sub DeleteException_Click()
      NonWorkingDays.RemoveItem NonWorkingDays.ListIndex
      ListCount = ListCount - 1
      DataChanged = True
End Sub

Sub SortList()
'Sort List based on first column
Dim Ind1 As Long
Dim Ind2 As Long
Dim SwapMade As Boolean
Dim strDate1 As String, strDate2 As String
Dim StartDate As Date, FinishDate As Date, Reset As String
      If ListCount >= 2 Then
         Do
            SwapMade = False
            For Ind1 = 0 To ListCount - 2
                Ind2 = Ind1 + 1
                strDate1 = NonWorkingDays.List(Ind1, 0)
                strDate2 = NonWorkingDays.List(Ind2, 0)
                If IsDate((strDate1)) And _
                           (CDate(strDate2)) Then
                    If CDate(strDate1) > CDate(strDate2) Then
                        'Copy first row
                        StartDate = NonWorkingDays.List(Ind1, 0)
                        FinishDate = NonWorkingDays.List(Ind1, 1)
```

```
                    Reset = NonWorkingDays.List(Ind1, 2)

                    'Move second row to 1st
                    NonWorkingDays.List(Ind1, 0) = NonWorkingDays.List(Ind2, 0)
                    NonWorkingDays.List(Ind1, 1) = NonWorkingDays.List(Ind2, 1)
                    NonWorkingDays.List(Ind1, 2) = NonWorkingDays.List(Ind2, 2)

                    'Re-save first row in second row
                    NonWorkingDays.List(Ind2, 0) = Format(StartDate, "mmm d yyyy")
                    NonWorkingDays.List(Ind2, 1) = _
                                         Format(FinishDate, "mmm d yyyy")
                    NonWorkingDays.List(Ind2, 2) = Reset
                    SwapMade = True
                End If
            End If

        Next Ind1
    Loop Until SwapMade = False
    End If
End Sub

Private Sub UserForm_Terminate()
'Remove any dates that finish earlier than today
'Save data if any changes have been made
Dim Txt As New clsTextFile
Dim Line As Long
    For Line = 0 To ListCount - 1
        If IsDate(NonWorkingDays.List(Line, 1)) Then
            If CDate(NonWorkingDays.List(Line, 1)) < Date Then
                NonWorkingDays.RemoveItem Line
                ListCount = ListCount - 1
                DataChanged = True
            End If
        End If
    Next Line
End Sub
```

The above code is from the *frmNonWorkingDays1* code in the Module 16 Sample Code Iteration1.mpp file. Code for Iteration 2 is in UserForm *frmNonWorkingDays Iteration2* and so on. Note that the code is in 10 procedures and that each one on its own is not difficult. I will explain each procedure in turn.

```
Private Sub UserForm_Initialize()
Dim DataArray(100, 2) As String
Dim Row As Long
    DataArray(0, 0) = "Dec 25 2013"
    DataArray(0, 1) = "Dec 26 2013"
    DataArray(0, 2) = "No"
    ListCount=1
    NonWorkingDays.ColumnHeads = False
    NonWorkingDays.ColumnCount = 3
    NonWorkingDays.List() = DataArray
    SortList
End Sub
```

UserForm_Initialize runs when you first display the UserForm with the *.show* method. Use it to initialize controls. In Iteration 2 you add code to this procedure to read in existing calendar exceptions from a text file and display them in the *List* box.

DataArray is an array of strings with 3 columns and 101 rows. The index for each row and column starts at 0 so the *DataArray(100,2)* declaration does have 3 columns as the first column in the first row is accessed using the *DataArray(0,0)* declaration. For initial testing purposes, the code adds only one row of data with entries for all three columns.

I initialize the *DataArray* string by using Christmas 2013 dates since the three years before rest on, or partly on, a weekend.

The *NonWorkingDays.List() = DataArray* statement sets the ListBox to have the same data displayed as entered into the Array. The *ListCount* variable keeps track of the number of rows of data. The *ListCount* variable is especially important when you add code to save and read from text files.

```
Private Sub NonWorkingDays_Click()
    If Not Updating Then
        StartDate = NonWorkingDays.List(NonWorkingDays.ListIndex, 0)
        FinishDate = NonWorkingDays.List(NonWorkingDays.ListIndex, 1)
    End If
End Sub
```

Click on the *ListBox* code to trigger this event. The code copies the data in the selected row into the two edit boxes at the bottom of the UserForm so the user can edit the dates. You cannot edit data directly in a VBA ListBox.

```
Private Sub ExitForm_Click()
    frmNonWorkingDays.Hide
End Sub

Private Sub StartDate_AfterUpdate()
    If IsDate(StartDate) Then
        FinishDate = StartDate
    End If
End Sub
```

Click the *Exit* button to trigger the *Quit_Click* event and move your cursor away from the *StartDate* control by clicking somewhere else with the mouse or by pressing the **Tab** key to trigger the *StartDate_AfterUpdate* event. The *Exit* command button cannot be named *Exit* because *Exit* is a reserved word in VBA, hence the name *ExitForm*.

The *StartDate_AfterUpdate* event copies the *Start* date to the *Finish* date, but only if you enter a valid date. The *IsDate* function is a VBA function that tests the variant or string value passed to verify that it holds a valid date. If the date is valid, the *IsDate* function returns *True* and only then does the *Start* date get copied to the *Finish* date. The idea is to make data entry a little quicker and easier. If the date range is for one day only, then no *Finish* date is required. If the date range is more than a day, the *Finish* date needs only editing. Either way you make the user's work a little bit easier.

```
Private Sub ToggleWorking_Click()
    If NonWorkingDays.ListIndex >= 0 Then
        Select Case NonWorkingDays.List(NonWorkingDays.ListIndex, 2)
            Case "No"
                NonWorkingDays.List(NonWorkingDays.ListIndex, 2) = "Yes"
            Case "Yes"
                NonWorkingDays.List(NonWorkingDays.ListIndex, 2) = "Default"
            Case "Default"
                NonWorkingDays.List(NonWorkingDays.ListIndex, 2) = "No"
        End Select
        DataChanged = True
    End If
End Sub
```

Click the *Toggle* command button to trigger the *ToggleWorking_Click* event. In the interest of data accuracy, this event cycles through the three possible values of *No, Yes,* and *Default* to make sure there are no typing errors or entry of a different value again.

The *NonWorkingDays.List(NonWorkingDays.ListIndex, 2)* function accesses the *Working* column of the ListBox for the currently selected row. The *List* property returns all data for the ListBox. The *NonWorkingDays.ListIndex* function returns the row number of the currently selected row (the top row is row zero). Number 2 is the third column of the row as the first column is column zero, and therefore the *Working* column. The code tests the current value then cycles through all three valid options in turn.

When the user edits the data, you must set the *DataChanged* flag to be sure that you saved the edit when the UserForm terminates.

```
Private Sub Update_Click()
    Updating = True
    NonWorkingDays.List(NonWorkingDays.ListIndex, 0) = _
        Format(CDate(StartDate), "mmm d yyyy")
    NonWorkingDays.List(NonWorkingDays.ListIndex, 1) = _
        Format(CDate(FinishDate), "mmm d yyyy")
    DataChanged = True
    SortList
    Updating = False
End Sub
```

Click the *Update* command button to trigger the *Update_Click* event. The statement most difficult to understand is the *Updating = True* statement. In VBA UserForms, code in some events such as the *_Click* or the *_Update* event can trigger other events in turn, such as other click or update events. Triggering more than one event can produce unexpected and undesirable results. For example, when you update the StartDate TextBox the *Click* event for the ListBox can also fire. By setting a flag (in this case the *Updating* flag) to *True* and testing for it in other events, and then only doing anything if the *Updating* flag is *False,* you make sure that only one event's code is run at one time.

Again, the *Format* function formats the date into an international format that has a 3 character month name to avoid any chance of confusion between international d/m and m/d formats.

The *DataChanged* flag is set whenever a row of data is added or edited. That lets the *_Terminate* event know that it needs to re-save all data to the text file.

SortList is a call to the *SortList* procedure to sort the list of calendar exceptions by *Start* date. This makes the list easier to read and to check all relevant dates are included in the list.

```
Private Sub UpdateProjects_Click()
    'UpdatePCCCalendars
End Sub
```

Click the *UpdateProjects* command button to call the *UpdateProjects_Click* event. The code calls the *UpdatePCCCalendars* procedure to open all projects in the *Project Control Center* project to update their *Standard* calendar. Do not think about the *UpdateProjects* code for now, you will work on it in the third iteration. In fact, notice that the call to the *UpdatePCCCalendars* event currently has a quote mark in front of it. This means it is a comment and the *UpdatePCCCalendars* event is, therefore, a placeholder waiting for you to develop the procedure.

```
Private Sub AddException_Click()
    Updating = True
    NonWorkingDays.List(ListCount, 0) = Format(CDate(StartDate), "mmm d yyyy")
    NonWorkingDays.List(ListCount, 1) = Format(CDate(FinishDate), "mmm d yyyy")
    NonWorkingDays.List(ListCount, 2) = "No"
    ListCount = ListCount + 1
    DataChanged = True
    SortList
    Updating = False
End Sub

Private Sub DeleteException_Click()
    NonWorkingDays.RemoveItem NonWorkingDays.ListIndex
    ListCount = ListCount - 1
    DataChanged = True
End Sub
```

The *AddException_Click* and *DeleteException_Click* events add or remove a row of data in the ListBox. The *AddException* event sets the *Updating* flag again to prevent any other event from interrupting it. Then it uses code very similar to the *UserForm_Initialize* event to add a row of data from the *Edit* boxes. For international date compatibility, use a three-character month for the *Start* and *Finish* dates.

In both events, the *ListCount* variable increments or decrements to reflect the new number of rows of data and the *DataChanged* flag is set to *True* to make sure the text file gets updated when the UserForm closes.

The next procedure is the *SortList* code. Rather than explain this code line by line, I explain what it has to accomplish instead. The code itself is nothing new. The *SortList* code has to perform the following steps:

1. Sort rows only if the number of rows is greater than or equal to two; there is no need to sort a list of one row!

2. Use a simple *swap-two-list-rows-if-needed-until-the-list-is-sorted* algorithm. Set the *SwapMade* flag to *False* before the loop starts. Set the *SwapMade* flag to *True* whenever two values are swapped. If after the loop has finished

the *SwapMade* flag is *True*, then the sort probably has not finished so loop again. If the *SwapMade* flag is still *False* after looping through all rows, then the sort is complete and SortList can exit.

3. For each pair of *StartDate* values (for two consecutive rows) in the ListBox, if there are two valid *Start* dates compare their values and swap them if the second (lower) one is less than the first. If you do the swap, set the *SwapMade* flag to *True* to make sure looping continues until the system makes no swaps indicating the sort is complete.

```
Private Sub UserForm_Terminate()
'Remove any dates that finish earlier than today
'Save data if any changes have been made
Dim Line As Long
    For Line = 0 To ListCount - 1
        If IsDate(NonWorkingDays.List(Line, 1)) Then
            If CDate(NonWorkingDays.List(Line, 1))<Date Then
                NonWorkingDays.RemoveItem Line
                ListCount = ListCount - 1
                DataChanged = True
            End If
        End If
    Next Line
End Sub
```

You have arrived at the last procedure. Well done! Close the UserForm by clicking the **X** button in the top right corner of the UserForm or close the project with the UserForm in it to trigger the *UserForm_Terminate* event. Clicking the *Exit* command button simply hides the UserForm and does not trigger the *UserForm_Terminate* event. Until you add the *save to text* file code, this event just deletes all old dates. The code used is simply a variation of previous code; there is nothing new in it. If you have problems understanding the code, single step through it and test each variable after each step. If all else fails, send me an email!

With all this working code you now have a working UserForm to enter and edit calendar exceptions. Iteration 2 adds the *TextFile* class so the system reads and saves all calendar exceptions to a text file.

Hands On Exercise

Exercise 16-1

Learn to use the Update Calendars macro.

1. Open the file Module 16 Sample Code Iteration1.mpp

2. Select Debug ➢ Compile. If no error messages appear your code has compiled correctly on your system. If errors do appear, see if you can resolve them, there should only be minor differences between systems.

3. Go to the first line of each procedure and press the **F5** function key to add a breakpoint.

4. Display the UserForm by double-clicking it in Project Explorer.

5. Press the **F5** function key to run the form. Use the different buttons and every time you hit a breakpoint, single step through your code making sure you understand what each line of code does.

6. Once you are happy you understand each procedure, remove the breakpoint for it by clicking on it then pressing the **F9** function key again.

Add the Text Class to Store Calendar Exceptions

A text file is a useful place to save data such as calendar exceptions. Storing the data in the registry quickly becomes unwieldy and requires a lot of code specific to the data saved. Once written, a *Text* class is quickly reusable, and contains code that is easy to understand and maintain.

The *Text* class is the same one you created in Module 05 and updated in Module 12 to add *write to text* file functionality. To use it in another macro, use the Project Explorer in the Visual Basic Editor (VBE) to copy the *clsTextFile Class* module from the Sample Module 13 file, to your file. To copy a module, use your mouse to drag it while holding down the **Ctrl** key.

> **TIP:** Dragging data while holding the **Ctrl** key copies the selected file in Windows Explorer and selected text in all Office applications.

To add the text file as a data storage location, perform the following steps:

1. Copy the Class *clsTextFile* to your project.

2. Add code in the *UserForm_Initialize* event to replace the setup of the DataArray with code to read the text file into the DataArray.

3. Add code to the *UserForm_Terminate* event to save all data (after old exceptions have been deleted) to the text file, but only if the *DataChanged* flag is *True*.

For the *Calendar Exceptions* macro, you now need to replace the *DataArray* code used to test the UserForm with calls to the *Text* class and add calls to the *Text* class to save all data in the *Terminate* event when needed. This only affects the *UserForm_Initialize* procedure and the *UserForm_Terminate* procedures that now look like the following code:

```
Private Sub UserForm_Initialize()
Dim DataArray(100, 3) As Variant
Dim Row As Long
Dim Txt As New clsTextFile
    Txt.FilePath = ActiveProject.Path & "\NonWorking Dates.txt"
    Txt.FileOpenRead
    Do Until Txt.IsLastWord
        DataArray(ListCount, 0) = Txt.NextWord   'Start Date
        DataArray(ListCount, 1) = Txt.NextWord   'Finish Date
        DataArray(ListCount, 2) = Txt.NextWord   'Working?
        ListCount = ListCount + 1
    Loop
    Txt.FileClose
    NonWorkingDays.ColumnHeads = False
    NonWorkingDays.List() = DataArray
    NonWorkingDays.ColumnCount = 3
    SortList
End Sub
```

As you are saving the data in a .txt file, any other program can easily update it if you wish. You do need to make sure, however, that each row in the text file has a valid *Start* date, *Finish* date and *Working Status* value of *Yes* or *No*.

The *Txt.FilePath = ActiveProject.Path & "\NonWorking Dates.txt"* macro uses the path of the active project and the given file name to build a full path. When you first run the macro, the file name does not exist. The *Text* class handles this and simply sets the *IsLastWord* flag so the UserForm opens without fuss and displays an empty ListBox.

```
Private Sub UserForm_Terminate()
'Remove any dates that finish earlier than today
'Save data if any changes have been made
Dim Txt As New clsTextFile
Dim Ind As Long
    'Delete dates older than today
    For Ind = 0 To ListCount - 1
        If IsDate(NonWorkingDays.List(Ind, 1)) Then
            If CDate(NonWorkingDays.List(Ind, 1)) < Date Then
                NonWorkingDays.RemoveItem Ind
                ListCount = ListCount - 1
                DataChanged = True
            End If
        End If
    Next Ind

    'If any data has changed, save all data to the text file again
    If DataChanged Then
        Txt.FilePath = ActiveProject.Path & "\NonWorking Dates.txt"
        Txt.FileOpenWrite
        For Ind = 0 To ListCount - 1
            Txt.WriteLine NonWorkingDays.List(Ind, 0) _
                & "," & NonWorkingDays.List(Ind, 1) & "," _
                & NonWorkingDays.List(Ind, 2)
        Next Ind
        Txt.FileClose
```

```
    End If
End Sub
```

The first part of the _Terminate event is the same as previously written. The second block of code is new. Because the *Txt class* variable now exists for this procedure, its *FilePath* property needs to be set again. When you open the file for write using the *FileOpenWrite* method, the system creates the file if it does not exist and overwrites the file if it does.

The *WriteLine* method accepts a string created out of all three columns in the ListBox. The *For Ind* loop makes sure you export every row to the text file.

That is it! I hope you noticed that the code consists of pieces of code you have already used. Increasingly, you will find that you develop macros from the same bits of code and simply bolt them together in different ways. When you get to this realization and achieve the ability to do it, you have crossed the watershed for learning Project VBA.

Hands On Exercise

Exercise 16-2

Learn more about the Update Calendars macro.

1. Open the file Module 16 Sample Code Iteration2.mpp.
2. Select Debug ➢ Compile.
3. Add a breakpoint to the different procedures in the text class.
4. Run the UserForm again.
5. Single step through each procedure in the text class.
6. Once you understand what each procedure does, remove its breakpoint.

Apply Calendar Changes to All Projects

This iteration does the calendar editing to all projects in the Project Control Center. The code for the *UpdatePCCCalendars* procedure is:

```
Sub UpdatePCCCalendars()
Dim prjPCC As Project
Dim prj As Project
Dim Tsk As Task
Dim Path As String
Dim StartDate As Date, FinishDate As Date
Dim Working As String
```

```
Dim ListIndex As Long
'Set project variable to Project Control Center
   Set prjPCC = ActiveProject

   For Each Tsk In prjPCC.Tasks
      If Not Tsk Is Nothing Then
      'test for empty tasks

      'Extract File path from the Hyperlink and open it

         FileOpen Name:=GetPathFromURL(Tsk.HyperlinkAddress), _
            ReadOnly:=False, noAuto:=True, openpool:=pjDoNotOpenPool
         Set prj = ActiveProject

         'Loop through all rows in the ListBox
         'Set Calendar period to working status
         Do
            If frmNonWorkingDays1.NonWorkingDays. _
                  List(ListIndex, 0) = "" Then
               Exit Do
            End If
            StartDate = CDate(frmNonWorkingDays1 _
               .NonWorkingDays.List(ListIndex, 0))
            FinishDate = CDate(frmNonWorkingDays1 _
               .NonWorkingDays. List(ListIndex, 1))
            Working = frmNonWorkingDays1. _
               NonWorkingDays.List(ListIndex, 2)

            Select Case Working
               Case "No"
                  prj.BaseCalendars("Standard").Period(StartDate, _
                     FinishDate).Working = False
               Case "Yes"
                  prj.BaseCalendars("Standard").Period(StartDate, _
                     FinishDate).Working = True
               Case "Default"
                  prj.BaseCalendars("Standard").Period(StartDate, _
                     FinishDate).Default
            End Select
            ListIndex = ListIndex + 1
         Loop
         FileClose pjSave
      End If
   Next Tsk
End Sub

Function GetPathFromURL(URL as String) as String
Dim Path as String
   Path = Tsk.HyperlinkAddress
   If Left(Path, 1) = "." Then
      Path = prjPCC.Path & "\" & Path
   End If
   Path = Replace(Path, "/", "\")
   Path = Replace(Path, "%20", " ")
   GetPathFromURL = Path
End Function
```

Once again all this code is very similar to previous procedures on which we worked. What the *UpdatePCCCalendars* procedure has to do is:

1. Set a project variable to point to the *Project Control Center* project. This allows you to access its tasks while other projects are open.

2. Loop through all *Project Control Center* tasks.

3. Extract the file path from the hyperlink and open the project to which the hyperlink points.

4. For each row in the ListBox on the UserForm update the calendar of the active project. The calendar period can be set to *Working, Nonworking,* or *Default.*

5. Close and save the project.

I explained all the code in this procedure in earlier sections and modules. All that remains is for you to remove the single quote from the *UpdateProjects_Click* event so that you call the *UpdatePCCCalendars* event. The event should now look like the following:

```
Private Sub UpdateProjects_Click()
    UpdatePCCCalendars
End Sub
```

Hands On Exercise

Exercise 16-3

Learn more about the Update Calendars macro.

1. Open the file Module 16 Sample Code Iteration3.mpp.

2. Select Debug ➢ Compile.

3. Add a breakpoint to the start of the *UpdatePCCCalendars* procedure.

4. Run the UserForm again.

5. Single step through the procedure until you are confident that you understand how it works.

Add the Macro to the Project Control Center Toolbar

The last iteration is very simple, duplicate code to add a command button to the *Project Control Center* toolbar to display the *UserForm NonWorkingDays* macro to complete the code. You can put the macro called to display the UserForm after Iteration 3 in the *UpdateStandardCalendar* module. It should look like:

```
Public Sub ShowFrmNonWorkingDays()
    frmNonWorkingDays.Show
End Sub
```

The extra code in the *GlobalToolbar* module in the Global.mpt file should be as follows:

```
Set MyButton = Nothing
Set MyButton = MyBar.Controls("UpdateCalendars")
If MyButton Is Nothing Then
    Set MyButton = MyBar.Controls.Add(Type:=msoControlButton)
    With MyButton
        .Style = msoButtonCaption
        .Caption = "UpdateCalendars"
        .OnAction = "ShowFrmNonWorkingDays"
    End With
End If
```

For Project 2010 menu code, add the following for an extra button:

```
& "<mso:button id=""Update Calendar"" label=" _
    & """Show what is driving the selected Task"" " _
    & "onAction=""ShowFrmNonWorkingDays"" />" _
```

Make sure you save all modules before testing your code.

Hands On Exercise

Exercise 16-4

Learn more about the Update Calendars macro.

1. Edit the code so that you update only selected projects in the Project Control Center. To do this you need to use the *Application.ActiveSelection.Tasks* property to return all selected tasks so you can loop through them.

2. Design then build a macro to update resource calendars as well. You will need to add an extra column to the ListBox for the calendar name (*Resource* or *Base* calendar) and then have a text file for each calendar or save the calendar name with each exception.

Module 17

Display Predecessor and Successor Tasks

Learning Objectives

After completing this module, you will be able to:

- Work with task links in Project VBA

- Use a macro to filter for all tasks preceding or succeeding a selected task

- Understand and develop recursive code

Inside Module 17

Working with Task Dependencies

Microsoft Project lets you create links between tasks so the software can calculate task *Start* and *Finish* dates based on these links. This is the preferred way to manage dependencies between tasks rather than the alternative, which is to enter dates for these tasks. Entering constraints leads to large amounts of manual updating and, inevitably, inaccurate schedules when the manual updating remains undone.

Schedulers often need to review all preceding and succeeding tasks for a particular task so they can review what is driving, or being driven by, a particular task. The macro in this module works with the currently selected task in the active project and displays all its preceding and succeeding tasks based on existing links. I call the macro *LinkedTasks*, which is useful for any schedule, and best suited to live in the Global.mpt file.

Designing the LinkedTasks Macro

The *LinkedTasks* macro performs all of the following:

- Requires the user to select the task on which to report. This task can be in any active project file, so it works using the *ActiveCell.Task* object.

- Expands all summary tasks to display all subtasks so link lines are visible in the Gantt chart.

- Needs code to clear the *Flag20* custom field then set *Flag20* to *Yes* against every task that precedes or succeeds the originally selected task.

- If a linked-to task is a *Summary* task, then it sets *Flag20* to *Yes* for all subtasks as well.

- Creates the *Flag20* filter to display only tasks with *Flag20* = *Yes*.

- Applies the *Flag20* filter to show only preceding and succeeding tasks, which is the desired outcome.

The difficulty in this macro is that you must work not only with immediate predecessors and successors of the selected task, but also with all of the predecessor's predecessors and all of the successor's successors, until your macro reaches the end of a chain of predecessor and successor tasks. To help make this problem clearer, I first walk through the logic needed to manually find all successors. These steps are as follows:

1. From the selected task, find the first successor.

2. Flag the successor and then find the first successor to the first successor.

3. Repeat the procedure to find the first successor to the first successor of the first successor and so on until reaching a task with no successors.

4. Find the second successor of the selected task.

5. Flag the successor and then find the first successor of the second successor.

6. Find the first successor of the first successor of the second successor and so on until reaching a task with no successors.

Besides ending up with a headache from trying to sort out which tasks have already been included and which have not, the solution rapidly becomes too complex. However, there is a surprisingly simple solution. If you select any one task, for all successors do the following:

1. Set its *Flag20* field to *Yes* (provided you have not already tested this task).

2. Loop through all its successors and process them.

3. Set *Flag20* for all its subtasks to *Yes* if the current task is a *Summary* task.

So, the simplest solution is to repeat these three steps for every successor. Thankfully, VBA provides a feature called **recursive programming** that does exactly this. VBA allows you to call a routine and then let the routine call itself. The same code runs as many times as necessary using only a small amount of extra memory overhead for each procedure call. We can now state the solution as the following steps:

1. Set its *Flag20* field to *Yes* (provided you have not already tested this task).

2. Call the successors procedure again using the task Id of the successor task if a successor for the current task exists.

3. Set *Flag20* for all its subtasks to *Yes* if the current task is a *Summary* task.

Your code now happily loops through all successors of all successors until there are no more successors to find. Add a similar procedure to work instead with predecessors and you have your solution. The solution, therefore, requires three procedures:

1. A main *LinkedTasks* procedure that does the following:

    * Shows the *All Tasks* filter and expands all *Summary* tasks

    * Clears *Flag20* for all tasks

    * Runs the first iteration of the *DepPred* and *DepSucc* procedures

    * Creates and then applies the *Flag20* filter

    * Reselects the original task

2. A *DepPred* procedure processes all predecessors for the original task. It must accept a *Task* object parameter to process and, in turn, it passes a predecessor's *Task* object when it next calls itself.

3. A *DepSucc* procedure processes all successors for the original task. It must accept a *Task* object parameter to process and, in turn, it passes a successor's *Task* object when it next calls itself.

The *TaskDependency* object is critical to the *LinkTasks* macro.

i) Note that the *TaskDependency* object became available in Project 2000, so this macro does not work in Project 98.

Understanding the TaskDependency Object

In Microsoft Project, all tasks have a *TaskDependencies* collection. The *TaskDependencies* collection holds one *Task-Dependency* object for every link **To** the task and **From** the task. In other words, if you have three tasks (Task1, Task2 and Task3) linked together in a chain, the middle task, Task2, has two links, so two *TaskDependency* objects. Task 1 and Task3 have one *TaskDependency* object each.

Each *TaskDependency* object has two methods: *Add* and *Delete*. With these methods you can add and delete links between tasks. For our *LinkedTasks* macro, the *TaskDependency* properties are more useful than the aforementioned methods. The key properties are:

- **From** property that returns a *Task* object of the preceding task

- **To** property that returns a *Task* object of the succeeding task

One thing you must keep in mind is that the *TaskDependencies* collection includes all predecessors and successors. To distinguish between the predecessor and successor, test the ID of the returned **From** and **To** *Task* objects.

In Figure 17 - 1, examine the first TaskDependency for Task2. For the first TaskDependency the *From* task is *Task1* and the *To* task is *Task2*. Therefore, when looking at the dependencies for Task2, if the *To* task ID is the same as the Task2 ID then the dependency is a predecessor. Similarly, if the *From* task ID is the same as the Task2 ID then we know that the dependency is a successor. With this understanding, you can quickly determine whether a TaskDependency is a predecessor or successor.

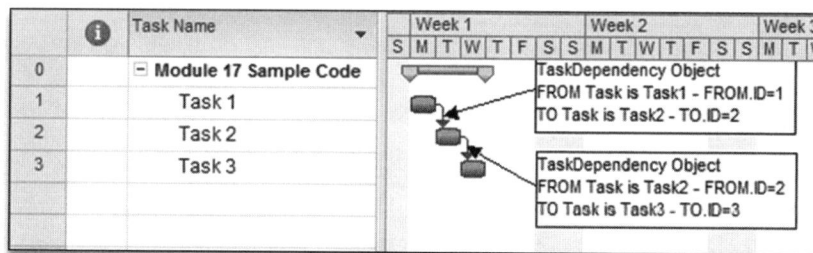

	ⓘ	Task Name ▾	Week 1		Week 2		Week 3	
			S M T W T F S	S M T W T F S	S M T W	
0		⊟ Module 17 Sample Code		TaskDependency Object FROM Task is Task1 - FROM.ID=1 TO Task is Task2 - TO.ID=2			
1		Task 1					
2		Task 2					
3		Task 3		TaskDependency Object FROM Task is Task2 - FROM.ID=2 TO Task is Task3 - TO.ID=3			

Figure 17 - 1: TaskDependency Objects with their From and To Properties

Understanding the TaskLinks Macro Code

The Module 17 Sample Code.mpp file contains the necessary code ready for you to copy to your Global.mpt file. The code is as follows:

```
Option Explicit
'This macro goes up all predecessors and down all successors 'to the active task and
sets Flag20 for each one.
'The macro creates a filter for Flag20 to display only flagged
'tasks.

Sub LinkedTasks()
Dim TD As TaskDependency
Dim Tsk As Task
```

```
      On Error Resume Next
      Set Tsk = ActiveCell.Task
      If Tsk Is Nothing Then
         MsgBox "Blank row selected", vbCritical
         End
      ElseIf Tsk.TaskDependencies.Count = 0 Then
         MsgBox "There are no Dependencies to show", vbInformation
         End
      End If
      FilterApply Name:="All Tasks"
      Application.OutlineShowAllTasks
      SelectAll
      SetTaskField Field:="Flag20", Value:="No", AllSelectedTasks:=True
      EditGoTo Tsk.ID

      DepPred Tsk          'Detect all predecessors
      Tsk.Flag20 = False   'Force Successors to be tested
      DepSucc Tsk          'Detect all successors

      'Create then apply Filter. Reset Flag20 field to No
      FilterEdit Name:="Flag20", Create:=True, _
         OverwriteExisting:=True, TaskFilter:=True, _
         FieldName:="Flag20", Test:="Equals", Value:="Yes", ShowSummaryTasks:=True
      FilterApply Name:="Flag20"
      EditGoTo Tsk.ID
      SelectRow
End Sub

Sub DepPred(Tsk As Task)
Dim Dep As TaskDependency
Dim SumT As Task
Dim SubT As Task
      If Tsk.Flag20 = False Then
         Tsk.Flag20 = True
         For Each Dep In Tsk.TaskDependencies
            If Dep.From.ID <> Tsk.ID Then
               DepPred Dep.From
            End If
         Next

         'Include any links to parent summary task
         If Tsk.OutlineLevel >= 2 Then
            Set SumT = Tsk.OutlineParent
            SumT.Flag20 = True
            For Each Dep In SumT.TaskDependencies
               If (Dep.From.ID <> SumT.ID) Then
                  DepPred Dep.From
               End If
            Next
         End If

         'If Tsk is a Summary task, include all sub tasks
         If Tsk.Summary Then
            For Each SubT In Tsk.OutlineChildren
               DepPred SubT
            Next SubT
```

```
            End If
        End If
End Sub


Sub DepSucc(Tsk As Task)
Dim Dep As TaskDependency
Dim subT As Task
    If Tsk.Flag20 = False Then
        Tsk.Flag20 = True
        For Each Dep In Tsk.TaskDependencies
            If (Dep.To.ID <> Tsk.ID) Then
                DepSucc Dep.To

            End If
        Next

    'Include any links to sub tasks if this
    'task is a summary task
        If Tsk.Summary = True Then
            For Each subT In Tsk.OutlineChildren
                For Each Dep In subT.TaskDependencies
                    If (Dep.To.ID <> subT.ID) Then
                        subT.Flag20 = True
                        DepSucc Dep.To
                    End If
                Next
            Next
        End If

    'Test for successors to Summary Task of Tsk
        If Tsk.OutlineLevel >= 2 Then
            DepSucc Tsk.OutlineParent
        End If
    End If
End Sub
```

Let's take a closer look at the code. Most of it is simple, but the recursive code needs careful thought.

```
Sub LinkedTasks()
Dim TD As TaskDependency
Dim Tsk As Task
    On Error Resume Next
    Set Tsk = ActiveCell.Task
    If Tsk Is Nothing Then
        MsgBox "Cursor must be on a valid task", vbCritical
        End
    ElseIf Tsk.TaskDependencies.Count = 0 Then
        MsgBox "There are no Dependencies to show", vbInformation
        End
    End If
    FilterApply Name:="All Tasks"
    Application.OutlineShowAllTasks
    SelectAll
    SetTaskField Field:="Flag20", Value:="No", AllSelectedTasks:=True
```

```
    EditGoTo Tsk.ID
```

First, the code confirms the validity of the active task and ends the macro if the task is blank or there are no dependencies. Next, it shows all tasks and removes any filter by selecting the *All Tasks* filter. Finally, the startup block of code needs to reset all *Flag20* values to *No* before once again selecting the original task.

```
DepPred Tsk            'Detect all predecessors
Tsk.Flag20 = False     'Force Successors to be tested
DepSucc Tsk            'Detect all successors
```

Tsk is a *Task* object variable pointing to the original task. The procedure successively calls *DepPred* and then *DepSucc* to find all predecessors and successors of the passed *Task* object *Tsk*. Between calling *DepPred* and calling *DepSucc* it resets the *Flag20* values , otherwise *DepSucc* sees the *Tsk* task as previously tested because *DepPred* previously set *Flag20* = *True*. Without resetting the values between the two calls, *DepSucc* will not look for all successors.

```
'Create then apply Filter. Reset Flag20 field to No
FilterEdit Name:="Flag20", Create:=True, _
    OverwriteExisting:=True, TaskFilter:=True, _
    FieldName:="Flag20", Test:="Equals", Value:="Yes", ShowSummaryTasks:=True
FilterApply Name:="Flag20"
EditGoTo Tsk.ID
SelectRow
```

To guarantee that the procedures do not crash on false assumptions that a *Flag20* filter exists and works correctly, the code creates or re-creates a *Flag20* filter to only display tasks and summary tasks with *Flag20* set to *Yes*.

The code applies the newly-created filter then selects the original task, by selecting the entire task row making the original task obvious to the user in the display.

> **Tip:** To show all tasks again, use the keyboard shortcut **F3** to apply the *All Tasks* filter. Applying the *Flag20* filter again shows all predecessors and successors of the original task until you re-run the macro using another task or until the *Flag20* field is changed by other means.

```
Sub DepPred(Tsk As Task)
Dim Dep As TaskDependency
Dim sumT As Task
Dim SubT As Task
    If Tsk.Flag20 = False Then
        Tsk.Flag20 = True
        For Each Dep In Tsk.TaskDependencies
            If Dep.From.ID <> Tsk.ID Then
                DepPred Dep.From
            End If
        Next
```

Different tasks may be linked via numerous link paths, so to significantly speed the macro up for large schedules, test *Flag20* and do nothing if the task has already been processed (*Flag20 = True*).

Set *Flag20* to *True* to include the current task in the result and then test for any additional predecessors and call *Dep-Pred* again if it finds additional predecessors. This recursive feature calls *DepPred* once for every predecessor without requiring you to keep track of what is happening.

```
'Include any links to parent summary task
If Tsk.OutlineLevel >= 2 Then
    Set SumT = Tsk.OutlineParent
    SumT.Flag20 = True
    For Each Dep In SumT.TaskDependencies
        If (Dep.From.ID <> SumT.ID) Then
            DepPred Dep.From
        End If
    Next
End If
```

If the current task is a subtask (OutlineLevel>=2) then check to see if the parent summary task has any predecessors as well.

```
If Tsk.Summary Then
    For Each SubT In Tsk.OutlineChildren
        DepPred SubT
    Next SubT
End If
```

If the predecessor is a summary tab, then we must check all predecessors of the summary task's sub-tasks as well.

```
Sub DepSucc(T As Task)
Dim Dep As TaskDependency
Dim subT As Task
    If Tsk.Flag20 = False Then
        Tsk.Flag20 = True
        For Each Dep In Tsk.TaskDependencies
            If (Dep.To.ID <> Tsk.ID) Then
                DepSucc Dep.To
            End If
        Next
```

The *DepSucc* procedure has a very similar structure to *DepPred* except that the first part looks for successors rather than predecessors. Like *DepPred*, *DepSucc* calls itself recursively, once for each new successor it finds. The **To** property always passes a *Task* object of linked-**To** task.

```
'Include any links to sub tasks if this task is a summary task
   If Tsk.Summary = True Then
      For Each subT In Tsk.OutlineChildren
         For Each Dep In subT.TaskDependencies
            If (Dep.To.ID <> subT.ID) Then
               subT.Flag20 = True
               DepSucc Dep.To
            End If
         Next
      Next
   End If
```

If the current task is a summary task, then check for successors to any of its child or subtasks, recursively calling *DepSucc* to handle each successor.

```
'Test for successors to Summary Task of T
If Tsk.OutlineLevel >= 2 Then
   DepSucc Tsk.OutlineParent
End If
```

DepSucc contains additional code to test whether the current task's summary task has any successors.

Now we need a temporary toolbar to display when opening the project with the *LinkedTasks* code and a procedure to copy the module to the Global.mpt file. The code for both procedures follows as well as a procedure to delete the *Linked Tasks* toolbar when your project closes:

```
Private Sub Project_Open(ByVal pj As Project)
Dim myBar As CommandBar
Dim myButton As CommandBarButton
   On Error Resume Next
   Set myBar = CommandBars("Linked Tasks ")
   If Not (myBar Is Nothing) Then
      Set myButton = myBar.Controls("Show Linked Tasks")
   End If

   'Only if macros not already copied to Global.mpt
   If myButton Is Nothing Then
      Set myBar = CommandBars.Add(Name:=" Linked Tasks ", _
            Position:=msoBarFloating)
      myBar.Visible = True
      Set myButton = myBar.Controls.Add(Type:=msoControlButton)
      With myButton
         .OnAction = "CopyToGlobal"
         .Style = msoButtonCaption
         .Caption = "Copy to Global.mpt"
      End With
      Set myButton = myBar.Controls.Add(Type:=msoControlButton)
      With myButton
         .OnAction = "Macro ""LinkedTasks"""
         .Style = msoButtonCaption
         .Caption = "Linked Tasks"
```

```
      End With End If
   EditGoTo Date:=Date
End Sub

Private Sub Project_BeforeClose(ByVal pj As Project)
'Closes the Toolbar
   On Error Resume Next
   Application.DisplayAlerts = False
   Application.OrganizerDeleteItem pjToolbars, "Global.Mpt", "Linked Tasks "
   Application.DisplayAlerts = True
End Sub

Sub CopyToGlobal()
Dim myBar As CommandBar
Dim myButton As CommandBarButton
   On Error Resume Next
   Set myBar = CommandBars("Global Macros")

   If myBar Is Nothing Then
      Set myBar = CommandBars.Add( _
            Name:="Global Macros", _
            Position:=msoBarFloating)
   End If
   myBar.Visible = True
   Set myButton = myBar.Controls.Add( _
            Type:=msoControlButton)
   With myButton
      .OnAction = "LinkedTasks"
      .Style = msoButtonCaption
      .Caption = "Show Linked Tasks"
   End With
   Application.OrganizerMoveItem pjModules, _
      ActiveProject.Name, "Global.Mpt", "LinkedTasksCode"
End Sub
```

The *Project_Open* procedure runs automatically when you open your project. *Project_Open* creates a new toolbar called *Linked Tasks* and adds one button to copy the code to the Global.mpt file and creates a new button on the *Global Macros* toolbar. By now, your *Global Macros* toolbar should look like Figure 17 - 2.

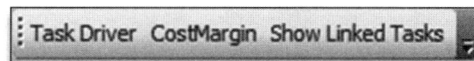

Figure 17 - 2: Global Macros toolbar In Project 2007 or earlier

The *CopyToGlobal* procedure repeats previous code. It copies the module with your *LinkedTasks* code in it. You must rename the module *CopyToGlobal* for the code to work. It then creates an extra button to run the *LinkedTasks* code. After running the *CopyToGlobal* module you can run the *LinkedTasks* macro from any active project. In Project 2010 the buttons appear in the *Add-Ins* tab.

Hands On Exercise

Exercise 17-1

Test the *LinkedTasks* macro code.

1. Get the code working and copied to the Global.mpt file.

2. Test that *LinkedTasks* works for a small schedule and a large one with many tasks.

3. Edit the code so that applying the *Flag20* filter highlights linked tasks rather than hiding unrelated tasks.

4. Click Format ➢ Bar Styles and create a new bar style for tasks with *Flag20* set.

5. Create a new procedure and toolbar button to clear *Flag20* so bar styles revert to normal.

Note: Steps #4-5 allow bars with *Flag20* set to *Yes* to appear differently in the Gantt chart.

6. Click Format ➢ Gridlines and add horizontal dotted lines to the Gantt bars so your eye can follow the level a bar is on to its task name.

Exercise 17-2

For Project 2010 users, edit the code used in Module 5 to include a button to run the *LinkedTasks* macro from a ribbon tab.

Module 18

Miscellaneous Useful Code

Learning Objectives

After completing this module, you will be able to:

- Outline tasks using VBA

- Reorganize your tasks in different sequences

- Use formulas in custom fields

- Work with hyperlinks

- Work with subprojects in a master project

- Speed up your code execution

- Use the Windows API to open and save files

Inside Module 18

Indenting Tasks Using VBA

A frequently-asked question in the Microsoft Project programming newsgroup is, "How do I indent tasks based on an indent value in imported data?" For example, if you import data from Excel containing a column with the outline level in it, you can import the data with your tasks indented correctly using two different methods:

- If the data is in Excel or another supported data format, insert a heading row for the data. For the *Task Name* column, name it the *Name* column. For the column containing the task *Outline Level* information, name it the *Outline Level* column. Now open the Excel file using Microsoft Project and create a new map that maps the *Name* column in Excel to the *Name* column in Project, and maps the *Outline Level* column in Excel to the *Outline Level* column in Project.

- If the data is not in a numeric format that easily moves to the *Outline Level* column, use VBA to interpret the data and indent tasks directly. For example if you have an outline numbering system but no level number, then you can use VBA code to determine each task's *Outline Level* number and indent the task correctly.

Figure 18 - 1 shows some sample data imported into the *Text1* field. The *Outline Number* column shows that all tasks are at the same outline level.

Task Name	Text1	Outline Number
Task1	1	1
Task2	2	2
Task3	2.1	3
Task4	2.2	4
Task5	2.2.1	5

Figure 18 - 1: Data in Project before Indenting

Notice in Figure 18 - 1 that the *Text1* field contains no periods for the two top level tasks (numbers 1 and 2). I designed the code to use a procedure to count the number of periods and another procedure to loop through all tasks, indenting them as required.

The code for these two procedures is as follows:

```
Sub IndentTasks()
Dim Tsk As Task
Dim Level As Long
    'Loop through all Tasks indenting as required
    For Each Tsk In ActiveProject.Tasks
        Level = NumberOfPeriods(Tsk.Text1)
        If Not Tsk Is Nothing Then
            Do Until Tsk.OutlineLevel = Level
                Tsk.OutlineIndent
            Loop
        End If
    Next Tsk
End Sub
```

```
Function NumberOfPeriods(OutlineNumber As String) As Long
'Return the number of periods in the Text1 column plus 1
Dim instr1 As Long
Dim instr2 As Long
Dim Level As Long
    Level = 1
    instr1 = 1
    Do
        instr2 = InStr(instr1, OutlineNumber, ".")
        If instr2 = 0 Then
            Exit Do
        Else
            instr1 = instr2 + 1
            Level = Level + 1
        End If
    Loop
    NumberOfPeriods = Level
End Function
```

The *IndentTask* routine is a simple variation of previous loops shown in this workbook. You find the key feature in the following code:

```
Level = NumberOfPeriods(Tsk.Text1)
If Not Tsk Is Nothing Then
    Do Until Tsk.OutlineLevel = Level
        Tsk.OutlineIndent
    Loop
End If
```

In the *NumberOfPeriods* function, *Instr* is a VBA function that searches for one string within another, and returns the start character position for the search string. It optionally accepts a start character position from which to start searching. You set this in the code using the *instr1* variable. If you single step through the *Instr* code, you see that it very effectively counts the number of periods in the *OutlineNumber* string variable. *Instr* returns *zero* if it cannot find the search string in the main string after the start character number. When it returns a zero (instr2=0), then the system exits the loop and sets the function's return value to the level count with the *NumberOfPeriods = Level* statement.

The *NumberOfPeriods* function returns the number of periods in the *Text1* string that the macro passed to it. The *Level* variable counts the number of periods. The *Tsk.OutlineLevel* method provides the current outline level and the *Tsk.OutlineIndent* method indents the *Tsk* task. The code continues to loop until it indents the current task to the value required by the number of periods in *Text1*. Figure 18 - 2 shows the result.

Task Name	Text1	Outline Number
Task1	1	1
⊟ **Task2**	**2**	**2**
Task3	2.1	2.1
⊟ **Task4**	**2.2**	**2.2**
Task5	2.2.1	2.2.1

Figure 18 - 2: Code result

You must make sure the *Outline* value in *Text1* is valid. For example, the code fails if 2.1 is followed by 2.1.1.1.

Versions of Microsoft Project since 2003 provide another way to indent tasks. You can set the *OutlineLevel* value directly and the task indents automatically. Strangely enough, Project 2003 VBA Help states that the *OutlineLevel* property is read-only; however, this is not true and Project 2007 help onwards say Read/Write. This method should not work and yet it does in Project 2003. For both safety and compatibility issues, I recommend that you use the *OutlineIndent* method instead. To provide you with all the options, the alternative method is as follows:

```
Sub IndentTasksAlternative()
Dim Tsk As Task
    'Loop through all Tasks indenting as required
    For Each Tsk In ActiveProject.Tasks
        If Not Tsk Is Nothing Then
            Tsk.OutlineLevel = NumberOfPeriods(Tsk.Text1)
        End If
    Next Tsk
End Sub
```

Reorganizing Task Sequences

Reporting on projects sometimes requires you to report tasks in different sequence than their native order. You may have a requirement to re-number the tasks on your report. The problem, therefore, is to temporarily renumber tasks and then restore the original numbering. One solution is to sort the file and then to close the file without saving the sorting changes. If your VBA code is in the file, then this solution is messy and slow. Another solution is to take these steps in your code:

1. Copy the current task ID numbers to a custom task *Number* field, such as *Number1*.

2. Sort tasks as required such as by date, with the *Renumber* option selected and produce the report.

3. Re-sort and renumber all tasks using the original ID numbers in the *Number1* field.

Following is the code to perform these three steps:

```
Sub ReNumber()
Dim Tsk As Task
    'Loop through all Tasks copying the ID number
    For Each Tsk In ActiveProject.Tasks
        If Not Tsk Is Nothing Then
            Tsk.Number1 = Tsk.ID
        End If
    Next Tsk

    'Sort and print the project
    Sort key1:="Start", Ascending1:=True, ReNumber:=True, Outline:=False
    Application.FilePrintPreview

    'Re-sort by the original ID number
    Sort key1:="Number1", Ascending1:=True, ReNumber:=True, Outline:=False
End Sub
```

Creating Formulas in Custom Fields

It is not usually safe to assume that non-enterprise views, tables, filters, or formulas needed by your code actually exist in any project. Therefore, it is always a good idea to recreate them in your code. To add a formula to a custom field use the *CustomFieldSetFormula* and *CustomFieldProperties* methods. The following code shows an example of how a formula can be set and the summary options configured:

```
Sub AddFormula()
    CustomFieldSetFormula FieldID:=pjCustomTaskText2, _
        Formula:="[Duration]/60/HoursPerWeek & ""w"""
    CustomFieldProperties FieldID:=pjCustomTaskText2, _
        Attribute:=pjFieldAttributeFormula, SummaryCalc:=pjCalcFormula
End Sub
```

The resulting formula looks like this:

$$[Duration]/60/HoursPerWeek \& "w"$$

This formula calculates the duration of each task as a number of weeks. To get a double-quote to appear in the string for the formula ("w"), you need to type two sets of double-quotes as in ""w"". VBA interprets "" in your string as a single double-quote (") in the final string.

Working with Hyperlinks

You previously worked with VBA code that reads hyperlinks in the *Project Control Center* code. In the Project Control Center, each task contains a hyperlink to a .mpp file. The code reads the path to the file from the hyperlink and then uses the path to open the file. In this section, I describe how the system stores hyperlinks and how to add a hyperlink to a task.

You can store hyperlinks for tasks, resources, and assignments. In addition there is a *Hyperlink Base* field in the *Properties* dialog. To access this field for Project 2010 click the *File* tab and click the *Info* tab, then click the *Project Information* pick list and select the *Advanced Properties* item on the list. For Project 2007 or earlier, click File ➤ Properties. The *Hyperlink Base* field provides a common location for all your hyperlinks in the project. If you provide a value in the *Hyperlink Base* field, all hyperlinks are relative to the base address. For example, if a *Hyperlink* base is *G:\Projects* then a hyperlink to *MyBusinessCase.Doc* refers to the full path *G:\Projects\MyBusinessCase.Doc*. To read the *Hyperlink Base* field, use the code:

```
MyBase = ActiveProject.BuiltinDocumentProperties("Hyperlink Base")
```

> The *BuiltinDocumentProperties* method is used to retrieve or set all file properties such as *Subject* and *Author* by replacing "Hyperlink Base" in the above code with "Subject" etc.

The following components make up a hyperlink:

- A name that the system displays as the hyperlink

- The address for the hyperlink

- A sub address for the hyperlink

- A ScreenTip displayed when you hover your mouse pointer over the hyperlink

The sub address component may not be familiar to you. A sub address lets you refer to a specific location in a file, such as a bookmark in a Word document or a named range in an Excel workbook, as in the following examples:

- #My Excel File.xls#A20#

- #My Excel File.xls#NamedRange#

- #My Word Document.Doc#BookmarkName#

- #My project file.mpp#20#

Use the # (hash) character to separate an address from a sub address. Within Microsoft Project files, the sub address can be the ID number of any existing task. The limiting factor is that ID numbers change, so it would be better to use the Unique ID instead. Unfortunately, you cannot specify a Unique ID as a sub address in a hyperlink!

> A task's Unique ID can be very useful to Project VBA developers. If you need to use a unique value for any task, resource, or assignment, use the object's UniqueID. Unique ID's are unique for any individual project file and never change.
>
> However, cutting and pasting a task creates a new task and subsequently a new Unique ID. Inserting a project into a master project creates new tasks within the master so again creating new Unique IDs (within the master project, but the sub-project retains its original Unique IDs).

To avoid creating new Unique IDs use click and drag to move a task and never cut and paste. This is especially important when using timesheets in Project Server. You can also use the *Reorganizing Tasks* code described earlier in this module.

In Microsoft Project VBA, you can create, edit, and delete hyperlinks for any task, resource, or assignment. Table 18 - 1 shows the key methods and properties used with hyperlinks.

Name	Method or Property	Description
EditClearHyperlink	Method	Remove a hyperlink
EditHyperlink	Method	Edit a hyperlink
FollowHyperlink	Method	Opens the file in the address with the appropriate application and then jumps to the sub address if provided
HyperlinkAddress	Property – Read/Write	Address of hyperlink (Required)
HyperlinkHREF	Property – Read/Write	Hyperlink Address and Sub Address separated with a # in between them
HyperlinkSubAddress	Property – Read/Write	Sub Address of hyperlink (optional)
HyperlinkScreenTip	Property – Read/Write	Screen tip shown when mouse hovers over hyperlink
InsertHyperlink	Method	Inserts a hyperlink to the parent task, resource or assignment

Table 18 - 1: Hyperlink Methods and Properties

Working with Subprojects

Some macros need to work with data from consolidated projects that hold many subprojects. There is a simple loop to iterate through all tasks in all subprojects, which is as follows:

```
Projects()
Dim SubProj As Project
Dim Tsk As Task
    'Loop through all Tasks in all subprojects
```

```
    For Each SubProj In ActiveProject.SubProjects
        For Each Tsk In SubProj.Tasks
            If Not Tsk Is Nothing Then
                'Task Code
            End If
        Next Tsk
    Next SubProj
End Sub

Sub Sub_
```

The *SubProjects* property returns a collection of all subprojects inserted in the active project. Remember that with sub-projects, all data lives in the inserted file, not the consolidated file.

Making Your Code Run Faster

Microsoft Project VBA code runs surprisingly fast, but there are times, especially in larger schedules, where code takes a long time to run. The following tips help you make your VBA code run faster:

- Never work with tasks by selecting the tasks one at a time. Always use *Task, Resource,* or *Assignment* objects instead.

- To work on a subset of tasks, for example all tasks with no successor, create a filter to show only the tasks you want to work with, then the *SelectAll* method to select all tasks followed by:

```
For Each Tsk in Application.ActiveSelection
```

- To iterate through only the sub set of tasks. Finish by removing the filter and selecting a single task.

- Do not move the cursor, because this slows down a macro while the screen updating catches up.

- If you are adding or editing many tasks or assignments, set the *Calculation* mode to *Manual* within your code, and then reset it to *Automatic* afterwards. Better still, read the calculation mode first, change it if necessary, and then return the application to the previous state which is likely the user's preference. With calculation set to *Manual*, Microsoft Project recalculates the schedule only once (when you reset to *Automatic*), saving processing time in the application. To set calculation to *Manual* then back to *Automatic* use:

```
Application.Calculation=pjManual
Application.Calculation=pjAutomatic
```

- Updating the screen takes time. Use **Application.ScreenUpdating = False** to pause screen updating and **Application.ScreenUpdating = True** to restart screen updating.

> If you want to display some form of progress indicator while you stop the screen from refreshing, or if your version of Project does not support the *ScreenUpdating* method, then display a blank project while your code works on your project in the background. Display progress messages for only those items that need refreshing. Once the code finishes, close the blank project to reveal your updated file.

If you work with other applications such as Excel, use Excel templates as much as possible for the bare bones of the application. Keep macros that do formatting in the same Excel template and then call the Excel macros from your Project VBA code. This technique minimizes the amount of code working between application processes which is slow. Running code within the same application process is much faster.

- If you write code that loops through many tasks in your schedules, do not call functions or other procedures inside the loop's code. Calls to functions and procedures activate overhead processing that slows down code execution. While making a few calls in your code results in no perceptible execution slowdown, making a call for each one of 5,000 can noticeably slow your code execution. Instead, include all code in the same procedure within the loop. This may lead to an overly long procedure and code that is more difficult to maintain, but it runs faster!

With today's powerful computers, most macros run more than fast enough. The speed issues you are likely to encounter happen when you work with large schedules or with macros performing lots of work with other applications.

Timing Code Execution

If you want to speed up your code it helps if you can measure how long it is taking to run! The following code returns the time it takes to execute code:

```
Sub TimingCode()
Dim Tim As Single
Dim str As String
Dim L As Long
    Tim = Timer
    For L = 1 To 500000
        str = Format((L ^ 0.5) * (L ^ 0.5), "0.00") & " secs"
    Next L
    Debug.Print "The Loop took " & Timer - Tim
End Sub
```

The *Timer* function is a VBA function that returns the number of seconds as a single variable type. By saving the value of the *Timer* function at the beginning of the loop and then comparing it at the end of the loop, you get an accurate time measurement. I set the loop to a large number because the code runs very fast, even though it is doing square roots and multiplication. This large number of loop iterations makes the code execution take a few seconds. Converting the number to a string also adds more work, which takes more time for the code to execute.

Hands On Exercise

Exercise 18-1

Work with some of the useful code examples.

1. Experiment with the *Outline Tasks* code. Add a breakpoint to the code and single step through it to see how it works.

2. Review all the methods and properties starting with *Outline*. In the *Immediate* window type *ActiveCell.Task* then type a capital O from your computer keyboard and look for *Outline*. Select any one of the *Outline* methods then press the **F1** function key for Help on it.

3. Add timing code to some of your macros and run several tests to record the average time. See if you can speed up your code execution. Examine loops for opportunities to speed your code up.

Using the Windows API to Open and Save Files

Excel has two great methods for users to browse for file names, which are the **GetOpenFilename** and **GetSaveAsFilename** methods. Unfortunately, Microsoft Project does not have the same file methods as Excel. In fact, Project does not even have the *FileDialog* methods enabled in Microsoft Office, which is a shame! This leaves you, the Project VBA programmer, with two options:

- Add a reference to Excel and use Excel's *File* methods. This works, but there is no *GetFolder* option. When moving a macro to different computers with different versions of Excel, problems may occur.

- Use Windows API's to open the dialog boxes you see and use them in all Microsoft Office applications.

In Module 20, you will learn how to use Excel *File* methods, so in this section I focus on using Windows API's only. Windows API's are pieces of code built into Windows that programmers can call in their programs to avoid re-coding basic file system functionality. There are three calls that interest us:

- Getting a file-open name

- Getting a file-save-as name

- Getting a folder name

When you write code that calls a Windows API, you must use care to get it to work. I have good news and bad news for you on this topic:

- **Bad news** – The code required to call a Windows API is very low-level and very complex. Coding against Windows APIs is not something you can do in a hurry, and if your code works incorrectly, it can crash your program and even Windows itself.

- **Good news** – Programmers more knowledgeable than I have already written most of the code a typical Project VBA programmer ever needs. When you search the Web for the code you want you will find a number of sites with working code that you can copy and use. I based the code in the Module 25 Sample Code.mpp file on code I acquired from **http://www.msdn.microsoft.com**.

The code in Module 25 Sample Code.mpp in the *clsBrowse* module is very complex and there are several good reasons why it is not worth your time to try and understand it:

- It is working code on the Web that you can download and use for free.

- The next version of Visual Studio will integrate with and allow direct coding of Microsoft Project using Visual Studio languages such as VB. These languages have much simpler calls to *File Open* dialogs using the Dot Net Framework that do not use Windows API's. Coding calls to a Windows API is a skill set required by a continuously decreasing number of people.

Instead of explaining the Windows API code, I want to explain how to use the *clsBrowse* class provided in the Module 25 Sample Code.mpp file. Assuming you have copied the *clsBrowse* module into your project, the following topics provide examples of using basic *clsBrowse* features.

Using File Open

```
Sub BrowseFileOpen()
Dim Browse As New clsBrowse
    With Browse
        .DialogTitle = "My File Open Dialog"
        .Filter = "Project Files|*.mpp"
        .ShowOpen
        If .FileName = "" Then
            MsgBox "You clicked the Cancel Key"
        Else
            MsgBox "You selected file:" & vbCrLf _
                   & .FileName
        End If
    End With
End Sub
```

The name of the *Class* module is *clsBrowse* so *Dim Browse As New clsBrowse* assigns and then creates a fresh copy of *clsBrowse*. One of the great features of classes is that the system displays all properties and methods in an *IntelliSense* pick list when you type the name of your class variable followed by a period character. Figure 18 - 3: IntelliSense pick list

shows the *Browse IntelliSense* pick list when I am ready to select the *DialogTitle* item. You use the *DialogTitle* property to set the title for the dialog.

```
Sub BrowseMultipleFileOpen()
Dim Browse As New clsBrowse
Dim Fil As Long
Dim str As String
    With Browse
        MsgBox "Hold the Ctrl Key down to select more than one file", vbInformation + vbOKOnly
        .DialogTitle = "My Multiple File Open Dialog"
  DialogTitle        t Files|*.mpp"
  Directory             = True
  ExistFlags
  Extension             = "" Then
  FileName             licked the Cancel button or pressed the Esc Key"
  FileNames
  FileTitle            lected files:" & vbCrLf
                    o .FileNames.Count
            str = str & .FileNames(Fil) & vbCrLf
        Next Fil
        MsgBox str
      End If
    End With
    Set Browse = Nothing
End Sub
```

Figure 18 - 3: IntelliSense pick list

The *ShowOpen* method uses the properties you set and shows a *File Open* dialog. If you press the **Escape** key or click the *Cancel* button, the *.Filename* property returns "". Otherwise, the *.FileName* property returns the selected file displayed using *MsgBox* in the code above.

```
Sub BrowseMultipleFileOpen()
Dim Browse As New clsBrowse
Dim Fil As Long
Dim str As String
   With Browse
      MsgBox "Hold the Ctrl Key down to select more " _
          &"than one file", vbInformation + vbOKOnly
      .DialogTitle = "My Multiple File Open Dialog"
      .Filter = "Project Files|*.mpp"
      .AllowMultiSelect = True
      .ShowOpen
      If .FileTitles(1) = "" Then
         MsgBox "You clicked the Cancel button or " _
              & "pressed the Esc Key" + vbOKOnly
      Else
         str = "You selected files:" & vbCrLf
         For Fil = 1 To .FileNames.Count
            str = str & .FileNames(Fil) & vbCrLf
         Next Fil
         MsgBox str
      End If
   End With
   Set Browse = Nothing
End Sub
```

The only difference between the preceding code and the previous example is that I set the *AllowMultiSelect* property to *True*. This enables the user to press and hold either the **Ctrl** key or the **Shift** key to select multiple files. This returns a *Filenames* collection that holds all files selected and the following code loops through all selected file names:

```
For Fil = 1 To .FileNames.Count
   str = str & .FileNames(Fil) & vbCrLf
Next Fil
```

> **i**
>
> All properties retain their values until the system terminates the class. This means that if you want to display the *ShowOpen* dialog a second time without *AllowMultiSelect* enabled, you need to reset it to *False* before calling *ShowOpen* again.

Using File Save as

```
Sub BrowseFileSaveAs()
Dim Browse As New clsBrowse
   With Browse
      .DialogTitle = "My File Save As Dialog"
      .Filter = "Project Files|*.mpp"
      .ShowSave
      If .FileName = "" Then
         MsgBox "You clicked the Cancel button or " _
            &"pressed the Esc Key"
      Else
         MsgBox "You selected file:" & vbCrLf _
               & .FileName
      End If
   End With
   Set Browse = Nothing
End Sub
```

The *BrowseFileSaveAs* code displays a browse dialog that lets the user browse to a folder and enter a file name as the *Save As* file name. What is different in this code example is that I use the *ShowSave* method instead of the *ShowOpen* method.

Using Get Folder

```
Sub BrowseGetFolder()
Dim Browse As New clsBrowse
   With Browse
      .DialogTitle = "My File Save As Dialog"
      .BrowseForFolder
      If .Directory = "" Then
         MsgBox "You clicked the Cancel button or " _
            & "pressed the Esc key", _
            vbInformation + vbOKOnly
```

```
        Else
            MsgBox "You selected folder:" & vbCrLf _
                   & .Directory
        End If
    End With
    Set Browse = Nothing
End Sub
```

Sometimes you need a user to select a folder. For example, you might want to work with all files in a nominated folder. The *BrowseGetFolder* method shows a *Select Folder* dialog using the *BrowseForFolder* method. It returns the selected folder in the *.Directory* property.

Applying the clsBrowse Class to a New Project

Using the *clsBrowse* code is simple if you follow these steps:

1. Copy the *clsBrowse* module into your project file in Project Explorer in Project's VBE.

2. Copy one of the procedures above and edit the property settings to suit your needs.

> **i** To set an initial folder for the file dialogs, set the *.Directory* property.

> **Hands On Exercise**

Exercise 18-2

Use the *clsBrowse* class.

1. Copy the *clsBrowse* class from Module 25 Sample Code.mpp into a project file.

2. Add the *clsBrowse* class to one of your own projects. Use a *File Open* or *File Save as* dialog. If you do not have a suitable project, create a new project to test the code.

3. Create a new *Sub* procedure in a new module.

4. Add the *Browse* declaration code detailed above.

5. Create the code to request a filename to *open*, a file name to *save to* and a folder to use to *save to* with three separate calls to the *Browse* class object.

READING AND WRITING DATA WITH PROJECT DATABASES

Learning Objectives

After completing this section, you will be able to:

- Read data from project databases to create multi-project reports

- Write data to a project database to create a new project

- Read data from a Project Server database to create automated project reports

Developing Project Database Code

Many organizations choose to save their projects in databases to facilitate multi-project reporting. Often it can take a lot of time, effort, and money to create new reports or to change existing reports. This section focuses on creating VBA code, mostly in Excel, to read and write data to a project database. The goal is for you to learn how to use the sample code to easily create powerful, flexible reports with minimal effort using an excellent reporting tool, Microsoft Excel.

I include code samples for working with projects saved both in Access databases and SQL Server databases. Because the code for working with both database types is the same, except for the code connecting to them, all code is for SQL Server after the first example for Microsoft Access. Note that Project 2007 onwards no longer supports saving to stand-alone databases like Microsoft Access. Use Project Server if you want to store projects in an SQL server database.

> Microsoft Project .mpd database files are the same as Access .mdb files. You can open .mpd files in Access by changing the file type to *All files (*.*)* in the *File Open* dialog, then selecting your .mpd file.

Project Server stores all its projects in a SQL Server database. Because of this, the last module of this section shows you how to read data from a Project Server database to create a powerful weekly report.

> **Warning:** Project Server 2007 and 2010 uses a very different data structure from Project Server 2003, so the code for Project Server 2003 will not work with Project Server 2007. Project Server 2007 onwards has a separate reporting database. This reporting database and SQL Server's new reporting tools allow easy custom reporting.

> To integrate other applications directly with Project Server use the Project Server Interface (PSI) APIs. For more information reference the book *Developer's Guide to Microsoft Project Server 2010* from MSProjectExperts for all PSI development.

Downloading the Sample Files

See the URL in the front of the book for the download site which contains sample Microsoft Project files, with one file per module. These files contain all of the sample code in this workbook. Download all these sample files so they are available to you while you work through each module.

The Project 2000-2003 file format is suitable for use with any recent version of Microsoft Project, from 2000 to 2010.

Note: Sample files are in Project 2000-2003 format, so if you have Project 2007 or later, open the files then Save As into your version's format. You will need to save in Project 2010 format to enable all 2010 features.

If Project will not open the files, in Project 2007 or earlier follow these steps:

1. In Project select Tools ➤ Options

2. Click the *Security* tab

3. Click the *Legacy Formats* section

4. Select the *Allow loading files with legacy or non default file formats* option

In Project 2010 onwards:

1. Click File ➤ Options

2. Click the *Trust Center* tab

3. In the *Trust Center* window click the *Legacy Formats* tab

4. Select the *Allow loading files with legacy or non-default file formats* option

Module 19

Importing Data from Other Sources

Learning Objectives

After completing this module, you will be able to:

- Import data from Excel into Microsoft Project

- Import data from an Access database into Microsoft Project

- Import data from an SQL Server database into Microsoft Project

Inside Module 19

244

Importing Data from an Excel Workbook

The quickest way to import data from an Excel workbook into a Microsoft Project file is using Project's Import Wizard. To run the Import Wizard, complete the following steps:

1. In Microsoft Project, click File ➤ Open.

2. Click the *Files of type* pick list and select *Microsoft Excel Workbooks (*.xls).*

3. Select your Excel file then follow the steps displayed by the Import Wizard.

4. To map the Excel fields to Project fields, create or edit an Import/Export map.

The simplest way to import tasks, resources, and assignments from Excel is to use a Project Excel template. To create a Project Excel template:

1. In Microsoft Project, click File ➤ Save as.

2. Click the *Files of type* pick list and select *Microsoft Excel Workbook (*.xlsx)* for Excel 2007 and later or *Excel 97-2003(*.xls)* for earlier versions of Excel.

3. Type a name for your template and click the *Save as* button.

4. In the Export Wizard click the *Next* button.

5. Select the *Project Excel Template* option.

6. Click the *Finish* button to save the project as a Project Excel template.

Microsoft Project creates the Project Excel template file and recognizes it when you import the data from Excel. The advantage of the Excel template method is that task, resources and their assignments are all included in the one import. Sometimes, however, the format of the data you want to import is not suitable for the Import Wizard, and you need VBA code to interpret and import your Excel data. The following code imports tasks, resources, and assignments from a Project Excel template:

```
Sub ImportFromExcel
'Open the file in Excel
'Read Task column offsets
'Import all Tasks Creating names and durations. Find earliest start date.
'Re-visit all tasks adding predecessors or date constraints
'If no predecessor and not summary task then add constraint if date exists
'Read Resource column offsets
'Import all Resources
'Read Assignment column offsets
'Make Assignments of Resources on Tasks
'   If Work provided, ignore units
'Update % Work complete if provided
'Tidy up
End Sub
```

Before the following code can work on your system, you must:

- Add a reference in the Project VBE to Microsoft Excel.

- Match column names to names in the *Switch* statements in the code if they are different.

- Make sure all predecessors are valid, which means if you pasted them into the *Predecessors* column in Microsoft Project they would work as you expect.

- Use units for duration and work, for example 5d or 2h.

The VBA code for each of the Comments follows:

```
Sub ImportFromExcel()
Dim xlApp As Excel.Application
Dim xlR As Excel.Range
Dim ExcelPath As String
Dim Tsk As Task
Dim Res As Resource
Dim Assgn As Assignment
Dim Units As Single
Dim Level As Long
Dim EarliestDate As Date
Dim colID As Integer
Dim colTaskName As Integer
Dim colDuration As Integer
Dim colStart As Integer
Dim colOutlineLevel As Integer
Dim colPredecessors As Integer
Dim colResName As Integer
Dim colMaxUnits As Integer
Dim colWork As Integer
Dim colUnits As Integer
Dim colPercentWork As Integer

Const TaskSheetName = "Task_Table"
Const ResourceSheetName = "Resource_Table"
Const AssignmentSheetName = "Assignment_Table"

    On Error Resume Next

'Open the file in Excel
    Set xlApp = CreateObject("Excel.Application")
    xlApp.Visible = True
    ExcelPath = xlApp.GetOpenFileName(FileFilter:="*.xl*,*.xl*", _
               Title:="Find Excel Workbook")
    If Dir(ExcelPath) = "" Then
       MsgBox "File not found, macro ended", vbCritical
       End
    End If
    xlApp.Visible = False      'Hide Excel so Project is visible again
    xlApp.Workbooks.Open ExcelPath

    'Use the Start date of Task 1 for the new Project's Start Date
    Set xlR = xlApp.Workbooks(1).Worksheets(TaskSheetName).Range("A2")
    Application.FileNew   'Create new project

'Read Task column offsets
    Set xlR = xlApp.ActiveWorkbook.Worksheets(TaskSheetName).Range("A1")
```

```
        Do Until IsEmpty(xlR)
            Select Case xlR.Text
                Case "ID"
                    colID = xlR.Column
                Case "Name"
                    colTaskName = xlR.Column
                Case "Duration"
                    colDuration = xlR.Column
                Case "Start"
                    colStart = xlR.Column
                Case "Outline Level"
                    colOutlineLevel = xlR.Column
                Case "Predecessors"
                    colPredecessors = xlR.Column
            End Select
            Set xlR = xlR.Offset(0, 1)
        Loop

'Import all Tasks Creating names only and reading earliest start dates.
    Set xlR = xlApp.ActiveWorkbook.Worksheets(TaskSheetName).Range("A2")
    If colStart > 0 Then
        EarliestDate = CDate(xlR.Offset(0, colStart))
    End If
    Do Until IsEmpty(xlR)
        If colTaskName > 0 Then
            Set Tsk = ActiveProject.Tasks.Add(xlR.Offset(0, colTaskName - 1).Text)
        Else
            Set Tsk = ActiveProject.Tasks.Add
        End If

        If colDuration > 0 Then
            Tsk.Duration = DurationValue(xlR.Offset(0, colDuration - 1).Text)
            Tsk.Estimated = False
        End If

        If colStart > 0 Then 'Check for earliest date
            If CDate(xlR.Offset(0, colStart)) < EarliestDate Then
                EarliestDate = CDate(xlR.Offset(0, colStart))
            End If
        End If
        Tsk.OutlineLevel = xlR.Offset(0, colOutlineLevel - 1).Value
        Set xlR = xlR.Offset(1, 0)
    Loop
    ActiveProject.ProjectStart = EarliestDate

'Re-visit all tasks adding predecessors or date constraints
    Set xlR = xlApp.ActiveWorkbook.Worksheets(TaskSheetName).Range("A2")
    Do Until IsEmpty(xlR)
        Set Tsk = ActiveProject.Tasks(xlR.Offset(0, colID - 1).Value)

        'If no predecessor and not summary task then add constraint if date exists
        If colStart > 0 Then
            If colPredecessors = 0 Or IsEmpty(xlR.Offset(0, colPredecessors - 1)) _
                    And Not Tsk.Summary Then
                Tsk.ConstraintType = pjSNET
                Tsk.ConstraintDate = CDate(xlR.Offset(0, colStart - 1))
            Else
                Tsk.Predecessors = xlR.Offset(0, colPredecessors - 1).Text
            End If
```

```
         End If

      Set xlR = xlR.Offset(1, 0)
   Loop

'Read Resource column offsets
   Set xlR = xlApp.ActiveWorkbook.Worksheets(ResourceSheetName).Range("A1")
   Do Until IsEmpty(xlR)
      Select Case xlR.Text
         Case "Name"
            colResName = xlR.Column
         Case "Max Units"
            colMaxUnits = xlR.Column
      End Select
      Set xlR = xlR.Offset(0, 1)
   Loop

'Import all Resources
   Set xlR = xlApp.Workbooks(1).Worksheets(ResourceSheetName).Range("A2")
   Do Until IsEmpty(xlR)
      Set Res = ActiveProject.Resources.Add(CStr(xlR.Offset(0, colResName - 1)))
      Res.MaxUnits = Val(xlR.Offset(0, colMaxUnits - 1))
      Set xlR = xlR.Offset(1, 0)
   Loop

'Read Assignment column offsets
   Set xlR = xlApp.ActiveWorkbook.Worksheets(AssignmentSheetName).Range("A1")
   Do Until IsEmpty(xlR)
      Select Case xlR.Text
         Case "Task Name"
            colTaskName = xlR.Column
         Case "Resource Name"
            colResName = xlR.Column
         Case "Units"
            colMaxUnits = xlR.Column
         Case "Work"
            colWork = xlR.Column
         Case "% Work Complete"
            colPercentWork = xlR.Column
      End Select
      Set xlR = xlR.Offset(0, 1)
   Loop

'Make Assignments of Resources on Tasks
   Set xlR = xlApp.Workbooks(1).Worksheets(AssignmentSheetName).Range("A2")
   Do Until IsEmpty(xlR)
      Set Tsk = ActiveProject.Tasks(CStr(xlR.Offset(0, colTaskName - 1)))
      Set Res = ActiveProject.Resources(CStr(xlR.Offset(0, colResName - 1)))
      Units = Val(xlR.Offset(0, colMaxUnits - 1))
      If xlApp.WorksheetFunction.IsText(xlR.Offset(0, colMaxUnits - 1)) Then
         Units = Units / 100    'Divide by 100 if units in text format
      End If
      Set Assgn = Tsk.Assignments.Add(ResourceID:=Res.ID, Units:=Units)

'    If Work provided, fix duration so units are recalculated
      If Not IsEmpty(xlR.Offset(0, colWork - 1)) Then
         Tsk.Type = pjFixedDuration
         Assgn.Work = xlR.Offset(0, colWork - 1) * 60
         Tsk.Type = pjFixedUnits
      End If
```

248

```
'Update % Work complete if provided
      If colPercentWork > 0 Then
         Assgn.PercentWorkComplete = xlR.Offset(0, colPercentWork - 1).Value
      End If
      Set xlR = xlR.Offset(1, 0)
   Loop

'Tidy up
   EditGoTo ID:=1
   xlApp.ActiveWorkbook.Close False      'Don't save changes
   xlApp.Quit
   Set xlApp = Nothing
End Sub
```

In Module 13, I showed you how to work with Excel. This code uses exactly the same techniques. The *xlApp.GetOpenFilename("*.xls,*.xls",, "Find Excel Workbook")* code gets Excel to prompt the user to find the Excel file to import. Before opening the file, use the *Dir* command to confirm the selected file exists and that the user has not clicked the *Cancel* button. Set *xlApp* to *not visible* again so that the focus is on Microsoft Project and the new project you are creating.

In the above example I start showing how to make code more flexible and robust. Instead of having constants defining which column data is in, I write code to find which column data such as *Name* or *Duration* is in and save the column number for later use. This means it does not matter if a user inserts extra columns or changes the column order as the code handles this. The following code looks for and records the column numbers of data the macro expects:

```
'Read Task column offsets
   Set xlR = xlApp.ActiveWorkbook.Worksheets(TaskSheetName).Range("A1")
   Do Until IsEmpty(xlR)
      Select Case xlR.Text
         Case "ID"
            colID = xlR.Column
         Case "Name"
            colTaskName = xlR.Column
         Case "Duration"
            colDuration = xlR.Column
         Case "Start"
            colStart = xlR.Column
         Case "Outline Level"
            colOutlineLevel = xlR.Column
         Case "Predecessors"
            colPredecessors = xlR.Column
      End Select
      Set xlR = xlR.Offset(0, 1)
   Loop
```

xlR is used to refer to a cell, in the above case cell *A1*, in the task sheet whose name is in the *TaskSheetName* constant. The following code imports all relevant task information:

```
'Import all Tasks Creating names only and reading earliest start dates.
   Set xlR = xlApp.ActiveWorkbook.Worksheets(TaskSheetName).Range("A2")
   If colStart > 0 Then
```

```
            EarliestDate = CDate(xlR.Offset(0, colStart-1))
        End If
    Do Until IsEmpty(xlR)
        If colTaskName > 0 Then
            Set Tsk = ActiveProject.Tasks.Add(xlR.Offset(0, colTaskName - 1).Text)
        Else
            Set Tsk = ActiveProject.Tasks.Add
        End If

        If colDuration > 0 Then
            Tsk.Duration = DurationValue(xlR.Offset(0, colDuration - 1).Text)
            Tsk.Estimated = False
        End If

        If colStart > 0 Then 'Check for earliest date
            If CDate(xlR.Offset(0, colStart)) < EarliestDate Then
                EarliestDate = CDate(xlR.Offset(0, colStart))
            End If
        End If
        Tsk.OutlineLevel = xlR.Offset(0, colOutlineLevel - 1).Value
        Set xlR = xlR.Offset(1, 0)
    Loop
    ActiveProject.ProjectStart = EarliestDate

'Re-visit all tasks adding predecessors or date constraints
    Set xlR = xlApp.ActiveWorkbook.Worksheets(TaskSheetName).Range("A2")
    Do Until IsEmpty(xlR)
        Set Tsk = ActiveProject.Tasks(xlR.Offset(0, colID - 1).Value)

        'If no predecessor and not summary task then add constraint if date exists
        If colStart > 0 Then
            If colPredecessors = 0 Or IsEmpty(xlR.Offset(0, colPredecessors - 1)) _
                    And Not Tsk.Summary Then
                Tsk.ConstraintType = pjSNET
                Tsk.ConstraintDate = CDate(xlR.Offset(0, colStart - 1))
            Else
                Tsk.Predecessors = xlR.Offset(0, colPredecessors - 1).Text
            End If
        End If

        Set xlR = xlR.Offset(1, 0)
    Loop
```

The code is easy to understand once you understand the function of the *xlR.Offset(0, colTaskName - 1).Text* code. *xlR* is an Excel *Range* variable which is set to *A2* in the *Task_Table* worksheet, the *Resource_Table* worksheet, and the *Assignment_Table* worksheet. The *Offset* method points to a number of rows and columns from the preceding range object. *Offset(0,0) indicates no offset*, *but .Offset(0, colTaskName-1)* code offsets zero rows down and *colTaskName-1* columns to the right, where *colTaskName* is a variable with the column number of the *Task Name* column. The *xlR.Offset(0, colTaskName - 1).Text* code returns the task name for the current row.

The *Set xlR = xlR.Offset(1, 0)* code points the *xlR* Excel *Range* object to the cell below the current cell. This code, combined with the *Do Until IsEmpty(xlR)* code, loops through all rows of data. The *IsEmpty(xlR)* code returns *False* when *xlR* finally points to an empty cell, so ending the loop.

Because you cannot add a predecessor to a task that does not exist, I first create all tasks, add their durations (if provided) and indent tasks using the *Outline Level* column if it exists. If the relevant *col* variable is *zero* then no column exists in Excel for that data.

In a second read through all tasks I finally add predecessors (if provided). Predecessor data needs to be in exactly the same format as in the *Predecessors* column in Microsoft Project.

```
'Read Resource column offsets
   Set xlR = xlApp.ActiveWorkbook.Worksheets(ResourceSheetName).Range("A1")
   Do Until IsEmpty(xlR)
      Select Case xlR.Text
         Case "Name"
            colResName = xlR.Column
         Case "Max Units"
            colMaxUnits = xlR.Column
      End Select
      Set xlR = xlR.Offset(0, 1)
   Loop

'Import all Resources
   Set xlR = xlApp.Workbooks(1).Worksheets(ResourceSheetName).Range("A2")
   Do Until IsEmpty(xlR)
      Set Res = ActiveProject.Resources.Add(xlR.Offset(0, colResName - 1).Text)
   Res.MaxUnits = Val(xlR.Offset(0, colMaxUnits - 1))
      Set xlR = xlR.Offset(1, 0)
   Loop
```

You handle importing resources the same way you import tasks. In the preceding code sample, only the *Resource Name* and *Maximum Units* fields are imported. Again I search for all column headings so a change of column sequence does not stop the code running and ignores any extra data.

```
'Read Assignment column offsets
Dim colWork As Integer
Dim colUnits As Integer
Dim colPercentWork As Integer

   Set xlR = xlApp.ActiveWorkbook.Worksheets(AssignmentSheetName).Range("A1")
   Do Until IsEmpty(xlR)
      Select Case xlR.Text
         Case "Task Name"
            colTaskName = xlR.Column
         Case "Resource Name"
            colResName = xlR.Column
         Case "Units"
            colMaxUnits = xlR.Column
         Case "Work"
            colWork = xlR.Column
         Case "% Work Complete"
            colPercentWork = xlR.Column
      End Select
      Set xlR = xlR.Offset(0, 1)
   Loop

'Make Assignments of Resources on Tasks
   Set xlR = xlApp.Workbooks(1).Worksheets(AssignmentSheetName).Range("A2")
   Do Until IsEmpty(xlR)
      Set Tsk = ActiveProject.Tasks(CStr(xlR.Offset(0, colTaskName - 1)))
```

```
        Set Res = ActiveProject.Resources(CStr(xlR.Offset(0, colResName - 1)))
        Units = Val(xlR.Offset(0, colMaxUnits - 1))
        If xlApp.WorksheetFunction.IsText(xlR.Offset(0, colMaxUnits - 1)) Then
            Units = Units / 100    'Divide by 100 if units in text format
        End If
        Set Assgn = Tsk.Assignments.Add(ResourceID:=Res.ID, Units:=Units)

'   If Work provided, ignore units
        If Not IsEmpty(xlR.Offset(0, colWork - 1)) Then
            Tsk.Type = pjFixedDuration
            Assgn.Work = xlR.Offset(0, colWork - 1) * 60
            Tsk.Type = pjFixedUnits
        End If

'Update % Work complete if provided
        If colPercentWork > 0 Then
            Assgn.PercentWorkComplete = xlR.Offset(0, colPercentWork - 1).Value
        End If
        Set xlR = xlR.Offset(1, 0)
    Loop
```

Adding assignments is a little different from adding tasks and resources because you add an assignment to either a task or a resource. The preceding code sample adds assignments to a task since that more accurately reflects the manual steps you take when you assign a resource to a task. To make the code easier to understand and maintain, I added separate variables for the task, the resource and the assignment. Although you can create assignments with one long statement, the resulting code is confusing and difficult to maintain and debug.

One small trap here is that if you export project data to Excel, Project saves assignment units as a text string. When you enter a percentage manually in Excel, you enter 50% as 0.5 with a format of % and the text displayed is still 50%. In Excel VBA you can use all of the built-in worksheet functions. Here I use the *IsText* function to test the *Units* cell. If it is text, I divide by 100. Why? Because if the cell has 50% as text, *Val*("50%") returns *50*. We want 0.5, hence the need to divide by 100.

The *Tsk, Res*, and *Assgn* objects require the *Set* command. The *Units* variable is of *Single* type and uses the *Val* function to convert the data in the spreadsheet. Using *Val* handles a % sign without causing an error. The *Set Assn = Tsk.Assignments.Add(ResourceID:=Res.ID, Units:=Units)* statement adds an assignment to the *Tsk* task with the *Res* resource at the units specified in the *Units* variable. Note that you need only the resource ID so you could save the ID number rather than the resource *Res* variable; however, the *Resource* variable is more flexible as you can refer to all properties and methods when using it.

If there is work specified in the *Work* column, the next block of code sets the *Task Type* to *Fixed Duration*, edits the *Work*, and then restores the *Task Type* to *Fixed Units*. The result is an assignment with the original *Duration* and *Work* but with recalculated *Units*. Note that *Work* and *Duration* are always stored in minutes.

The code could import and save the original *Task Type*, and then restore it after editing the *Work*, but because both the project and the tasks are all new, *Fixed Units* is the standard default *Task Type* which is most flexible and useful. The *Tidy Up* code closes the workbook without saving changes, and then quits Excel and clears the *xlApp* variable.

Excel is a useful format to pass data in between applications. With Project VBA you can import any data in Excel, in any format or structure into Project.

Importing Data from an Access Database

People commonly use an Access database as an intermediate storage location when working with other databases. It is easy to import data from Access .mdb files or from any application that uses the Access Jet Engine. The code for this section requires the following to work:

- Download the Module 19 sample code.mdb file from our website and save it to a known location.

- Create a reference in the Project VBE to a Microsoft ActiveX Data Objects library, also known as ADO. Figure 19 - 1 shows the *References* dialog with the latest version of the ADODB library selected. Any version is usable, but the newer the better.

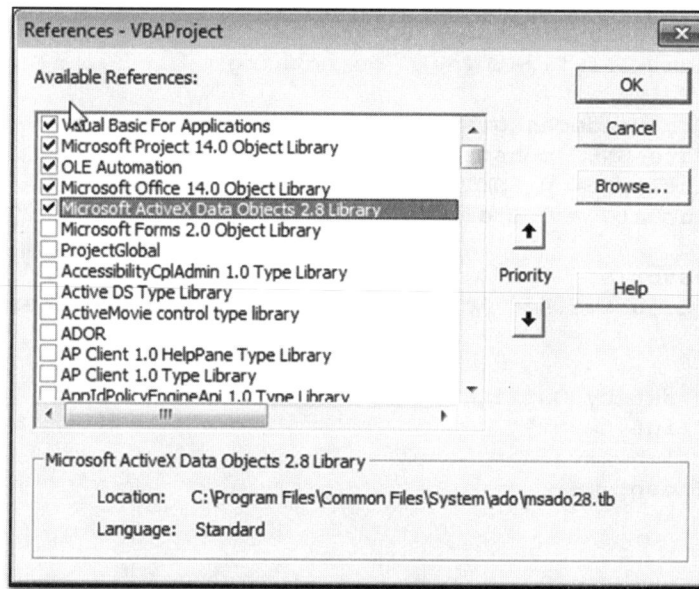

Figure 19 - 1: Set a reference to an ADODB library

Assuming that you have exactly the same data used previously in the Excel file and stored the data in an .mdb file in three tables instead of three worksheets, then the code is as follows:

```
Sub ImportFromAccess()
Dim Conn As New ADODB.Connection
Dim rs As ADODB.Recordset
Dim MdbPath As String
Dim Tsk As Task
Dim Res As Resource
Dim Ass As Assignment
Dim Units As Single
Dim Level As Long
Dim FirstTask As Boolean
Dim Files As New clsBrowse

'Create Connection to the .mdb file
    With Files
        .DialogTitle = "Please Find .mdb file"
        .Filter = "Access Files|*.mdb"
        Files.ShowOpen
        Conn.ConnectionString = "Provider=Microsoft.Jet.OLEDB.4.0;Data Source=" _
```

```
                              & Files.FileName & ";Persist Security Info=False"
      Conn.Open
   End With

'Setup up new Project file
   Application.FileNew

'Import all Tasks
'   If a Task has a Predecessor ignore its dates
   Set rs = New ADODB.Recordset
   rs.Open "SELECT * FROM Task_Table ORDER BY ID", Conn
   ActiveProject.ProjectStart = rs![Start Date]
   FirstTask = True
   Do Until rs.EOF
      Set Tsk = ActiveProject.Tasks.Add(CStr(rs![Task Name]))
      Tsk.Duration = rs!Duration * 8 * 60
      If FirstTask Then   'If first Task, do nothing
         FirstTask = False
      ElseIf (IsNull(rs!Predecessors)) Then
         'Set Start date SNET constraint
         Tsk.ConstraintType = pjSNET
         Tsk.ConstraintDate = CDate(rs![Start Date])
      Else
         'Set predecessor
         Tsk.TaskDependencies.Add ActiveProject.Tasks(rs!Predecessors)
      End If

'      Indent Tasks as set by Outline Level
      Level = rs![Outline Level]
      Do Until Tsk.OutlineLevel >= Level
         Tsk.OutlineIndent
      Loop

'      Add Notes
      If Not IsNull(rs!Notes) Then
         Tsk.Notes = rs!Notes
      End If
      rs.MoveNext
   Loop
   rs.Close

'Import all Resources
   rs.Open "SELECT * FROM Resource_Table ORDER BY [Resource Name]", Conn
   Do Until rs.EOF
      Set Res = ActiveProject.Resources.Add(CStr(rs![Resource Name]))
      Res.MaxUnits = rs![Max Units] / 100
      rs.MoveNext
   Loop
   rs.Close

'Make Assignments of Resources on Tasks
   rs.Open "SELECT * FROM Assignment_Table ORDER BY [Task Name]", Conn
   Do Until rs.EOF
      Set Tsk = ActiveProject.Tasks(CStr(rs![Task Name]))
      Set Res = ActiveProject.Resources(CStr(rs![Resource Name]))
      Units = rs!Units
      Set Ass = Tsk.Assignments.Add(ResourceID:=Res.ID, Units:=Units)

'   If Work provided, ignore units
      If Not IsNull(rs!Work) Then
```

```
            Tsk.Type = pjFixedDuration
            Ass.Work = rs!Work * 60
            Tsk.Type = pjFixedUnits
        End If
        rs.MoveNext
    Loop
    rs.Close

    'Tidy up
    Set rs = Nothing
    Conn.Close
    Set Conn = Nothing
End Sub
```

To import data from a database using OLEDB, create and open a connection object and then set up and open a Recordset with the data you want. Importing data from a Recordset requires that you know the names of the source fields and how to navigate through the Recordset. In the above code, navigation steps one record at a time using the *MoveNext* method to move from one record to the next. Look at the above code, then copy and edit it to import data from your database.

Importing Data from an SQL Server Database

SQL Server is a common data source for projects. You may have workflow software that provides you with basic tasks or timesheet data that you want to import into Microsoft Project. Except for the code connecting to SQL Server, the code required to import data from SQL Server is very similar to that for Access. The code for this topical section requires you to do the following before it can work:

- Create an SQL Server database with the same tables, fields, and data as you did for the Access .mdb sample, or modify the code to work with your specific database.

- Create a reference in the VBE to a Microsoft ActiveX Data Objects library, also known as MDAC or ADODB library, as previously shown in Figure 19 - 1.

You will also need the following prerequisites for your SQL Server database:

- The computer name of your SQL Server.

- The name of the database you created to test your code.

- Tables and data setup as the code expects. For example, there must be a table called *Task_Table*.

- You must be an SQL Server user with at least Read access to the tables.

The following code imports data from an SQL Server database:

```
Sub ImportFromSQLServer()
Dim Conn As New ADODB.Connection
Dim rs As ADODB.Recordset
Dim MdbPath As String
Dim Tsk As Task
Dim Res As Resource
Dim Assn As Assignment
Dim Units As Single
Dim Level As Long
```

```
Dim FirstTask As Boolean

'Create Connection to the .mdb file
   Conn.ConnectionString = "Provider=sqloledb;" _
      & "Data Source=ServerName;" _
      & "Initial Catalog=ProjectVBA2010;" _
      & "Integrated Security=SSPI;"
   Conn.Open

'Setup up new Project file
   Application.FileNew

'Import all Tasks
'   If a Task has a Predecessor ignore its dates
   Set rs = New ADODB.Recordset
   rs.Open "SELECT * FROM Task_Table ORDER BY ID", Conn
   ActiveProject.ProjectStart = rs![Start Date]
   FirstTask = True
   Do Until rs.EOF
      Set Tsk = ActiveProject.Tasks.Add(CStr(rs![Task Name]))
      Tsk.Duration = rs!Duration * 8 * 60
      If FirstTask Then   'If first Task, do nothing
         FirstTask = False
      ElseIf (IsNull(rs!Predecessors)) Then
         'Set Start date SNET constraint
         Tsk.ConstraintType = pjSNET
         Tsk.ConstraintDate = CDate(rs![Start Date])
      Else
         'Set predecessor
         Tsk.TaskDependencies.Add ActiveProject.Tasks(rs!Predecessors)
      End If

'      Indent Tasks as set by Outline Level
      Level = rs![Outline Level]
      Do Until Tsk.OutlineLevel >= Level
         Tsk.OutlineIndent
      Loop

'      Add Notes
      If Not IsNull(rs!Notes) Then
         Tsk.Notes = rs!Notes
      End If
      rs.MoveNext
   Loop
   rs.Close

'Import all Resources
   rs.Open "SELECT * FROM Resource_Table " & "ORDER BY [Resource Name]", Conn
   Do Until rs.EOF
      Set Res = ActiveProject.Resources.Add(CStr(rs![Resource Name]))
      Res.MaxUnits = rs![Max Units] / 100
      rs.MoveNext
   Loop
   rs.Close

'Make Assignments of Resources on Tasks
   rs.Open "SELECT * FROM Assignment_Table " & "ORDER BY [Task Name]", Conn
   Do Until rs.EOF
      Set Tsk = ActiveProject.Tasks(CStr(rs![Task Name]))
      Set Res = ActiveProject. _
```

256

```
                  Resources(CStr(rs![Resource Name]))
        Units = rs!Units
        Set Assn = Tsk.Assignments.Add(ResourceID:=Res.ID, Units:=Units)

'   If Work provided, ignore units
        If Not IsNull(rs!Work) Then
            Tsk.Type = pjFixedDuration
            Assn.Work = rs!Work * 60
            Tsk.Type = pjFixedUnits
        End If
        rs.MoveNext
    Loop
    rs.Close

'Tidy up
    Set rs = Nothing
    Conn.Close
    Set Conn = Nothing
End Sub
```

The only difference between this and the Access example is the code connecting to SQL Server. You do not need to browse for a .mdb file, but you must edit the connection string to match the name of your SQL Server database server and database name.

Your SQL Server administrator will probably set up a database on a test server for you when developing code to ensure it's easy to find and then change server names so when the time comes to run on the production server it is easy to find and change.

You can download several files from our website (as described in the section introductions) to help you create the SQL Server database as explained in Table 19 - 1. In addition there are several sites that have connection strings for different databases on the web. http://www.connectionstrings.com/ is one such example.

File Name	Use
Module 19.sql	SQL Server script that creates a database and all required tables.
Test Sample Module 19 Tasks.csv	Test data for you to import into the *Task_Table* table.
Test Sample Module 19 Resources.csv	Test data for you to import into the *Resource_Table* table.
Test Sample Module 19 Assignments.csv	Test data for you to import into the *Assignment_Table* table.

**Table 19 - 1: Files you can use to
create a test database in SQL Server**

You may need the help of your SQL Server database administrator (DBA) to set up a test SQL Server database if you do not know how to do this or do not have sufficient rights on the system.

Hands On Exercise

Exercise 19-1

Import data from various sources.

1. Download and use the test data from our VBA download site, or use some data of your own and get the import routine most useful to you to work for you.

2. Single step through the code to make sure you understand what it does.

3. Edit the *ImportFromExcel* routine to ensure that you do not add *Task* constraints if the *Start* date in Excel is the same as the earliest date (the project *Start* date).

Module 20

Reading and Writing Data in a Project Database

Learning Objectives

After completing this module, you will be able to:

- Understand and use the PJDB.HTM file

- Loop through all projects in a database

- Read data from a database file for multi-project reports

- Create project schedules by writing data directly into a project database

Inside Module 20

Using the PJDB.HTM File

Project 2007 onwards does not support saving projects to ODBC databases (except Project Server) or even to the .mpd Microsoft Access database format. Project 2007 onwards can read from those sources. Project 2010 original release has an ODBC button in the *Save as* dialog, but this is a bug. Clicking it lets you select a DSN to write to a database, but the process does not work, instead displaying an error. Expect a hotfix or Service Pack to remove the ODBC button from the *Save as* dialog. Use of the PJDB.HTM file is, therefore, limited to Project 2003, 2002 and 2000. This module is useful to users of these earlier versions who must remember that this code will not work in Project 2007 onwards.

Whenever a full project saves to a database, descriptions of the created tables' structure are in a file called PJDB.HTM. Use it as your guide when reading and writing data from and to a project database, a .mdb file, an SQL Server database, or any other ODBC-compliant database. The PJDB.HTM file is located in one of Project's program folders and on the Project CD. Locate this file on your system before you dig into this module as I use information from the PJDB.HTM file to do some basic tasks. By default the English Language installation location for Project 2003 is:

C:\Program Files\Microsoft Office\OFFICE11\1033

> Before Microsoft Project 2003, the file name was PRJDB.HTM. In Project 2003, the name changed to PJDB.HTM. This module uses the later version of the name PJDB.HTM.

The PJDB.HTM file structure consists of two parts. Part 1 describes the project database and focuses on the "how to" side of working with a project database. It includes the following topics:

- About the Project Database

- Database Permissions and Configuration

- How Information is Stored in the Project Database

- Working with Projects in the Project Database

- Adding and Changing Rows in the Database

- Creating Project Schedule Data

- Customizing Project Data

- Managing Other Data in the Database

- Database Processing Order, Conventions, and Abbreviations

Part 2 describes every field in every table in the project database. The PJDB.HTM file topics provide vital information for correctly using a project database. In many cases, flags in different tables need to be set for edits to work. The PJDB.HTM file explains the required edits to flags and provides sample SQL code to make them happen. The PJDB.HTM file describes almost anything you can do to a project database; therefore, you do not need to rely on other information sources.

The PJDB.HTM explains that, for time phased data, the system stores this information in a Binary Large Object (BLOB) by default. To retrieve timescaled data stored in the database in a text readable format, complete these steps in Microsoft Project:

1. Click Tools ➢ Options.

2. Click the *Save* tab.

3. Select the *Expand time phased data* option in the database.

4. Click the *OK* button.

5. Resave your project to your database.

Reading the time phased data accurately from the Project database is difficult because Project stores the data in one of the binary fields by default. Even with the *Expand time phased data* option set, fully accurate data requires checking resource calendars as well. I recommend that you do not read and write time phased data in the database. Instead, open the project and use the *TimeScaleData* method in Project VBA. Please note that storing timescaled data in text form adds considerable size to your project database and slows down file open and close.

Tip: Open your .mdb or .mpd files in Microsoft Access and click Tools ➢ Database Utilities ➢ Compact and Repair at least once a month. Continual editing of schedules is likely to bloat the database file size. This process also repairs any minor corruptions. Always remember to make a backup copy of your database before compacting it.

Warning: Failure to follow instructions to the letter in the PJDB.HTM file can cause corruption for the project and possibly corruption for the entire database! Do all testing of new code in a test database and maintain regular backups of production databases before you run code on them.

All of the following topical sections use an Access .mdb file. Except for the connection string, all remaining code works equally well on SQL Server. To change the connection string to work with SQL Server, copy the SQL Server connection code shown previously in Module 19.

While PJDB.HTM provides you with a data dictionary enhanced with sample code, you can also download an Entity Relationship Diagram (a diagram showing all tables and common fields) for the Project 2003 database from Microsoft at http://www.msproj.com/1002

Looping Through all Projects in a Database

One of the most common action programmers want to accomplish with a project database is to loop through all of the projects it contains. The following code outputs the titles of all projects you have stored in the database to the *Immediate* window:

```
Sub ReadProjectTitles()
Dim Conn As ADODB.Connection
Dim rs As ADODB.Recordset
Dim Files As New clsBrowse

'Create Connection to the database file
   Set Conn = New ADODB.Connection
   With Files
       .DialogTitle = "Please Find database file"
       .Filter = Array("Access Files|*.mdb", "Project Database|*.mpd")
       .ShowOpen
       If .FileName <> "" Then
           Conn.ConnectionString = "Provider=Microsoft.Jet.OLEDB.4.0;" _
               & "Data Source=" &.FileName & ";Persist Security Info=False"
           Conn.Open
       Else
           MsgBox "Macro halted by user, nothing done", vbInformation
           End
       End If
   End With

'Read all Project Titles
   Set rs = New ADODB.Recordset
   rs.Open "SELECT PROJ_NAME, PROJ_PROP_TITLE " & "FROM MSP_Projects " & _
           "ORDER BY PROJ_NAME", Conn

   Do Until rs.EOF
      Debug.Print "Name used to save project: " ; rs!PROJ_NAME, _
              "Name of Project Summary Task: " ; rs!PROJ_PROP_TITLE
      rs.MoveNext
   Loop
   rs.Close

'Tidy up
   Set rs = Nothing
   Conn.Close
   Set Conn = Nothing
End Sub
```

In Module 19 I showed you how to browse for and then open an Access database file. In Microsoft Project 2003 and earlier, you can save projects either to a .mdb file or to a .mpd (Microsoft Project Database) file. The two file types are exactly the same format; in fact, you can even open the .mpd file in Access. However, you need a way to let the user select whether to open .mdb files or .mpd files. The preceding code gives the user two file types to choose from in the *File Type* pick list. You need to specify the two types in an Array using the following code:

Filter = Array("Access Files|*.mdb", "Project Database|*.mpd").

Files.FileName <> "" confirms that the user has not clicked the *Cancel* button. *rs.Open "SELECT PROJ_NAME, PROJ_PROP_TITLE FROM MSP_Projects ORDER BY PROJ_NAME", Conn* reads the data from the database. The Pjdb.htm file tells you the name of the project table (MSP_PROJECTS) and the names of the fields (PROJ_NAME and PROJ_PROP_TITLE). *PROJ_NAME* is the name you enter for the project when you save the project file to the data-

263

base. *PROJ_PROP_TITLE* is the name you enter in the Project Summary Task's *Name* field, or the title you enter by clicking File ➤ Properties.

The PJDB.HTM file lists the field names in uppercase letters, but you do not need to observe that standard because field names are not case-sensitive. I covered the remaining code in previous modules.

Reading Data from a Database

In this example, I explain how to write Excel VBA code to read all assignment data for all projects in the database and to display this information as a *WhoDoesWhatWhen* report. The process for developing this code is as follows:

- Develop a view in Access/SQL Server to collect all required data.

- Create Excel VBA code to generate the report in a new Excel workbook and then read the data from the database.

Creating the Database View

The *Database* view pulls data from the *Projects, Tasks, Resources*, and *Assignments* tables. It sets the sort order by resource, by project, and then by *Start* date. The Excel code reads the column titles and inserts them into the Excel workbook in the same order as the view. What's nice about this is that editing the view to add or remove data automatically updates the report next time you run it. Note that as described in the PJDB.HTM file, *Work* is stored in thousandths of minutes and *Duration* as tenths of minutes.

The SQL code for the *WhoDoesWhatWhen* view is in the Module 20.mpd file, which you can download. This code is as follows:

```
SELECT MSP_PROJECTS.PROJ_ID,
    [ASSN_WORK]/60000 AS [Work (h)],
    MSP_RESOURCES.RES_NAME AS [Resource Name],
    MSP_TASKS.TASK_NAME AS [Task Name],
    MSP_PROJECTS.PROJ_PROP_TITLE AS [Project Title],
    MSP_TASKS.TASK_START_DATE AS Start,
    MSP_TASKS.TASK_FINISH_DATE AS Finish,
    [TASK_DUR]/600/8 AS [Dur (d)],
    MSP_TASKS.TASK_PCT_COMP AS [% Comp]
FROM MSP_TASKS INNER JOIN
    (MSP_RESOURCES INNER JOIN
    (MSP_PROJECTS INNER JOIN MSP_ASSIGNMENTS ON
    MSP_PROJECTS.PROJ_ID = MSP_ASSIGNMENTS.PROJ_ID)
    ON MSP_RESOURCES.RES_UID = MSP_ASSIGNMENTS.RES_UID) ON
    MSP_TASKS.TASK_UID = MSP_ASSIGNMENTS.TASK_UID
WHERE (((MSP_RESOURCES.RES_NAME) Is Not Null))
ORDER BY MSP_RESOURCES.RES_NAME,        MSP_PROJECTS.PROJ_PROP_TITLE,
MSP_TASKS.TASK_START_DATE
```

Note that the SQL code provides aliases for the columns for easier reading.

Creating the Excel VBA Macro

Create a new workbook in Excel from which to run the following macro:

```
Sub WhoDoesWhatWhen()
Dim FileName As String
Dim Conn As ADODB.Connection
Dim rs As ADODB.Recordset
Dim fld As ADODB.Field
Dim R As Range
Dim Off As Long

'Create Connection to the database file
    Set Conn = New ADODB.Connection
    FileName = Application.GetOpenFilename( _
        "Access Files (*.mdb), *.mdb,Project Databases (*.mpd),*.mpd")
    If FileName <> "False" Then
        Conn.ConnectionString="Provider=Microsoft.Jet.OLEDB.4.0;" _
            & "Data Source=" & FileName
        Conn.Open
    Else
        MsgBox "Macro halted by user, nothing done", vbInformation
        End
    End If

'Create Excel Report
    Workbooks.Add
    Set R = Range("A1")
    With R
        .Value = "Who Does What When"
        .Font.Bold = True
        .Font.Size = 14
    End With
    With R.Range("A2")
        .Value = "As of: " & Format(Date, "Long Date")
        .Font.Italic = True
        .Font.Size = 12
    End With
    Set R = Range("A4")

'Read Data
    Set rs = New ADODB.Recordset
    rs.Open "SELECT * FROM WhoDoesWhatWhen", Conn
    For Each fld In rs.Fields
        R.Offset(0, Off) = fld.Name
        Off = Off + 1
    Next fld
    R.CurrentRegion.Font.Bold = True

    R.Offset(1,0).CopyFromRecordset rs
    rs.Close

'Adjust column widths
    Range(R.Range("B1"), R.End(xlToRight)).EntireColumn.AutoFit
```

```
'Tidy up
    Set rs = Nothing
    Conn.Close
    Set Conn = Nothing
End Sub
```

One of the first things you discover about the preceding code is just how fast it runs! You could have 20 projects in a database and the code exports the data into a report in Excel within seconds. This code has all the makings of a true multi-project reporting tool.

> **i** If you save multiple projects in a database, there is a risk of having all your schedule eggs in one basket. Make sure your backup process is thorough!

You might want to modify the Excel workbook report to do one of the following:

- Filter out completed assignments

- Limit the view to assignments starting in the next 3 months

Edit the code in the *Read Data* section as follows:

```
'Read Data
    Set rs = New ADODB.Recordset
    rs.Open "SELECT * FROM WhoDoesWhatWhen", Conn
    For Each fld In rs.Fields
        R.Offset(0, Off) = fld.Name
        Off = Off + 1
    Next fld
    R.CurrentRegion.Font.Bold = True

    R.Offset(1,0).CopyFromRecordset rs
    rs.Close
```

The *Set rs = New ADODB.Recordset* statement creates a new object in memory to work with your data. A recordset is a set of records (rows) in your database. The *rs.Open "SELECT * FROM WhoDoesWhatWhen", Conn* statement opens the new recordset. It includes the data in all columns, specified by the * asterisk notation, from the *WhoDoesWhatWhen* query or view using the *Conn* connection. The connection provides the database path for Access, or the server name and database name for SQL Server.

A recordset object holds information about the data in it including the details of each field or column of data. The *Rs.Fields* statement is a collection of all the fields in the recordset. The *For Each fld In rs.Fields* statement sets the field *fld* variable to each field in turn. *Off* is a counter that the system uses to offset the range variable so each field ends up in its own column in the worksheet.

The *R.Offset(0, Off) = fld.Name* statement copies the field's name into the relevant cell. To help you understand this code, single step through it and then hover your mouse over each bit to read its values. In the *Immediate* window, when this line is the next to be executed Project highlights in yellow in the VBE. Type *? R.Offset(0, Off).Address* and then press the **Enter** key. The VBE will print the address to which the code is referring at that time. By looking at the current value of the *Off* variable, you quickly understand how this code works. Remember that a little experimentation on your part is worth a thousand of my words.

The *R.CurrentRegion.Font.Bold = True* statement applies bold formatting to the row of titles. The *R.Range("A2").CopyFromRecordset rs* statement is a very powerful statement. It automatically copies the data in the *rs recordset* object into Excel starting at the address pointed to by *R.Offset(1,0)*. This address is the cell below R. Since R is still pointing to the first title cell, *R.Offset(1,0)* is the cell immediately below the first field title.

You can use the basics of this macro as a basis for other macros to create multi-project reports on projects in a database. I recommend that you get help from people experienced in using Access or SQL Server databases, so you can report on just the data you want. A big bonus from using this code is that you can edit the query in Access or in the SQL Server view, and the code automatically adjusts to output on the information you now want without revising a line of code or updating macros on everyone's computers.

Writing Data to a Database

Project administrators often need to create new schedules based on information in a legacy system. If you have only a few tasks, using the code for importing data from Excel can work well. However, once the number of tasks gets above a certain number, which is dependent on the speed of your computer and network, using Excel can be slow. You may also want to create a new schedule in a database on your network from a computer that does not have Microsoft Project installed. In these cases, a useful technique is to create the schedule in a database and then open it in Microsoft Project.

Next I show you how to add tasks, resources, and assignments to the database. By working carefully with the PJDB.HTM file you can add anything else you want, but leave the creation of time phased data for VBA macros in Microsoft Project.

To add data to a project database, you can use any development system you want, from Visual Basic to ASP or to a variant of C. In this example, I use Excel VBA as it is the language most readers are likely to know and use. For the Excel VBA code to work, you must have the following:

- An Access database containing at least one project or one with the table structure already in place (the system creates table structures automatically when you save the first project in a new database).

- A copy of the PJDB.HTM file readily available.

- A reference in your code to the Microsoft ActiveX Data Objects library. Although any version will do, it is better to have the latest version. At the time of writing, 2.8 is the latest version number.

Following are the comments for this code:

```
'Create Connection to the database file
'Get next highest project number
'Create a new Project and Project Summary task
'Create new Tasks
'Create a new Task Link
'CREATE a new Task Text1 field
'Create a new Resource
'Create a new Assignment
'Tidy Up
```

The code to add a simple project to the database using Excel VBA is as follows:

```
Sub CreateProject()
Dim FileName As String
Dim Conn As ADODB.Connection
Dim rs As ADODB.Recordset

Dim fld As ADODB.Field
Dim SQL As String
Dim ProjNum As Long

'Create Connection to the database file
    Set Conn = New ADODB.Connection
    FileName = Application.GetOpenFilename("Project Databases (*.mpd),*.mpd," _
         & "Access Files (*.mdb), *.mdb")
    If FileName <> "False" Then
        Conn.ConnectionString = _
             "Provider=Microsoft.Jet.OLEDB.4.0;" & "Data Source=" & FileName
        Conn.Open
    Else
        MsgBox "Macro halted by user, nothing done", vbInformation
        End
    End If
    Set rs = New ADODB.Recordset

'Get next highest project number
    SQL = "SELECT Max([PROJ_ID])+1 AS ProjNum FROM MSP_PROJECTS;"
    rs.Open SQL, Conn
    ProjNum = rs!ProjNum
    rs.Close


'Create a new Project and Project Summary task
    SQL = "INSERT INTO MSP_PROJECTS ( PROJ_ID, " _
         & "PROJ_NAME, PROJ_INFO_START_DATE, " & "PROJ_EXT_EDITED ) " _
         & "VALUES (" & ProjNum & ", 'My Project', " & "#1/1/2011#, '1');"
    Conn.Execute SQL
    SQL = "Insert into MSP_TASKS " _
         &"(PROJ_ID,TASK_UID,TASK_ID,TASK_NAME," & "EXT_EDIT_REF_DATA ) " _
         & "values (" & ProjNum & ",0,0,'My Project','1' )"
    Conn.Execute SQL

'Create new Tasks
    SQL = "Insert into MSP_TASKS " _
         & "(PROJ_ID,TASK_UID,TASK_ID,TASK_NAME," _
         & "TASK_DUR,TASK_OUTLINE_LEVEL, EXT_EDIT_REF_DATA ) " _
         & "VALUES (" & ProjNum & ", 1, 1,'My Task 1', 4800, 1, '1')"

    Conn.Execute SQL
    SQL = "Insert into MSP_TASKS " _
         & "(PROJ_ID,TASK_UID,TASK_ID,TASK_NAME," _
         & "TASK_DUR,TASK_OUTLINE_LEVEL, EXT_EDIT_REF_DATA ) " _
         & "VALUES (" & ProjNum & ",2,2,'My Task 2', 9600,1,'1' )"
    Conn.Execute SQL
```

```
'Create a new Task Link
   SQL = "Insert into MSP_LINKS (PROJ_ID,LINK_UID,LINK_PRED_UID," _
        & "LINK_SUCC_UID,EXT_EDIT_REF_DATA ) " _
        & "values (" & ProjNum & ",1,1,2,'1' );"
   Conn.Execute SQL

'Create a new Task Text1 field
   SQL = "INSERT INTO MSP_TEXT_FIELDS (PROJ_ID,TEXT_CATEGORY,TEXT_REF_UID," _
        & "TEXT_FIELD_ID,TEXT_VALUE) " _
        & "VALUES (" & ProjNum & ",0,1,188743731,'My Text1' )"
   Conn.Execute SQL
   SQL = "UPDATE MSP_PROJECTS " _
        & "SET PROJ_EXT_EDITED_TEXT='1' WHERE Proj_ID=" & ProjNum & ";"
   Conn.Execute SQL

'Create a new Resource
   SQL = "Insert into MSP_RESOURCES (PROJ_ID,RES_UID,RES_ID,RES_NAME," _
        & "RES_TYPE,EXT_EDIT_REF_DATA ) " _
        & "VALUES (" & ProjNum & ",1,1,'My Resource',-1,'1' )"
   Conn.Execute SQL

'Create a new Assignment
   SQL = "Insert into MSP_ASSIGNMENTS " _
        & "(PROJ_ID,ASSN_UID,RES_UID,TASK_UID," _
        & "ASSN_UNITS,ASSN_WORK,EXT_EDIT_REF_DATA)" _
        & "values (" & ProjNum & ",1,1,1,0.5,240000,'1' )"
   Conn.Execute SQL

'Tidy Up
   Conn.Close
   Set Conn = Nothing
End Sub
```

Note that the project created in the .mpd file will have to be opened in Project 2003 as it has been externally edited (you created it, not Microsoft Project). Attempting to open the new project in Project 2007 produces an error.

Connecting to the Access database is nothing new for you. The first block of code to add data to the database is as follows:

```
'Get next highest project number
   SQL = "SELECT Max([PROJ_ID])+1 AS ProjNum FROM MSP_PROJECTS;"
   rs.Open SQL, Conn
   ProjNum = rs!ProjNum
   rs.Close
```

In all the tables, the **PROJ_ID** number is an essential piece of information. This number must be unique to your new project, so your first task is to read the maximum PROJ_ID number and increment it by 1 to create an ID for your new project. The SQL statement performs that step. The only field and row returned is the new project number. This technique guarantees a unique number. The code saves the new number in *ProjNum* for use whenever you need the PROJ_ID number.

```
'Create a new Project and Project Summary task
    SQL = "INSERT INTO MSP_PROJECTS ( PROJ_ID, " _
            & "PROJ_NAME, PROJ_INFO_START_DATE, " _
            & "PROJ_EXT_EDITED ) " _
            & "VALUES (" & ProjNum & ", 'My Project', " _
            & "#1/1/2011#, '1');"
    Conn.Execute SQL
    SQL = "Insert into MSP_TASKS " _
            &"(PROJ_ID,TASK_UID,TASK_ID,TASK_NAME," _
            & "EXT_EDIT_REF_DATA ) " _
            & "values (" & ProjNum & ",0,0,'My Project','1' )"
    Conn.Execute SQL
```

All sections essentially repeat the first section, so let's look at what is in the PJDB.HTM file and how that translates into VBA code. In PJDB.HTM, the *Creating a new, non-enterprise project* section contains a list of all tables and fields that require values to add an item. A new project is unique because it requires a row of data in the *MSP_PROJECTS* table and in the *MSP_Tasks* table. The system requires a Project Summary task, Task 0 (zero) that holds data for the Project Summary Task.

Most of the instructions on adding a task, resource, or assignment provide the sample SQL code for you to edit and use. However, the new Project topic does not. The first SQL statement above carries the minimum information you must provide to create a new Project record in the *MSP_PROJECTS* table.

One interesting and vital field that must contain a value is the *PROJ_EXT_EDITED* field. Microsoft Project stores all its data in binary fields that are not available for editing and extracts these values to the database fields for you to read. If you add a new record or edit an existing record, then you must set the *PROJ_EXT_EDITED* flag in *MSP_PROJECTS* so that Project knows that you have changed the data deliberately. The next time you open the record, it knows to update the binary data based on the text data in the record. Each table has an *EXT_EDITED* field and in some tables, like the *MSP_TEXT_FIELDS* table, it requires you to set an extra flag in the table as well. If you ignore these flag fields, the system will ignore your updates to the database, and at worst will corrupt the project.

The *#m/d/yyyy#* format is the date format for an Access database. For SQL Server, a good international date format is the *'yyyy-mm-dd'*. *Conn.Execute* is the format in which SQL executes the SQL statement using the *Conn* connection object. The next instruction adds a task to the *MSP_TASKS* table. Any task with a UID and ID of zero is a Project Summary Task (Task 0) and there can only be one for each project.

By carefully reviewing the PJDB.HTM file, and looking at data Microsoft already put into the database, it is not too difficult to determine the additional data you must add.

> When you add a new project to the *MSP_PROJECTS* table, all flags default to zero. For your project to have the options you expect, you need to set the *PROJ_OPT* fields to the desired settings. The easy way to determine the correct settings is to copy the settings from another project already saved into the database using Microsoft Project.

While creating this sample macro, I found that I needed to set the *RES_TYPE* field to *-1* when adding a resource to force the resource to be a *Work* resource rather than a *Material* resource. Oddly, this is contrary to what the PJDB.HTM file says. Otherwise, I have not found any other discrepancies in the file. If you are even slightly in doubt, then copy the values from projects, tasks, resources, and assignments that you find in projects that you saved to the database using Microsoft Project.

Hands On Exercise

Exercise 20-1

Read and write data with a database.

1. Read the PJDB.HTM file to get familiar with the contents.

2. Create a .mpd file by saving a .mpp project in the .mpd file format.

3. Save two more projects to the same .mpd file but with different project titles.

4. Create queries in Access to read queries from the .mpd database to show all milestones across all projects. Use the queries detailed above.

5. If it is useful for you, develop a macro to create a project in a database.

Note: If you wish, you can save the projects in an SQL Server database.

Module 21

Using OLE DB

Learning Objectives

After completing this module, you will be able to:

- Understand how to use OLE DB drivers

- Understand the limitations of OLE DB drivers

- Read data from a Project .mpp file using OLE DB

Inside Module 21

Understanding OLE DB

OLE DB is a Microsoft technology used for reading data from just about any source. Microsoft Project automatically installs an OLE DB driver you can use to read .mpp files directly from another application. Microsoft first provided OLE DB drivers when it released Microsoft Project 2000, but with limitations. Table 21 - 1 explains what features each version of Project provides.

Microsoft Project Version	Features Provided
98	No OLE DB driver available
2000	Read Only data for Tasks, Resources, Assignments (not time phased)
2002	Many more tables such as calendars and custom fields, as well as time phased data. Unfortunately, the dates and times values it returns for daily time phased data are incorrect
2003	All data available with correct daily time phased data
2007 and later	No OLE DB driver available

Table 21 - 1: OLE DB drivers for Project versions

Using the OLE DB Driver for Your Project Version

In one of Microsoft Project's program folders, look for the **PJOLEDB.HTM** file (called **PRJOLEDB.HTM** in Project 2002 and 2000). This file contains the OLE DB information you need including sample code. Once you connect to a .mpp file using OLE DB, reading its data is very similar to reading data from any other data source.

Pay close attention to the *Limitations* section in the pjoledb.htm file. Read this section first as it will save you time and frustration! The key aspects of OLE DB are:

- It provides read access only, so you cannot write to .mpp files.

- It does not support multi-table queries; therefore, you can read from only one table at a time. It does support *Shaped* data sets as a way around this limitation. (See the example later in this module).

- You can read Recordsets in forward-only mode. OLE DB neither supports the *MovePrevious, MoveFirst*, and *MoveLast* methods, nor does it support the *RecordCount* property.

- The WHERE clause of your SQL statements does not support ANY, LIKE, and IS NOT.

- It does not support the *Sum, Avg, Min, Max, Count*, and *StDev* aggregate functions.

OLEDB Drivers and Project 2007 Onwards

Microsoft Project 2007 onwards does not include an OLE DB driver. Your only options for reading .mpp data from Project 2007 onwards are:

- Save your projects as .xml files and read the .xml file directly.

- Save your project's information to a database using VBA and then read from the database.

- Open the project in Microsoft Project and use automation to read data.

- Use Project Server and read data using its PSI programming interface or read data directly from the Reporting Database in SQL Server. Module 19 teaches you how to read data from SQL Server.

Connecting to a .mpp File Using OLE DB

Before OLE DB code can work, you must add a reference to a Microsoft ActiveX Data Object library. At the time of writing, the 2.8 refresh is the latest version. The following code connects to a .mpp file you select and then closes the connection and returns a message indicating the successful connection. The following code runs in Excel VBA, but it works for VBA in any Office application. It can also run with little change in VB or VB.Net.

```
Sub OLEDBConnect()
Dim Conn As ADODB.Connection
Dim FileName As String
   On Error Resume next
   FileName = Application.GetOpenFilename(FileFilter:= _
        "Project Files (*.mpp),*.mpp", Title:="Find Project file to report on")
   If Dir(FileName) <> "" Then
       Set Conn = New ADODB.Connection
'Connect to Project 2003
       Conn.ConnectionString = "Provider=" & _
       "Microsoft.Project" & ".OLEDB.11.0;" & "PROJECT NAME=" & FileName

       Conn.Open
       If Err Then
          MsgBox "Could not connect to the Project file." & _
             vbCrLf & "Error: " & Err.Description, vbCritical + vbOKOnly
       Else
          MsgBox "Successful Connection", vbInformation + vbOKOnly
            Conn.close
       End If
   End If
End Sub
```

The *GetOpenFilename* function is the same one used in earlier modules to let the user browse to a file. The *Dir()* statement tests whether the user clicked the *Cancel* button or entered an invalid file. The *Conn.ConnectionString = "Provider=Microsoft.Project.OLEDB.11.0;PROJECT NAME="* & *FileName* connection string is a Project 2003 requirement. To connect when you have Project 2002 installed, edit the version number from 11 to 10. To connect when you have Project 2000 installed, edit the version number from 11 to 9. The remaining code displays a message depending on the success of the connection. If the connection open succeeds, the code closes the connection.

The next routine shows a more complete example which reads tasks, resources, and time phased data for each resource. Module 21 Sample Code.xls contains the sample code for this module:

```
Sub ReadData()
Dim rs As ADODB.Recordset
Dim cnnProject As ADODB.Connection
Dim strSelect As String
Dim R As Range
Dim Path As String
Dim strConn As String
    On Error Resume Next
    Path = Application.GetOpenFilename("Project Files (*.mpp), *.mpp", , _
            "Select file to report on")
    If Dir(Path) = "" Then
        MsgBox "File invalid or macro halted by user", vbInformation
        Exit Sub
    End If

    strConn = "Provider=Microsoft.Project.OLEDB.11.0;" & "Project Name=" & Path

    Set rs = New ADODB.Recordset
    Set cnnProject = New ADODB.Connection

    cnnProject.Open strConn & ";"
    If cnnProject Is Nothing Then
        MsgBox "Could not connect to the Project file." _
            & vbCrLf & "Error: " & Err.Description, vbCritical + vbOKOnly
    End If
    'Copy Task details
    strSelect = "Select TaskUniqueID, TaskName " &"FROM Tasks Order by TaskID"
    rs.Open strSelect, cnnProject
    Set R = [A3]
    R.CurrentRegion.Offset(2, 0).ClearContents
    Do Until rs.EOF
        R.Range("A1") = rs!TaskName
        R.Range("B1") = rs!TaskUniqueID
        Set R = R.Offset(1, 0)
        rs.MoveNext
    Loop
    rs.Close

    'Copy Resource details
    strSelect = "Select ResourceUniqueID, ResourceName " _
            & "FROM Resources Order by ResourceName"
    rs.Open strSelect, cnnProject
    Set R = [D3]
    R.CurrentRegion.Offset(2, 0).ClearContents
    Do Until rs.EOF
        R.Range("A1") = rs!ResourceName
        R.Range("B1") = rs!ResourceUniqueID
        rs.MoveNext
        Set R = R.Offset(1, 0)
    Loop
    rs.Close
```

```
'Copy Daily details
'rsProjectResourcesTimephased.Open _
    "ResourceTimephasedByDay", cnnProject

On Error Resume Next
strSelect = "Select ResourceUniqueID, " _
        & "ResourceTimeStart, " _
        & "ResourceTimeFinish, ResourceTimeWork " _
        & "FROM ResourceTimephasedByDay " _
        & "ORDER BY ResourceTimeStart"
rs.Open strSelect, cnnProject
Set R = [G3]
R.CurrentRegion.Offset(2, 0).ClearContents
With rs
    Do Until .EOF
        If Val(rs!ResourceTimeWork) > 0 Then
            R = rs!ResourceUniqueID
            R.Offset(0, 1) = rs!ResourceTimeStart
            R.Offset(0, 2) = rs!ResourceTimeFinish
            R.Offset(0, 3) = _
                    rs!ResourceTimeWork / 60000
            Set R = R.Offset(1, 0)
        End If
        rs.MoveNext
    Loop
End With
rs.Close

'Copy Weekly details
strSelect = "SELECT ResourceUniqueID, " _
        & "ResourceTimeStart, " _
        & "ResourceTimeFinish, ResourceTimeWork " _
        & "FROM ResourceTimephasedByWeek " _
        & "ORDER BY ResourceTimeStart"
rs.Open strSelect, cnnProject
Set R = [L3]
R.CurrentRegion.Offset(2, 0).ClearContents
With rs
    Do Until .EOF
        If Val(rs!ResourceTimeWork) > 0 Then
            R = rs!ResourceUniqueID
            R.Offset(0, 1) = rs!ResourceTimeStart
            R.Offset(0, 2) = rs!ResourceTimeFinish
            R.Offset(0, 3) = _
                    rs!ResourceTimeWork / 60000
            Set R = R.Offset(1, 0)
        End If
        rs.MoveNext
    Loop
End With
rs.Close

'Copy Monthly details
strSelect = "SELECT ResourceUniqueID, " _
        & "ResourceTimeStart, " _
        & "ResourceTimeFinish, ResourceTimeWork " _
```

```
                   & "FROM ResourceTimephasedByMonth "
    rs.Open strSelect, cnnProject
    Set R = [Q3]
    R.CurrentRegion.Offset(2, 0).ClearContents
    With rs
        Do Until .EOF
            If Val(rs!ResourceTimeWork) > 0 Then
                R = rs!ResourceUniqueID
                R.Offset(0, 1) = rs!ResourceTimeStart
                R.Offset(0, 2) = rs!ResourceTimeFinish
                R.Offset(0, 3) = _
                        rs!ResourceTimeWork / 60000
                Set R = R.Offset(1, 0)
            End If
            rs.MoveNext
        Loop
    End With
    rs.Close
    cnnProject.Close
End Sub
```

The first code blocks should be familiar to you, so the first new code to discuss in this example reads *Task* data:

```
'Copy Task details
    strSelect = "Select TaskUniqueID, TaskName " _
        &"FROM Tasks Order by TaskID"
    rs.Open strSelect, cnnProject
    Set R = [A3]
    R.CurrentRegion.Offset(2, 0).ClearContents
    Do Until rs.EOF
        R.Range("A1") = rs!TaskName
        R.Range("B1") = rs!TaskUniqueID
        Set R = R.Offset(1, 0)
        rs.MoveNext
    Loop
    rs.Close
```

Using the *strSelect* variable is not required, but it makes for tighter code that is easier to understand. I took the field names directly from the pjoledb.htm file and its *Tasks* table description. Use the *rs.Open* statement exactly as you would to open a recordset from a database. If you have worked through each module in this workbook, you have previously seen and used all the code shown here! This macro simply repurposes old snippets of code in order to accomplish new functionality.

Lastly, you must learn how to create *Shaped* recordsets. This is not simple, as it requires advanced SQL code. If you do not have access to anyone with good SQL skills, then the following example provides you with a good starting point:

```
Public Sub GetShapedData()
Dim strSQL As String
```

```
Dim cnnProject As ADODB.Connection
Dim rsPrj As ADODB.Recordset
Dim rsTsk As ADODB.Recordset
Dim rsAsn As ADODB.Recordset
Dim R As Range
Dim FileName As String
Dim strConn As String
  On Error Resume Next
  Worksheets("Shaped OLEDB").Select

  Set cnnProject = New ADODB.Connection
  Set rsPrj = New ADODB.Recordset
  Set rsTsk = New ADODB.Recordset
  Set rsAsn = New ADODB.Recordset
  Set R = [A1]
  R = "Projects"
  R.Range("B1") = "Tasks"
  R.Range("C1") = "Resources"
  R.Range("A1:C1").Font.Bold = True

  Set R = [A2]
  R.CurrentRegion.Offset(1, 0).ClearContents
  FileName = Application.GetOpenFilename( _
       "Project Files (*.mpp), *.mpp")
  If Dir(FileName) = "" Then
    MsgBox "File invalid or macro halted by user", _
       vbInformation
    Exit Sub
  End If

  strConn = "Provider=MSDataShape;Extended Properties= _
       & "'Project Name=" & FileName & "';" _
       & "Persist Security Info=False;Data " _
       & "Provider=MICROSOFT.PROJECT.OLEDB.11.0"

  cnnProject.Open strConn

  strSQL = "SHAPE {SELECT * FROM Project} " _
       & "APPEND ((SHAPE {SELECT * FROM Tasks} " _
         & "APPEND ({SELECT * FROM Assignments} " _
           & "as rsAsn " _
           & "RELATE 'TaskUniqueId' TO " _
             & "'TaskUniqueId')) as rsTasks " _
         & "RELATE 'Project' TO 'Project')"
  rsPrj.Open strSQL, cnnProject
  If Err Then
    MsgBox "Could not open Shaped Recordset." _
       & vbCrLf & "Error: " & Err.Description
    Exit Sub
  End If

  Do While Not rsPrj.EOF
       Set rsTsk = rsPrj!rsTasks.Value
       Do While Not rsTsk.EOF
           Set rsAsn = rsTsk!rsAsn.Value
           Do While Not rsAsn.EOF
               R.Range("A1") = rsPrj("ProjectTitle")
```

```
                R.Range("B1") = rsTsk("TaskName")
                R.Range("C1") = _
                       rsAsn("AssignmentResourceName")
                R.Range("D1") = _
                       rsAsn("AssignmentStart")
                R.Range("E1") = _
                       rsAsn("AssignmentFinish")
                R.Range("F1") = _
                       rsAsn("AssignmentWork") / 60000
                Set R = R.Offset(1, 0)
                rsAsn.MoveNext
             Loop
             rsTsk.MoveNext
          Loop
       rsPrj.MoveNext
    Loop
    rsAsn.Close
    rsTsk.Close
    rsPrj.Close
    cnnProject.Close
End Sub
```

The new code for you in the above example is the SQL Code and its SHAPE command which appends related record-sets together. You can then iterate through each recordset, and by keeping them in sync, you can simulate linked tables. The example above reads data from the *Tasks*, *Resources*, and *Assignments* tables.

Make sure you select a Project .mpp file which has *Resource* assignments when the macro prompts you for a .mpp file.

Hands On Exercise

Exercise 21-1

Work with the Microsoft Project OLE DB.

1. Test the sample code with one of your .mpp files.

2. Single step through the code to help understand what it does.

3. Edit the *Resource* data to return data for a specific Unique ID.

4. Edit the time phased data to create a report in Excel that looks like the week-by-week *Resource Usage* view in Project. You will need Project 2002 or 2003 to do this.

Module 22

Accessing Project Server Data from Excel

Learning Objectives

After completing this module, you will be able to:

- Understand and use the PJSVRDB.HTM file

- Develop a weekly report from Project Server data

- Loop through all projects in the Project Server database

- Read milestone data for all projects in the Project Server database

- Read all Issues and Risks for a project

Inside Module 22

Understanding the PJSVRDB.HTM File

Project Server 2003 has a very different database structure to Project Server 2007 and later. Table 22 - 1 shows the basic differences and Project Server 2003 is most discussed in this topic.

Project Server 2003	Project Server 2007 and later
Schema described by PJSVRDB.HTM (not available for Project Server 2007 onwards)	Schema described in Project SDK (free download from Microsoft.com)
All information in one database	Information in 4 databases
Can use all tables for information	Only Reporting database is described in the schema and recommended for use

Table 22 - 1: Project Server Structures

Microsoft reserves the right to change the database structures for Project Server in any hotfix or service pack. However, they have made the project reporting database available for reporting purposes and provided a full schema (description) of the Reporting Database in the Project 2007 and 2010 Software Development Kits (SDK). By its very nature, a reporting database is Read-Only: the software overwrites any changes you might make to it next time you publish projects. To update Project Server data, use Project Server's PSI interface, described fully in *Developers Guide to Microsoft Project Server 2010*. This book describes reading data from Project Server databases and more.

Similar to the file called pjdb.htm that describes the Microsoft Project 2003 tables, Microsoft provides a file called **PJSVRDB.HTM** describing the tables in the Project Server Database. The pjsvrdb.htm file relates only to data in the Project Server 2003 tables, but does not address the separate Windows SharePoint Services database used for Risks, Issues, and Documents. Microsoft recommends that you do not work directly with SharePoint tables, choosing not to release a similar document to pjsvrdb.htm for the WSS database. When you work with Project Server, use both PJDB.HTM and PJSVRDB.HTM together as a reference set.

The tables in the Project Server 2003 database fall into four main groups:

- **Project data** – The Project Server database exposes native data about any project in a collection of tables labeled with the prefix "msp_." The system populates the project tables each time the project manager saves a project in the Project Server database.

- **Project Web Access data** – Once a project has been "published" to Project Web Access, the system stores the published data in a collection of tables labeled with the prefix "msp_web."

- **OLAP Cube data** – Each time the system processes the OLAP Cube, it stores the data in a collection of tables labeled with the prefix "msp_cube."

- **View data** – The system stores data used for the processing of business and presentation logic in Project Web Access in a collection of tables labeled with the prefix "msp_view."

It is very risky to update data in the Project Server tables. Microsoft provides a limited set of functionality through Project Server 2003's PDS programming interface and you can also use automation via Project Professional. The Microsoft product development team recommends using the new PSI interface introduced with Project Server 2007 to update projects.

The remaining topics in this module describe how to use Project Server 2007 onwards data, culminating in a powerful Excel report. The macros read data via Read-Only views.

Understanding the Project Server Reporting Database

Starting with Project Server 2007, Microsoft has supplied a separate *Reporting* database for reporting purposes. Each time you publish a project, behind the scenes the system copies data from the published database into the reporting database. This allows them to make changes to the project database structure and still provide a stable set of tables that you can report from. The reporting database also provides interim data storage for the Analysis Cube during cube building. The reporting database includes all tables you would expect, but also normalized time phased data. In addition, there are a number of built-in views that are very useful for reporting purposes. Most of these have names ending with _UserView, for example, *dbo.MSP_EpmProject_UserView*. This view includes all common fields and values for all custom project fields. This makes interrogating the list of projects using custom data very easy. There are similar UserViews for tasks, resources, assignments, time phased versions by day, timesheets, deliverables, issues, risks and all custom fields with lookup tables showing all their values.

Weekly Reporting on Project Server Data

Project Server holds lots of useful information for project stakeholders. Unfortunately, some project managers have a long list of excuses for not keeping their projects, issues, and risks up to date, making the Project Server data less useful than it should be!

If you could provide project managers with an Excel spreadsheet that, with a click, a button automatically filled out 80% of their weekly report, wouldn't this provide an incentive for project managers to update their projects, issues, and risks? I dedicate the rest of this module to creating such a spreadsheet to help you learn the basics of reading data from a Project Server 2007 onwards database; including *Issue* and *Risk* data from the Windows SharePoint Services (WSS) database.

Looping through All Projects

Eventually, you will want to loop through all incomplete projects in the Project Server database. For example, you may want to republish them all after changing custom fields in the Enterprise Global file. The following code loops through all incomplete projects in Project Server 2007 onwards and publishes each plan before closing them.

```
Sub LoopThroughAllProjects()
Dim Conn As New ADODB.Connection
Dim rs As ADODB.Recordset
'Create Connection to the .mdb file
   Set Conn = New ADODB.Connection
   Set rs = New ADODB.Recordset
   Conn.ConnectionString = "Provider=sqloledb;" _
      & "Data Source=YourSqlServerName;" _
      & "Initial Catalog=YourReportingDatabaseName;" _
      & "Integrated Security=SSPI;"
   Conn.Open
```

```
'Open Recordset with all projects in.
   Rs.Open "Select ProjectName " _
      & "FROM dbo.MSP_EpmProject_UserView " _
      & "WHERE (ProjectPercentComplete < 100) " _
      & "ORDER BY ProjectName" , Conn

'Open and Publish each project
   Do Until rs.EOF
      FileOpen "<>\" & rs!ProjectName
      Application.PublishProjectPlan
      FileClose pjDoNotSave
      Rs.MoveNext
   Loop

'Tidy up
   rs.Close
   conn.Close
End Sub
```

To build the recordset open statement, you must look up the field names in the Project SDK. To avoid seeing all old projects, I only include incomplete projects.

In the previous code example, the *Open* and *Publish* statements are the only ones we have not used before. To open a project from the Project Server database, you must first open Microsoft Project Professional and log in to Project Server. To open any project from Project Server 2010, use the following code:

```
FileOpen "<>\ProjectName"
```

Starting Project Professional and Logging in to Project Server

In order for the previous example to work, you must already have Project Professional open and logged in to Project Server. If you need to start Project Professional from another application and want to log in to Project Server, the usual *CreateObject* statement does not work. With *CreateObject*, you cannot pass the Project Server address or login details; consequently the system starts Project Professional in *Offline* mode when you start it with the *CreateObject* command. The following code starts Project Professional in *Online* mode, reports the online status, and then exits the application.

```
Sub StartProject()
'Requires Reference to Microsoft Project
Dim projApp As MSProject.Application
   On Error Resume Next
   'Start Project
   Shell "winproj.exe /s http://ServerName/ProjectServerName/"
   Do Until Not (projApp Is Nothing)                'Wait for Project to connect
      DoEvents
      Set projApp = GetObject(, "MSProject.Application")
   Loop
   Debug.Print projApp.Name
```

287

```
    Debug.Print projApp.Profiles.ActiveProfile.ConnectionState
    projApp.Quit
    Set projApp = Nothing
End Sub
```

The *Shell "winproj.exe /s http://ServerName/ProjectServerName/"* code opens Project Professional and logs in to Project Server using Windows authentication. Shell is a VBA command that lets you start an application and pass parameters as part of the command line. The */S* parameter for *winroj.exe* allows you to pass the Project Server address. You can also pass a user name and a password using */U* and */P* parameters. Omitting */U* and */P* forces a login using Windows authentication.

Shell runs the application command you pass, then returns control right back to the calling code. This means that your code tries to connect to Project Professional before it has started and logged in. The *Do Until Not (projApp Is Nothing)* statement keeps your code looping until the *Set ProjApp* statement succeeds, or until after Project Professional has successfully started and logged in.

The *DoEvents* statement passes control to Windows so it can catch up with any actions it has queued, including getting Project Professional started and logged in to Project Server. While you do not need this functionality for the weekly report, it is valuable for many applications that need to start Project Professional in *Online* mode and to connect with Project Server.

Setting up the Excel Report

The basic Excel report for Project Server projects includes the following features:

* Separate worksheets for milestones, current tasks, issues and risks. Each sheet has a named cell where the system copies data.

* A fifth worksheet, *Setup*, is for temporary data. Initially it contains the list of Project titles in Project Server to populate the pick list in the *Milestones* worksheet. A separate cell holds which project the user selected from the Combo Box on the *Milestones* worksheet.

The macro reads all column titles and data directly from the Project Server database each time it runs. Download the file Module 22 Sample Code.xls from the website. The workbook has the worksheets already set up and contains all the VBA code. You must edit the Project Server computer and database names in the code to match your own names to get the code to work. Either your database administrator will provide the server and database names or you need to find them from the SQL Server Management System.

Reading a List of All Project Titles

The *Milestones* worksheet contains a pick list for all Project titles, so the first step is to create a view in the Project Server 2007 database called *ProjectTitles*.

To make this code work, add the *ProjectTitlesPublished* view to your Project Server database. This requires your SQL Server administrator to add the view and make sure all Project Server users have Read-Only access to the view (and all other views that follow).

The *ProjectTitlesPublished* view has the following SQL code:

```
SELECT   ProjectUID,  ProjectName AS Title
```

```
FROM      dbo.MSP_EpmProject_UserView
WHERE     (ProjectPercentCompleted < 100)
ORDER BY ProjectName
```

The view returns the ProjectUID number and title for each incomplete project. You must use the ProjectUID to refer to data in other tables for the selected project. The system uses ProjectUID, not title, to define which task, resource, or assignment belongs to which project. ProjectUID is what is called A GUID: a unique (across all records in Project Server) 36 character string. It is the only reliable way of finding data for a project.

After you have the *ProjectTitlesPublished* view in place and your Project Server user account has Read access to it, with the *GetProjectTitles* code in place you are ready to add the pick list using the following three stages:

Stage 1: Prepare a spreadsheet

1. Create and save a new workbook with any name

2. Set macro security to *medium* or *low*

3. Name Sheet1 *Milestones*

4. Name Sheet2 *Current Tasks*

5. Name Sheet3 *Risks*

6. Name Sheet4 *Issues*

7. Name Sheet5 *Setup*

8. In the *Setup* worksheet, name cell A1 *Projects*

9. Name cell D1 *SelectedProject*

10. In the first four worksheets, name cell A4 with the same name as its worksheet. So cell A4 in the *Risks* worksheet is called *Risks*.

Stage 2: Add a Combo Box to your spreadsheet as shown in Table 22 - 2.

Step	Excel 2007 or later	Excel 2003 or earlier
Show the Excel Form Controls.	Click the Developer Tab ➤ Click the Insert icon.	Click View ➤ Toolbars ➤ Forms.

Table 22 - 2: Showing the Excel Form Controls

1. Click the *Combo Box* button.

2. Draw the Combo Box from cell H1 to cell L1 and make it 1 row tall.

3. Right-click the *Combo Box* object and select the *Format Control* option from the shortcut menu.

4. Click the *Properties* tab and select the *Don't move or size with cells* option. Also, deselect the *Print Object* option.

5. Click the *Control* tab and press the **Enter** key on your computer keyboard

6. Enter *ProjLink* in the *Cell link* field and then enter *20* in the *Drop down lines* field.

7. Click the *OK* button.

8. In the *Name* box in Excel (the white box at the left end of the *Formula* bar) enter the name *ProjectsDropDown* and press the **Enter** key.

Stage 3: Write the code

The third stage in creating the *Milestones* worksheet is writing the code to read the Project titles from the Project Server database into the pick list, as follows:

```
Sub GetProjectTitles()
'This routine is called by the Open event in the ThisWorkbook
'Excel Object. It updates the drop down list with the latest
'Project Titles in Project Server.
Dim Conn As ADODB.Connection
Dim rs As ADODB.Recordset
Dim R As Range
    Set Conn = New ADODB.Connection
    Conn.ConnectionString = "Provider=sqloledb;" _
                & "Data Source=ServerName;" _
                & "Initial Catalog=" _
                & "ProjectServerReportingDatabaseName;" _
                & "Integrated Security=SSPI;"
    Conn.Open

    Set rs = New ADODB.Recordset

    rs.Open "SELECT * FROM ProjectTitlesPublished", Conn

    'Create Report
    Set R = Range("Projects")
    R.CurrentRegion.ClearContents
    R.CopyFromRecordset rs
    R.Sort Key1:=R, Order1:=xlAscending, Header:=xlNo
    R.Range("A1:B1").EntireColumn.AutoFit

    'Reset Drop Down box
    Worksheets("Milestones").Shapes("ProjectsDropDown").Select
    With Selection
        .ListFillRange = "Setup!" & Range("Projects").Address _
            & ":" & Range("Projects").End(xlDown).Offset(0, 1).Address
        .LinkedCell = "Setup!" & Range("SelectedProject").Address
        .DropDownLines = 20
        .Display3DShading = False
    End With
    Range("A3").Select

    'Tidy up
    rs.Close
    Conn.Close
End Sub
```

As usual, I point out that you should be familiar with much of this code by now. The *rs.Open "SELECT * FROM ProjectTitlesPublished", Conn* statement gets all data from the *ProjectTitlesPublished* view using the *Connection Object* code created at the start of the routine. The system copies the data to the *Setup* worksheet to the cell labeled *Projects*.

The *Worksheets("Milestones").Shapes("ProjectsDropDown").Select* statement selects the pick list combo box so you can work on it. Normally you do not need to select objects before working on them, but the *Form Objects* worksheet is an exception.

The *.ListFillRange = "Setup!" " & Range("Projects").Address & ":" & Range("Projects").End(xlDown).Offset(0, 1).Address* statement builds a text string that looks like *"Setup!A1:B50"*. This code is an example where you must set a breakpoint and then hover your mouse over bits of the statement to see their values.

Run the *GetProjectTitles* macro and then click the pick list button to determine if the Project titles appear. If they do not appear on the pick list look for the likely causes of this problem:

- The code cannot connect to the Project Server database because you have not changed the server and project server names for your environment.

- You have not created the *ProjectTitlesPublished* view in SQL Server or do not have Read access to it.

- You have not set up the *SelectedProject* and *Projects* names on the required cells as described earlier.

- You have not named the Combo Box *ProjectsDropDown*.

Figure 22 - 1 shows how the pick list looks when built from the Project Server 2007 sample database.

Figure 22 - 1: Projects pick list

Your final step is to call the *GetProjectTitles* routine from the *Workbook_Open* event. Create this event exactly the same way that you did for Microsoft Project's *Project_Open* event. To create the *Workbook_Open* event:

1. Press **Ctrl+R** on your computer keyboard in the Excel VBE to display the Project Explorer.

2. Double-click the *ThisWorkbook* object in the Microsoft Excel Objects folder.

3. Select the *Workbook* option in the *Object* pick list at the top left of the code window. The default event added to the code window is *Workbook_Open*.

4. Enter the following code:

```
Private Sub Workbook_Open
   GetProjectTitles
End Sub
```

When your workbook opens, the system calls *GetProjectTitles* to refresh the list of Project titles from the Project Server database. Your user now has a current list of all projects in Project Server.

Reading Milestone and Current Task Data

This macro reads milestones into Excel for all projects in the Project Server database. The macro reads data from an SQL Server view and writes the data to an Excel worksheet. Provided the layout of each worksheet is the same, there is no need for four separate routines to read data. Instead, let's write one routine with parameters for the name of a cell for the relevant worksheet, with a copy of the connection object and the SQL code needed to read the data for that worksheet. Now you have one routine to do all the work. To prepare for this common routine, we need the following:

- A view in SQL Server to read the correct data. Ask your database administrator to add the view you want and to set the column alias to the column titles you want to see in Excel. The macro copies the column titles automatically to the Excel workbook. Include the *Proj_ID* field in the view, but make it the last column shown. The code tests the last column and hides it if its title is *Proj_ID*.

- A named cell in the correct worksheet where the leftmost column title will appear, usually A4.

Create the following SQL views in your Project Server database. The SQL code for the *Milestones* view is:

```
SELECT    TOP (100) PERCENT dbo.MSP_EpmProject_UserView.ProjectName,
          Tsks.ProjectUID, Tsks.TaskUID, Tsks.TaskName, Tsks.TaskStartDate,
          Tsks.TaskIndex
FROM   dbo.MSP_EpmTask AS Tsks INNER JOIN
          dbo.MSP_EpmProject_UserView ON Tsks.ProjectUID =
          dbo.MSP_EpmProject_UserView.ProjectUID
WHERE  (Tsks.TaskIsMilestone <> 0)
ORDER BY dbo.MSP_EpmProject_UserView.ProjectName, Tsks.TaskIndex
```

The SQL code for the *CurrentTasks* view is:

```
SELECT    TOP (100) PERCENT TaskName AS Name, TaskStartDate AS Start,
          TaskFinishDate AS Finish, TaskPercentCompleted AS [% Compl],
          TaskBaseline0StartDate AS [Baseline Start], TaskBaseline0FinishDate
          AS [Baseline Finish], TaskWork / 60 AS [Work], ProjectUID
FROM   dbo.MSP_EpmTask_UserView
WHERE  (TaskStartDate < GETDATE() + 14) AND (TaskPercentCompleted < 100)
```

The SQL code for the *Issues* view is as follows:

```
SELECT    TOP    (100)    PERCENT    Proj.ProjectName,    Iss.Title,    Iss.Discussion,
          Iss.Owner,    Iss.Resolution,    Iss.Status,    Iss.Priority,    Iss.DueDate,
          Iss.ProjectUID
FROM      dbo.MSP_WssIssue AS Iss INNER JOIN dbo.MSP_EpmProject_UserView AS Proj
          ON Iss.ProjectUID = Proj.ProjectUID
ORDER BY Proj.ProjectName, Iss.IssueID
```

The SQL code for the *Risks* view is as follows:

```
SELECT    TOP (100) PERCENT Proj.ProjectName, Risks.Title, Risks.Owner,
          Risks.Description AS Discussion, Risks.Status, Risks.DueDate,
          Risks.Category,    Risks.Probability,    Risks.Impact,    Risks.Cost,
          Risks.ContingencyPlan, Risks.TriggerDescription, Risks.ProjectUID
FROM      dbo.MSP_WssRisk         AS        Risks         INNER         JOIN
          dbo.MSP_EpmProject_UserView AS Proj ON Risks.ProjectUID =
          Proj.ProjectUID
ORDER BY  Proj.ProjectName, Risks.RiskID
```

The *Risks* and *Issues* views are sorted risks by Project title then *Risk/Issue* number. With the help of your DBA, it is easy to edit the fields and control the data display order. This in turn automatically changes the layout and content of the Excel report. Because the *Issues* and *Risks* views both refer to the WSS database by name, both views can live in the Project Server database. The idea behind putting as much information as possible in the views is that database administrators are usually more readily available to edit views than you are to edit code.

Writing the VBA Code for the Excel Report Macro

The comments for the common routine to import all data are:

```
Sub GetData
    'Clear old data
    'Copy headings and data from Project Server
    'Format Data
    'Tidy up and Hide Proj_ID column
End Sub
```

The code for these comments is:

```
Sub GetData(RangeName As String, Conn As ADODB.Connection, Sql As String)
Dim rs As ADODB.Recordset
Dim R As Range
Dim fld As ADODB.Field
Dim Off As Long
    Set rs = New ADODB.Recordset

    'Clear old data
    Set R = Range(RangeName)
    R.CurrentRegion.EntireColumn.Hidden = False

    'Copy headings and data from Project Server
    rs.Open Sql, Conn
    For Each fld In rs.Fields
        R.Offset(0, Off) = fld.Name
        Off = Off + 1
    Next fld

    With R.CurrentRegion
```

```
        .Font.Bold = True
        .VerticalAlignment = xlVAlignCenter
        .HorizontalAlignment = xlHAlignCenter
    End With
    R.Range("A2").CopyFromRecordset rs
    rs.Close

    'Format Data
    Set R = Range(RangeName)
    With R.CurrentRegion.Offset(1, 0)
        .WrapText = True
        .VerticalAlignment = xlVAlignTop
    End With
    With R.CurrentRegion.EntireColumn
        .WrapText = False
        .AutoFit
    End With

    'Tidy up and Hide Proj_ID column
    With R.End(xlToRight)
        If .Text = "ProjectUID" Then
            .EntireColumn.Hidden = True
        End If
    End With
    R.EntireColumn.ColumnWidth = 40
End Sub
```

The *RangeName* code for getting all *Milestones* data is *Milestones* and it typically refers to A4 in the *Milestones* worksheet. The first block of code works on all cells in the current region. When you press **Ctrl+Shift+8 (Ctrl+*)** on your computer keyboard in Excel, the software selects all cells until it reaches either a blank row or column or the edge of the worksheet. The *CurrentRegion* method returns the same cell area. Clearing a report after a previous run includes showing any hidden columns and deleting all data.

The remaining code is once again a variation on previous code. Single-step through the code and look at the variables and properties to see their values as the code execution progresses through the routine.

Before writing the final VBA code, let's review the prerequisites for this macro. The items already in place are:

- All SQL views to read the data. You can edit these views which in turn changes the data imported to our Excel report.

- The code to read all Project titles in a pick list.

- Named cells in the Excel workbook to mark where each set of data goes.

- A common routine (GetData) to read data for all worksheets.

There are two more routines required to complete the tool: *UpdateReport* and *ClearReport*. The *UpdateReport* routine calls *GetData* once for each worksheet and provides the SQL code and the database connection *Object*. The *ClearReport* routine is a utility function to clear all data from the report. The comments for this code are:

```
Sub UpdateReport
    'Delete Old Data
```

```
    'Setup database connection
    'Get Proj_ID and update Project title from Project List
    'Fill Worksheets
    'Delete <div>, </div>,  
    'Tidy Up
End Sub
```

The contents of some *Text* fields are stored as HTML code, so the *Delete <div>, </div>, * code removes the HTML tags to make the text more readable. Since the code only reads the text, removing the tags does not affect anything else. The *UpdateReport* code is as follows:

```
Sub UpdateReport()
Dim Conn As ADODB.Connection
Dim rs As ADODB.Recordset
Dim ProjGUID As String
Dim R As Range
Dim Sql As String
    'Delete Old Data
    ClearReport

    'Setup database connection
    Set Conn = New ADODB.Connection
    Conn.ConnectionString = "Provider=sqloledb;" _
            & "Data Source=(local);" _
            & "Initial Catalog=ProjectServer2007_Litware_Reporting;" _
            & "Integrated Security=SSPI;"
    Conn.Open

    'Get Proj_ID and update Project title from Project List
    ProjGUID = Left(Range("Projects").Offset( _
                    Range("SelectedProject").Value - 1, 1),38)
    Range("ProjectTitle") = "Project Title: " & _
        Range("Projects").Offset(Range("SelectedProject") - 1, 0).Text
    Range("ProjectTitle").Range("A2") = "As of: " & Format(Date, "Long Date")

    'Fill Worksheets
    Sql = "SELECT * FROM Milestones WHERE (ProjectUID='" & ProjGUID & "')"
    GetData "Milestones", Conn, Sql

    Sql = "SELECT * FROM CurrentTasks WHERE (ProjectUID='" _
        & ProjGUID & "')"
    GetData "CurrentTasks", Conn, Sql

    Sql = "SELECT * FROM Issues WHERE (ProjectUID='" & ProjGUID & "')"
    GetData "Issues", Conn, Sql

    Sql = "SELECT * FROM Risks WHERE (ProjectUID='" & ProjGUID & "')"
    GetData "Risks", Conn, Sql

    'Delete <div>, </div>,  
    With Range("Issues").CurrentRegion
        .Replace "<div>", ""
        .Replace "</div>", ""
```

```
        .Replace "< >", ""
    End With
    With Range("Risks").CurrentRegion
        .Replace "<div>", ""
        .Replace "</div>", ""
        .Replace " ", ""
    End With

    'Tidy Up
    Conn.Close
End Sub
```

Most of the preceding code should be familiar to you by now except for the *ProjGUID = Range("Projects").Offset(Range("SelectedProject") - 1, 1)* code. The pick list has a cell link property in which you designate a cell that the control uses to store the selected value. This value is a number for the selected project. For example, if you select the second project in the list, the linked cell contains the value 2. You now need code to translate the value 2 into the ProjectGUID for the selected project.

In the *Setup* worksheet your code stores a list of all Project ID's and their Project titles. The system displays the titles in the list, but does not display the ID's. If your code reads down to the second project in the *Setup* list, then your code can read the ProjectGUID and the Project title. That is the function of this code as it goes to the projects named cell A1 in the *Setup* worksheet and then goes down the number of cells in the *SelectedProject minus 1* linked cell. *Minus 1* because it offsets *start* at *zero*, not *one*.

The returned value is in the *Left* function purely as a security measure. Your code expects a 36 character GUID plus two curly brackets in the *Projects* list. So, just in case someone injects some malicious SQL code into a cell in the Project's range, forcing the code to only accept the first 38 characters adds a useful layer of protection. Good code security involves carefully forcing all data input by a user to a format that you expect. The likelihood of someone within your organization doing this is very remote; however good security is a habit and is the responsibility of everyone who can improve it.

Each call to *GetData* has three parameters: the name of the cell where *GetData* will write your data, the *Object Conn* connection, and the SQL code passed in the *Sql* string variable. Notice the simplicity of the SQL code to read issues or risks now that you have a SQL Server view in the background to do the difficult work. The SQL code is:

SELECT * FROM Risks WHERE (ProjectUID='" & ProjectUID & "')"

This code also explains why you need to include the *ProjectUID* field in the views. Your code must select only the issues or risks for the selected project. By placing the *ProjectUID* field last the *GetData* code can easily test for its presence and hide it because users do not need to see the *ProjectUID* data. If your *Issues* and *Risks* data includes more HTML tags than those for which we test here, simply add an extra *Replace* statement to delete them.

We now need a small routine to clear any existing data from the report before refreshing the data. Since you might edit the view to add new columns, change their order, or delete the column titles, *GetData* refreshes everything. The code to clear the report follows:

```
Sub ClearReport()
    With Range("Milestones").CurrentRegion
        .EntireColumn.Hidden = False
        .ClearContents
    End With
    With Range("CurrentTasks").CurrentRegion
        .EntireColumn.Hidden = False
        .ClearContents
    End With
    With Range("Issues").CurrentRegion
        .EntireColumn.Hidden = False
        .ClearContents
    End With
    With Range("Risks").CurrentRegion
        .EntireColumn.Hidden = False
        .ClearContents
    End With
End Sub
```

Note that the code shows any hidden columns as well so *GetData* starts with a completely clean worksheet.

Creating a Project Program Report

You now have an effective reporting tool for individual reports in Excel. With this, it is not difficult to create a different Excel report for a program of projects. To create a program report you need to complete the following steps:

1. Add a custom enterprise *Project* field in the Enterprise Global file in Project Server to enter the program name. Use a value list in this field to avoid typing errors.

2. Create views in SQL Server to select the data you want in the *Program* report.

3. Copy the Excel *Project* report for a *Program* report.

4. Edit the code to call the program views instead of the project views you used above.

Another version of the report you can create is one for all projects for a particular manager or corporate strategy. Add the necessary enterprise custom *Project* field in Project Server and the views in SQL Server and another useful report is nearly finished!

Hands On Exercise

Exercise 22-1

Work with the weekly report code.

1. Format the weekly report to make it more readable and attractive. Try adding a colored background and *Red*, *Yellow*, and *Green* flags for milestones to show whether they are behind schedule, or for issues and risks on their due dates.

2. Add a worksheet for comments needed in your weekly reports.

3. Add a macro button on the first worksheet to run the macro.

4. If you need to report by project program or all projects for different managers, create a new version of the Excel report.

Module 23

Using Project 2007 VBA

Learning Objectives

After completing this module, you will be able to:

- Understand new features in Project 2007 VBA

- Write code using the new features in Project 2007 VBA

- Convert the SQL Statements in Module 22 to the Project Server 2007 Reporting Database

Inside Module 23

Introducing Project 2007 VBA

Microsoft Project 2007 introduced a number of very useful new features. These new features include:

- Multiple undo

- Task drivers (the Task Investigator)

- Calendars

- Visual Reporting

- Cell Formatting

- Deliverables (Project 2007 Professional only)

Project 2007 VBA provides full support for these key features. There are also a number of other, smaller improvements, all of which Project 2007 VBA supports. I will only discuss the main feature groups listed above. To find what is new for Project 2007 VBA:

1. Open the Visual Basic Editor (VBE) for Project 2007.

2. Press **F1** for Help.

3. Search for the *What's New* topic.

In Project 2007 VBA, a number of objects, methods, and properties used in Project 2003 VBA (such as the Global Object) now have alternatives where Project 2007 does things differently from Project 2003. These members no longer have descriptions in the Help files, but Microsoft still supports them for compatibility. For example, the system now hides many project level fields such as *Start, Work,* and *Cost.* Instead you should use *ActiveProject.ProjectSummaryTask.Start,* etc.

To see these hidden members in the Object Browser:

4. In the VBE press the **F2** function key to open the Object Browser.

5. Right-click anywhere in the Object Browser window and then click the *Show Hidden Members* option.

To get full details of programming Project and Project Server 2007 download the Project Server 2007 SDK by searching for Project Server 2007 SDK at **www.microsoft.com**. The SDK includes full details on how to use the Project Server Interface (PSI) to control Project Server. PSI is a powerful development interface for programmers using Visual Studio.

The following link details all Object Model Changes for Project 2007 http://msproj.com/1003

Using Named Parameters

There are a number of new parameters and options for existing methods and objects in Project 2007 VBA. If a new parameter is optional, then Microsoft can safely add it to the end of the parameter list. However, if the new parameter is required, then it has to precede all optional parameters. This means that if you specify parameters by including a comma for each parameter, your code may fail in Project 2007 as you will have the wrong number or sequence of parameters.

The safest way to code all calls to objects and methods with parameters is to name the parameters. That way wherever you add new parameters their naming ensures your code will continue to work with each new release of Microsoft Project. An example of a named parameter is:

```
Sort Key1:="ID", Ascending1:=True
```

The parameters are all separated from their values by := (colon then an equals).

Undoing a Macro

If you ever ran a macro without saving your project first and then regretted it once you saw the results, then this feature is for you! Project 2007 has multiple levels of undo. The number of undo levels defaults to 20, but the following statement increases the levels to 30:

```
Application.UndoLevels = 30
```

Every time VBA code executes an undoable action, the system adds a new undo record onto the undo list. If your macro performs 50 undo actions, then with 30 undo levels 20 actions will be lost. Even if you increase the undo levels to 50, your user is likely to be very confused!

Project 2007 VBA allows you to group undoable actions together by giving them a single name (such as Formatting-Macro) and then that one name appears in the *Undo* list. The user can then undo all the actions of the macro in one easy undo.

To group many actions together, you need to create an Undo Transaction Set. To create an Undo Transaction Set copy and edit the following code:

```
Sub CreateUndoTransaction()
    Application.OpenUndoTransaction "Macro Changes"

    'Insert code that changes your project here

    Application.CloseUndoTransaction
End Sub
```

The following code is an edited example that simply adds 3 tasks to a project.

```
Sub CreateUndoTransaction()
    Application.OpenUndoTransaction "Macro Changes"

    ActiveProject.Tasks.Add "Macro Inserted Task 1"
    ActiveProject.Tasks.Add "Macro Inserted Task 2"
    ActiveProject.Tasks.Add "Macro Inserted Task 3"

    Application.CloseUndoTransaction
End Sub
```

Figure 23 - 1 shows a project where a user ran a macro to add 3 tasks. The macro creates a transaction called **Macro Changes** to capture all task additions. By clicking the *Undo* pick list button, you see *Macro Changes* at the top, as the most recent action. Click the *Macro Changes* item and the system removes all tasks inserted by the macro.

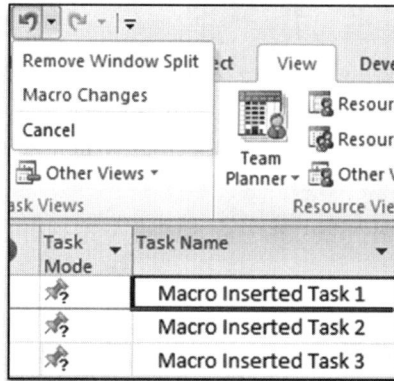

Figure 23 - 1: Undo list with the Macro Changes transaction

Rod Gill recommends that you capture the changes your macro makes to a project file in a VBA Undo Transaction which allows the user to easily undo the results of running the macro.

Managing Custom Fields

Project 2007 VBA handles custom fields in a slightly different manner than previous versions. You still manage local fields as with previous versions, but you must now manage all enterprise fields for Project Server 2007 in Project Web Access (PWA). The basic changes are as follows:

- Enterprise custom field details are Read-Only in Project Professional.

- You can create as many enterprise custom fields as you want (from PWA provided you have Admin rights).

- You can still customize local fields such as *Text1*, etc.

To read and write to the new enterprise custom fields you need to use the *GetField, SetField* and *FieldNameToField Constant* methods. To read a project level enterprise custom field called *Technical Reviewer* use the code:

```
Dim TechnicalReviewer as String
   TechnicalReviewer = ActiveProject.ProjectSummaryTask _
      .GetField(FieldNameToFieldConstant("Technical Reviewer"), pjProject)
```

To write to the same field use:

```
ActiveProject.ProjectSummaryTask.SetField _
    FieldNameToFieldConstant("Technical Reviewer"), "New Value", pjProject
```

The *GetField* method needs only a constant representing the field and the *SetField* method needs the same constant and the new value for the field. The field constant can be stored in a variable of type *Long*. As there are *Project, Task* and *Resource Enterprise* custom fields, a field type parameter specifies which type you are working with. It has the values *pjProject, pjTask* or *pjResource*.

This new method is not as simple as before, but you gain as many fields as you want using any name you want.

Controlling Visual Reports

Project 2007 VBA has a number of new objects and methods to support the new *Visual Reports* feature. The simplest way to learn about them is to record a macro as you create and view a *Visual Report*. The following recorded code creates a new report template and then displays it.

```
VisualReportsNewTemplate PjVisualReportsCubeType:=pjResourceTP
VisualReportsSaveCube strNamePath:="C:\CubesPath\Resource Usage.cub", _
    PjVisualReportsCubeType:=pjResourceTP
VisualReportsView _
    strVisualReportTemplateFile:="C:\Templates\My Resource\Usage.xlt"
```

Note that the new template method simply displays the *New* template view in Excel for the user to create the template.

Managing Calendars

Project 2007 offers new functionality to project schedulers. In previous versions, if shift times needed to change for all working days on a calendar, then every day was an exception. In Project 2007 *Exception* calendars allow you to define new base working hours so any edits (such as for vacations) can be seen as exceptions. There are two different types of calendar edits: *Exceptions* and *Work Week*. You use *Exception* edits to create sub-calendars. For example, if a construction company has different winter and summer working hours, you can create a *Winter* and *Summer Exceptions* calendar, each with different working hours.

If a resource is taking a week of vacation, add a new working week that includes the vacation period. Project VBA calls a working week entry an *EffectiveWeek*. A resource can have an *Exception* and a *Working Week* calendar that overrules the *Exception* edit as well.

The following code creates an *Exception* calendar for a resource to show extra working hours before Christmas and then adds a *Work Week* calendar for a vacation:

```
Sub AddException()
Dim cal As Calendar
   Set cal = ActiveProject.Resources("My Resource").Calendar

   ' Exception bitmask for Mon, Tue, Wed, Thu, Fri
   'is 00111110, or Hexadecimal 0x3E
   cal.Exceptions.Add Type:=pjWeekly, _
      Start:="1/12/2010", Finish:="24/12/2010", _
      Name:="BeforeXmas", DaysOfWeek:=&H3E&

   cal.Exceptions("BeforeXmas").Shift1.Start = #9:00:00 AM#
   cal.Exceptions("BeforeXmas").Shift1.Finish = #12:00:00 PM#
   cal.Exceptions("BeforeXmas").Shift2.Start = #1:00:00 PM#
   cal.Exceptions("BeforeXmas").Shift2.Finish = #4:00:00 PM#

   cal.Exceptions.Add Type:=pjDaily, Start:="25/12/2007", Finish:="3/1/2008", _
      Name:="Xmas vacation"
End Sub
```

The code specifies all dates in m/d/yyyy format. An error will occur if any exception conflicts or overlaps with another one. By default, creating an exception creates a nonworking period.

Formatting Cell Background Colors

Another feature in Project 2007 allows you to apply a background color to the cells in your project. There are two ways to set the background color of a cell as shown in the following code sample:

```
Font CellColor:=pjRed
ActiveCell.CellColor=pjBlue
```

Either way works, but we can use the *ActiveCell.CellColor* method to read the current cell background color as shown below:

```
Sub TestCellColor()
Dim ThisCellColor As String
Dim ColorIndex As Integer
   ColorIndex = ActiveCell.CellColor
   ThisCellColor = Choose(CSng(ColorIndex), "Black", "Red", _
      "Yellow", "Lime", "Aqua", "Blue", "Fuchsia", "White", _
      "Maroon", "Green", "Olive", "Navy", "Purple", "Teal", _
      "Grey", "Siver", "Automatic")
   MsgBox "The active cell's background color is: " _
      & ThisCellColor, vbInformation
End Sub
```

The *CellColor* property returns a number from *0* to *16*. If you look at the dropdown list for colors in the *Format ≻ Font* dialog then *0* is *Black, 1* is *Red* and so on down to the 17th item which is *Automatic*. The *Choose* function converts the number returned by the *CellColor* property to a string for the color.

Managing Deliverables

Deliverables are a new feature in Project Professional 2007 when used with Project Server 2007. The system allows you to create tasks, flag them as deliverables, and then use them to negotiate and track agreed dates when cross-project deliverables will occur. One project can create and update deliverables (called *Commitment* objects in Project VBA) and other projects can get and then accept changes to deliverables. Thus, using deliverables is a better and more realistic way of managing cross-project relationships.

The easiest way to see how VBA works with deliverables is to record a macro of you manually doing what you want. However the very nature of deliverables is that they will be used in different ways for different projects so apart from automatically updating all deliverables in a project I see little productive use for controlling deliverables with VBA. The following code updates every deliverable in the active project.

```
Sub UpdateDeliverables()
Dim Tsk As Task
Const NoDeliverable = "00000000-0000-0000-0000-000000000000"
    For Each Tsk In ActiveProject.Tasks
        If Not Tsk Is Nothing Then
            If Tsk.DeliverableGuid <> NoDeliverable Then
                DeliverableUpdate Tsk.DeliverableGuid, Tsk.Name, _
                    Tsk.Start, Tsk.Finish
            End If
        End If
    Next Tsk
End Sub
```

Note that deliverables belong to tasks and that the way to test for a deliverable is by testing its *Guid*.

Converting SQL Views from 2003 to 2007

Module 22 recommended that you create views in SQL Server to read data for reports. In Project Server 2007, the main databases will not have a schema available as Microsoft wants to reserve the right to edit the schema in service packs and future releases. In fact, Microsoft warned that editing data in any database is likely to cause problems. Publishing a project updates the *Reporting* database overwriting any changes you might make to it. You can, however, add extra tables to the *Reporting* database.

For all reporting needs in Project Server 2007, use the *Reporting* database. You must convert all previous views you created against SQL Server with Project Server 2003 in order to use the *Reporting* database for Project Server 2007. Microsoft simplified this conversion for you because *Issue* and *Risk* data is available in the *Reporting* database, so you no longer need to reference the *Windows SharePoint Services* database.

I created Project Server 2007 equivalents for all the views used in Module 22. In all samples, I include the original code as shown in Module 22 followed by the Project Server 2007 equivalent code. The same code should work in SQL Server 2000, 2005 and 2008.

```
--Project Server 2003
CREATE VIEW dbo.ProjectTitlesPublished
AS
SELECT    TOP 100 PERCENT PROJ_ID, PROJ_PROP_TITLE AS Title
FROM      dbo.MSP_PROJECTS
WHERE (PROJ_VERSION = 'Published')
ORDER BY PROJ_NAME

--Project Server 2007
CREATE VIEW dbo.ProjectTitlesPublished
AS
Select ProjectUID as Proj_ID,
    Left(ProjectName,Len(ProjectName)-10) as Title
From dbo.MSP_EpmProject
```

Project 2007 onwards does not have versions.

```
--Project Server 2003
CREATE VIEW dbo.Milestones
AS
SELECT tsks.PROJ_ID, tsks.TASK_UID,
    tsks.TASK_IS_MILESTONE, tsks.TASK_NAME,
    tsks.TASK_START_DATE
FROM MSP_TASKS as tsks
WHERE (((tsks.TASK_IS_MILESTONE)<>0))

--Project Server 2007
CREATE VIEW dbo.Milestones
AS
SELECT Tsks.ProjectUID, Tsks.TaskUID,
    Tsks.TaskName, Tsks.TaskStartDate
FROM dbo.MSP_EpmTask Tsks
WHERE (((Tsks.TaskIsMilestone)<>0))
```

Notice how using alias names for tables means that once the table name has been edited, most of the remaining SQL remains unchanged (give or take a few column name changes!)

```
--Project Server 2003
CREATE VIEW dbo.CurrentTasks
AS
SELECT tsks.PROJ_ID, tsks.TASK_UID,
    tsks.TASK_NAME, tsks.TASK_DUR,
    tsks.TASK_START_DATE, tsks.TASK_FINISH_DATE,
    tsks.TASK_PCT_COMP
FROM MSP_TASKS tsks
WHERE (((tsks.TASK_START_DATE)<GetDate()) AND
    ((tsks.TASK_PCT_COMP)<100))

--Project Server 2007
CREATE VIEW dbo.CurrentTasks
AS
SELECT tsks.ProjectUID, tsks.TaskUID,
    tsks.TaskName, tsks.TaskDuration/8 as Duration,
    tsks.TaskStartDate, tsks.TaskFinishDate,
    tsks.TaskPercentCompleted

FROM dbo.MSP_EpmTask as tsks
WHERE (((tsks.TaskStartDate)< GetDate()) AND
    ((tsks.TaskPercentCompleted)<100))
```

```
--Project Server 2003
CREATE VIEW dbo.Issues
AS
SELECT TOP 100 PERCENT UD.ntext3 AS Discussion, User1.tp_Title
    AS Owner, UD.nvarchar3 AS [Issue Title], UD.ntext4 AS
    Resolution, UD.nvarchar1 AS Status, UD.nvarchar4 AS
    Priority, UD.datetime1 AS [Due Date], Prj.PROJ_ID
FROM YourWSSdatabase.dbo.UserData UD
    INNER JOIN YourWSSdatabase.dbo.UserInfo User1
    ON UD.tp_SiteId = User1.tp_SiteID AND UD.int4 =
    User1.tp_ID INNER JOIN dbo.MSP_WEB_PROJECTS Prj
    ON UD.tp_ListId = Prj.WPROJ_ISSUE_LIST_NAME
WHERE (UD.tp_IsCurrent = 1)
ORDER BY UD.nvarchar3

--Project Server 2007
CREATE VIEW dbo.Issues
AS
SELECT Issues.Title, Issues.Discussion, Issues.Owner,
    Issues.Resolution, Issues.Status, Issues.Priority,
    Issues.DueDate, Issues.ProjectUID
FROM dbo.MSP_WssIssue as Issues
ORDER BY Issues.Title
```

As you can see, the *Issues* and following *Risks* views are simpler than in Project Server 2003.

```
--Project Server 2003
CREATE VIEW dbo.Risks
AS
SELECT TOP 100 PERCENT UD.nvarchar6 AS [Risk Title],
    User1.tp_Title AS Owner, UD.ntext3 AS Discussion,
    UD.ntext4 AS Resolution, UD.nvarchar1 AS Status,
    UD.datetime1 AS [Due Date], UD.nvarchar2 AS Category,
    UD.float1 AS Probability, UD.float2 AS Impact,
    UD.float3
    AS Cost, UD.ntext5 AS [Contingency Plan],
    UD.nvarchar5 AS [Trigger],
    UD.ntext6 AS [Trigger Description], Prj.PROJ_ID
FROM YourWSSdatabase.dbo.UserData UD INNER JOIN
    YourWSSdatabase.dbo.UserInfo User1 ON
    UD.tp_SiteId = User1.tp_SiteID AND
    UD.int4 = User1.tp_ID
    INNER JOIN dbo.MSP_WEB_PROJECTS Prj ON UD.tp_ListId =
    Prj.WPROJ_RISK_LIST_NAME
WHERE   (UD.tp_IsCurrent = 1)
ORDER BY UD.nvarchar3

--Project Server 2007
CREATE VIEW dbo.Risks
AS
SELECT Risks.Title, Risks.Owner,
    Risks.Description as Discussion,
    Risks.Status, Risks.DueDate, Risks.Category,
    Risks.Probability,  Risks.Impact, Risks.Cost,
    Risks.ContingencyPlan, Risks.TriggerDescription,
    Risks.ProjectUID
FROM dbo.MSP_WssRisk as Risks
ORDER BY Risks.Title
```

Another thing you want to do is rename the *PROJ_ID* field names in your VBA code to refer to *ProjectUID* instead. Project Server 2007 now uses full GUID's for each project, task resource and assignment. The idea is that each item will be unique within the Project Server databases and not just unique within each project. GUID's are text rather than the old numeric IDs so a GUID needs delimiting with single quotes.

If you want to change the name of a field in the final Excel report, then simply rename the field's alias in the *SQL Server* view. For example *Risks.Description as Discussion* renames the *Description* field so it becomes *Discussion* in Excel.

Hands On Exercise

Exercise 23-1

Use new features in Project 2007 VBA code. Note: For this exercise, you need Project 2007 Standard or Professional.

1. Take any existing macro and a wrap a VBA Undo Transaction around it. Confirm that the *Undo* command can undo every action in your macro.

2. In the VBE, press the **F2** function key to display the Object Browser. Search the project library for the word "Report" (without the quotes). Read the Help topics on *Report* objects and methods that interest you.

3. Develop a macro to add an *Exception* calendar for the *Standard* calendar to be four 9-hour working days Monday to Thursday, with four hours on Friday. Make this effective from the beginning of next month for one year.

4. If you have Project Professional 2007 connected to Project Server 2007, click *Project ➢ Project Information* and note the names of any custom enterprise fields. In a new macro, read and write to a custom enterprise field using the code in the *Managing Custom Fields* topic.

Module 24

Using Project 2010 VBA

Learning Objectives

After completing this module, you will be able to:

- Understand new features in Project 2010 VBA

- Write code using the new features in Project 2007 VBA

- Avoid bugs in the first release of Project 2010 VBA

Inside Module 24

Introducing Project 2010 VBA

Project 2010 comes with everything Project 2007 has, but adds objects, methods and properties to match new features. New features with VBA code include:

- Timeline View

- User Controlled Scheduling

- Team Planner (Project 2010 professional only)

- Inactive tasks

- The Fluent UI (Ribbon)

Project 2010 includes the *Office* ribbon to replace its old menus system. In Module 05, I demonstrate how to change the ribbon. Since VBA does not typically use menu options, the new ribbon has little effect on existing macros. The exception is code using the *SendKeys* command. In the first version of my VBA book I suggested that the *SendKeys* command was a dangerous tool and not to use unless absolutely necessary. Project 2010 and keyboard control changes reaffirm this!

There have been few changes to existing Project VBA methods, objects and properties, but I still advise basic defensive coding for reliability across all past and future Project versions -- named parameters being the most important coding style to adopt.

The following link details all Object Model Changes for Project 2010 http://msproj.com/1004

Using Named Parameters

Microsoft has renamed methods that have changed parameters to have **EX** appended to the name. For example in Project 2010 there is a new *CellColorEx* method. It sets or gets a cell's background color. The *CellColor* method still exists, but is not visible by default in the Object Browser and it is not in Help. The *CellColorEx* method works with Project 2010's 64,000 colors while the *CellColor* method only handles Project 2007's 16 colors.

There are a number of new parameters and options for existing methods and objects in Project 2010 VBA. If a new parameter is optional, then Microsoft can safely add it to the end of the parameter list. However, if the new parameter is required (rather than optional), then it has to precede all optional parameters. If a parameter becomes optional, it needs to follow all required parameters, again changing the parameter sequence. This means that if you specify parameters by including a comma for each parameter, your code may fail in some Project versions as you will have the wrong number or sequence of parameters.

With named parameters, provided you use common parameters and do not expect any of the new capabilities of the new *Ex* version of a method, code will work with the *original* and *Ex* versions of a method.

The safest way to code all calls to objects and methods with parameters is to name the parameters. That way wherever parameters' sequences differ between versions, parameter naming ensures your code will continue to work with all versions of Microsoft Project. Named parameters can be in any sequence and you only need to specify the parameters you need. An example of named parameters is:

```
Sort Key1:="ID", Ascending1:=True
```

The parameters are all separated from their values by := (colon then an equals).

Project 2010 VBA Compatibility

Project 2010 compatibility with other versions is good, but not quite as good as earlier versions. Obviously, features such as saving to .mpd files or ODBC, which no longer exist in Project 2007 or 2010, will not work when running code from earlier Project versions. Likewise, code for new features in Project 2010 such as the *Timeline* view, will not work when run in earlier versions. Apart from these considerations, the release version of Project 2010 has introduced some bugs. Specifically error handling for some methods does not work. One example is the *FileOpen* command: it no longer generates an error if it does not find a file that it has been asked to open.

> **i** The June 2010 Cumulative Update (CU) package for Project Professional and Project Standard fixes this problem. Visit http://msproj.com/1005 to download this CU and read what other bugs are fixed.

The easiest way to check for the latest method or how to code a new feature, is to record a macro of you manually doing what you want, and then inspecting the recorded code.

To learn all the changes to the VBA Object model visit http://msproj.com/1006

Controlling the Timeline View

The *Timeline* view is a great new view provided by Project 2010. Actions you may want to do with this view include: displaying it, adding tasks to it, and formatting it.

Displaying the Timeline View

To determine the correct code to display the *Timeline* view, I recorded a macro and the recorded code follows:

```
ViewApplyEx Name:="Time&line", ApplyTo:=1
```

With an *Ex* at the end of its name, the *ViewApplyEx* method has changed. Click on the method then press **F1** for Help to find the *ViewApplyEx* method:

- Added in Project 2010.

- Has *ApplyTo* and *BuiltInView* as two extra, optional parameters.

- *ApplyTo* allows you to apply the named view to either pane without having to select the pane first.

- Is a secondary view, but displayed on top rather than on the bottom.

- Either the *Timeline* view or the *Details* window can show, but never both.

- *ApplyTo*:=1 means show the *Timeline* view in the top window.

- The *BuiltInView* feature allows selecting a specific view to show with the named view regardless of the current view.

Adding Tasks to the Timeline View

Methods to control the *Timeline* view are all new to Project VBA, rather than changes. Therefore, there are no *Ex* suffixes. Recording the action of right-clicking a task and selecting the *Add to Timeline* option produces the code:

```
TaskOnTimeline
```

On its own, this command adds the active task to the *Timeline* view. Help tells us that there are various, useful parameters as shown in Table 24 - 1.

Parameter	Description
TaskID	The Unique ID of the task to add or remove. If not provided, the the system adds selected tasks.
Remove	Set to *True* to remove the task from the Timeline
TimelineViewName	Name of custom *Timeline* view. Defaults to "Timeline"
ShowDialog	Shows the *Add Tasks to Timeline* dialog

Table 24 - 1: Add Task to Timeline parameters

The code to add a task with Unique ID 100 then remove it is as follows:

```
TaskOnTimeline TaskId:=100

TaskOnTimeline TaskId:=100, Remove:=True
```

I recommend this code by providing the unique task ID, there is no need to select the task to be added first.

TimelineFormat is a method that lets you specify the number of lines of text and whether or not to show task details. The following code shows two lines of code and makes sure task details are visible:

```
TimelineFormat NumLines:=2, Minimized:=False
```

Handling User-Controlled Scheduling

User-controlled scheduling is new to Project 2010. It allows planners to enter text instead of dates. For example, where a delivery date is under negotiation, you can enter a *Start* and *Finish* date of *TBD* . Obviously to calculate a valid critical path date fields need correct dates, driven by links and durations.

The biggest change for manually scheduled dates is the new fields provided. Each date (including all baselines) now has two versions: *scheduled* and *text*. For example, *Start* now has *ScheduledStart* and *StartText*. After entering a text value such as *TBD*, a manually scheduled task keeps its original date, available in *ScheduledStart*. Once the task is set to *Auto Schedule*, *StartText* holds a copy of the scheduled date. The code to set selected tasks to auto mode is:

```
SetTaskMode Manual:=False
```

Selecting tasks before operating on them is not desirable, but forced on us in this case. Finally there are some useful flags for *Start*, *Finish* and *Duration* fields. The *ActiveCell.Task.IsStartValid* flag returns *true* if the field contains a valid date (instead of text such as *TBD*).

> **i** If you need to restore the cursor to the originally selected task, save the original task's ID first then re-activate with *EditGoto Id:=OriginalidNumber*.

Working with the Team Planner

The Team Planner is one way to review resource assignments and to level resource workloads. Project 2010 does not provide any methods to control the Team Planner, just one to format it: **EditTPStyle**

The *EditTPStyle* method edits the box and border colors of different types of tasks in the *Team Planner* view.

Miscellaneous New VBA Methods

There are a number of other methods added to Project 2010 VBA. Read all VBA Object model changes at the msdn address given at the beginning of this module.

I detail some of the other changes below in Table 24 - 2.

New VBA Method	Description
ProjectMove	Moves the project, just as if you clicked on the *Move Project* button on the *Project* tab of the Ribbon. Moves project start date, constraining dates and deadlines. This method is very useful when moving a project to a correct start date after creating a new project from a template.
ShareProjectOnline	Follows a url to a Microsoft.com page to learn more about sharing. However, at the time of writing, this page was unavailable.
OpenFromSharePoint	Opens a project from a SharePoint task list.
CleanupProjectfromCache	Clears the local copy of the project title you pass to it from the cache. If your local cache for projects saved in Project Server gets corrupted or needs regular clearing for reliability, this is the method for you!

Table 24 - 2: Some Miscellaneous new methods for Project 2010

Search VBA help for more information on these topics. By allowing your help to connect online you will be sure to receive the most up-to-date information.

SECTION 3

Developing Add-ins using Visual Studio Tools for Office

Learning Objectives

After completing the modules in this section, you will be able to:

- Know when to use Add-ins for Project

- Develop Add-ins for Project 2003 to 2010

- Learn which language best suits your needs

- Convert VBA code to C# or VB

When and Why to Develop Add-ins for Microsoft Project

A Project Add-in is a customized set of features that appears built-in to Microsoft Project. However, the features are coded using Visual Studio and distributed and deployed separately from Project.

Use an Add-in when:

- You need to incorporate features only available to .Net languages such as C# and VB.Net.

- You need to interact with other applications that VBA cannot work with.

- You need more code security so no one can edit or otherwise change your code (for example for shrink wrapped application extensions for sale).

- The bulk of your code processes information outside Project and you need more speed.

There is a near religious debate as to whether C# or VB.Net is the better language. For the purposes of this book, I am assuming that most readers are more familiar with VBA. Therefore, I use the development approach for Add-ins that starts by getting your code working in VBA then copy and pasting it into VB.Net for your Add-in. VB.Net is, therefore, easier to learn (for people who learned VBA first) and is the tool I recommend. C# developers are more likely to already be proficient in its use and can easily translate to C# and need no help from me! However I do provide sample C# code to get you started.

About Project and Add-ins

Add-ins for Project allow you to add custom features that appear built-in. I show the advantages for Add-ins compared to VBA in Table S3 - 1.

Advantages	Disadvantages
Takes advantage of the power of everything Visual Studio and managed code can offer	More complex tools that requires a higher skill set than Project VBA
Code security – Customers cannot copy or change your code	Slower to change – it takes more effort and skill to make changes
Faster accessing databases and other line of business applications	Slower to work with data in Project

Table S3 - 1: Advantages and Disadvantages of Add-ins for Project

As a generalization, there are two types of people writing Add-ins for Project:

1. Project VBA developers; and

2. Professional developers – often C# programmers.

This section addresses the needs of both groups.

Developer Tools you will need

To create an Add-in for Project, you need Visual Studio Professional or above. Table S3 - 2 details what versions of Visual Studio for what versions of Project Add-in.

Project Version	Visual Studio Version
Project 98 to 2002	Not supported
Project 2003 to 2007	Visual Studio 2008
Project 2007 to 2010	Visual Studio 2010

Table S3 - 2: Project and Visual Studio versions

Visual Studio 2005 does support working with Project, but it did not sufficiently integrate the creation of Add-ins to make the process easy. Visual Studio 2005 and 2008 require PIA's (Primary Interop Assemblies) that define and make available all of Project's automation features. Project PIA's install with Project, but you can include them in your installation package.

Visual Studio 2010 does away with PIA's and builds into the application all information formerly stored in PIA's. This simplifies your solution and deployment. All examples and figures use Visual Studio 2010, but all code examples work in Visual Studio 2008 except where I note.

Skills and Knowledge you need to develop a Project Add-in

This book assumes you have a working knowledge of Visual Studio; how to enter code, build solutions, debug and basic deployment solutions. There are plenty of sources you can find by searching the Internet. I focus primarily on showing you how to develop a Project Add-in using your existing Visual Studio, Project VBA and C# or VB skills.

You need to know and use VB (recommended for Visual Studio 2008) or C# for Visual Studio 2010. I discuss which language to use in more detail in Module 25.

You need VBA skills, so make sure you are comfortable with coding most of what you need in VBA first. While Add-ins offer added capabilities outside the Project VBA object model, they cannot do anything inside Project that VBA cannot, so all your VBA skills are essential to successful Add-in development. If you are a professional programmer with little knowledge of Project you will need someone who knows Project well to work with you. If you do not know Project VBA, the first 2 sections of this book are required reading, especially the modules relevant to your solution.

Module 25

Introducing VSTO Project Add-ins

Learning Objectives

After completing this module, you will be able to:

- Know what you can and cannot do with Project Add-ins

- Use a methodology to build your Project Add-ins

- Choose the most suitable programming language for your Project Add-in

Inside Module 25

Introducing VSTO Project Add-ins

You can build Project add-ins with Visual Studio Tools for Office, which allows you to add Windows forms, connect to web services and much more. However, when it comes to controlling Project, you can only add features you cannot change built-in features. You are also limited to what you can do manually. In fact, you can do everything that's possible with Project VBA, no more, no less.

When it comes to performance, add-ins run in a Windows process, so all interactions with Project are across an inter-process barrier that is slow depending on your hardware. For project-intensive programs, Project VBA is faster. However, if your solution deals with data external to Project, an add-in will be much faster overall. So be careful when deciding whether to develop an add-in or a macro if performance is important.

Visual Studio creates solutions, which it also calls projects. To avoid confusion, I refer to Microsoft Project, a project (in Microsoft Project) and add-ins (a project or solution in Visual Studio). Visual Studio Tools for Office is a set of tools in Visual Studio for programming solutions that work with Office applications. I use the acronym VSTO to represent Visual Studio Tools for Office in the following text.

Excel and Word have two types of add-ins: *Application* and *Document* add-ins. Microsoft Project only has an application type add-in. (*Document* add-ins act upon specific files while *Application* add-ins operate on any open files.)

What Skills and Knowledge you need to Know

A Project add-in developer should understand Project and know how it works. Even if you develop in C#, you need to know how to develop in Project VBA. Knowing VBA provides you with knowledge of the objects, methods and properties you must use to make any add-in work. Without this knowledge, getting Project add-ins to work is a long uphill battle. To develop a *VSTO* add-in you require knowledge of how to use Visual Studio and either VB or C#. I cover writing code to control Microsoft Project, I do not explain how to use Visual Studio or develop in C# or VB.

What your Development PC needs

To develop a *Project* add-in, your PC requires:

- Microsoft Project installed – the version you want your add-in to work with.

- Visual Studio Professional or above. Only Professional versions and above include VSTO tools.

- Any other applications your add-in needs to work with.

- All Service Packs and upgrades available for Visual Studio and Project.

Microsoft recommends that if you want to develop an add-in for Project then only install that version. So to develop for several different versions, use Microsoft's Virtual PC or any other virtual tool to create separate environments for each version of Project/Office for which you want to create an add-in.

Table 25 - 1 shows the project version and corresponding version of Microsoft Visual Studio.

Project Version for Add-in	Visual Studio Version Required
Project 2003	Visual Studio 2005
Project 2007	Visual Studio 2008
Project 2010	Visual Studio 2010

Table 25 - 1: Visual Studio version required for different Project versions

Skilled users of Visual Studio can delve into its depths to produce add-ins for different versions of Project using older versions of Visual Studio. However, the rest of us need to buy the appropriate version!

Methodology for Developing an Add-in

There are obviously many ways to go about developing any software solution. I offer a methodology that takes you one step at a time. If you start with little Project VBA knowledge and little or no skills with Visual Studio and VB or C#, then you have a very steep learning curve. When something does not work (and believe me, when you start off a lot of "things" won't work!) then life is significantly easier if you can take one step at a time, getting each step to work before moving to the next one. I offer such a method that I recommend you use until very familiar with the process.

The easy methodology for creating an add-in for Microsoft Project is:

1. Develop a VBA macro that does everything you need with Microsoft Project.

2. Once the VBA macro works, convert the code to VB or C#.

3. Add remaining code, such as forms, links to other line of business applications and more.

4. Conduct user acceptance testing.

5. Develop your deployment solution and release.

Using this methodology, a Microsoft Project user with VBA skills can perform step 1 then hand over the development to a professional developer to do the rest. Alternately, one person can perform all steps. In this book, I focus on steps 1, 2, 4 and 5.

Choosing your Programming Language

I am taking hold of the proverbial hot potato and near-religious war between the languages when recommending which is better for writing *Office* add-ins: C# or VB. The best answer, of course, is the language you can use most productively. I have mentioned C# and VB. You can also develop in any of the other .Net applications, but as C# and VB are by far the most popular, and anyone considering anything else is almost certainly a professional developer, I leave you to convert the sample code I provide for C# and VB into your preferred language.

I suggest C# for Visual Studio 2008, C# for Visual Studio 2010 and VB for either version of Visual Studio. Visual Studio 2010 provides some important improvements for C# when working with *Office* applications, so you need to consider them separately.

For the VBA programmer, VB is the easiest and quickest transition. C# is case sensitive, has at times a cryptic language and, after copy/pasting VBA code, requires far more edits to make the code compile.

Given our methodology of getting the application to work in VBA first, VB has a clear advantage because VBA and VB are very similar, making conversion simpler and quicker. VB has always had two powerful features that make for easier to understand and easier to develop code, both very familiar to VBA developers. These are named parameters and optional parameters. As an example, I use the *FileOpen* method.

FileOpen code in VB

In VBA this is:

```
FileOpen Name:="C:\My Project.mpp", ReadOnly:=True
```

In VB, once a variable for the Project application has been declared and set, the code is:

```
projApp.FileOpenEx(Name:="C:\My Project.mpp", ReadOnly:=True)
```

Code is not case sensitive. VB converts case to match Project's PIA information.

FileOpen code in C# for Visual Studio 2008

C# for Visual Studio 2008 and earlier has neither named parameters nor optional parameters. Therefore, the *FileOpen* code for C# 2008 is:

```
projApp.FileOpen ("C:\My Projectmpp",true,Type.Missing,
    Type.Missing,Type.Missing,Type.Missing,Type.Missing,Type.Missing,
    Type.Missing, Type.Missing,Type.Missing,
    MSProject.PjPoolOpen.pjDoNotOpenPool, Type.Missing,Type.Missing,
    Type.Missing);
```

I find that the code is not only very hard to read, but very awkward and slow to maintain and change. For example, what does *true* represent? The *MSProject.PjPoolOpen.pjDoNotOpenPool* constant is required as the *Type.Missing* parameter cannot convert to a meaningful parameter for *OpenPool*.

You can reduce the amount of code by creating a missing variable:

```
object missing=Type.Missing;
projApp.FileOpen ("C:\My Projectmpp",true,missing,missing,
    missing,missing,missing,missing,missing,missing,missing,
    MSProject.PjPoolOpen.pjDoNotOpenPool,missing,missing,missing);
```

This is more readable, but still difficult to understand and change. Moreover, all code is case sensitive meaning that *Missing* (capital M) creates a compilation error. I recommend that if you have Visual Studio 2008, VB is very much the more productive language to use. Otherwise upgrade to C# 2010. In this book I provide sample code for C# 2010 and VB.

FileOpen code in C# for Visual Studio 2010

With Visual Studio 2010, C# has optional and named parameters and the choice comes down to preference. The *FileOpen* code in C# for Visual Studio 2010 is:

```
projApp.FileOpen (Name: "C:\My Project.mpp", ReadOnly: True);
```

I can live with the above, but C# has a different syntax, such as requiring a semi-colon (;) to end each statement, declares variables differently and more. VBA developers will be more at home with VB. For all remaining C# code examples, I use C# for Visual Studio 2010. Finally, compiled code in both C# and VB run at exactly the same speed. Make your choice based on ease of learning and productivity.

Differences between VBA and VB or C#

Besides the syntax differences between VBA, VB and C#, there are a number of key differences of which the VBA programmer needs to be aware. These are in three areas: code structure and rules, code location, and deployment.

Code Structure Differences

Code differences are:

- VBA allows default properties. For example *ActiveProject.Tasks(1)* returns *1*, the ID of the task. In VB and C# default properties do not exist and you use *ActiveProject.Tasks(1).ID* to get a result.

- VBA allows you to declare a variable as a variant. VBA defines all undeclared variables by default as variants. VB and C# do not support variant and after copying and pasting your code, VB and C# convert all undeclared variables to objects. Objects behave differently than variants so make sure you explicitly declare all your variables.

- VBA passes parameters *by reference* by default (the system passes a pointer to the variable so the original variable parameter can be changed by the code in the procedure). VB and C# pass parameters *by value* by default (the system passes copies of the variable so code in the procedure cannot change the original value). Before converting your VBA code, make sure you specify all parameters as passed by reference or by value. If a parameter does not have *ByVal* or *ByRef* specified, pasting code into VB or C# causes *ByVal* to be specified.

- VBA requires parentheses when a value is returned to code as in *Find("String")*. When no value is expected, no parentheses are required, as in *Find "String"*. In VB and C# parentheses are always required.

- VBA uses the *Set* keyword to set an object variable to point to an object. VB and C# do not need or support the *Set* keyword.

- As you will see in Module 26, you cannot copy or convert VBA UserForms to VB or C#. You need to re-create all UserForms in Visual Studio using *Windows Forms*.

Code Locations

VBA code in Microsoft Project lives either in a .mpp file or in the Global.mpt file. With add-ins, all code lives in .vb files for VB or .cs files for C# in a folder you nominate when you create the solution. When you build (compile) your add-in the resultant executable files are stored in a sub-folder called *bin* for your solution.

Deployment Differences

VBA deployment means distributing the project file your VBA code is in, or pushing out a fresh copy of the Global.mpt file to everyone. With an add-in, there are a variety of deployment methods as I explain in Module 27.

Checking your Development Environment Works

First, you create a trivial add-in to confirm that you installed everything correctly and are ready to move on to more complex examples. I provide instructions for Visual Studio 2010 and Project 2010 with comments on parts that will only work on Project 2010. The interface for Visual Studio 2008 is not much different.

Visual Studio refers to projects and solutions interchangeably. A solution is everything that is required to meet your needs; for example, one project to do all the work and perhaps another project to manage installation. Details about the contents of a solution are in the *project name.sln* file. Unfortunately, as Visual Studio versions have come and gone, the line between projects and solutions has blurred. For example, there is a *Solution* name, rather than a *Project* name when you create a new "project" and there is a *Solution* explorer, rather than a *Project* explorer. Just remember that a solution can hold many projects.

To create our test, follow these instructions on your PC once you have your version of Project installed (with all Service Packs added) and your version of Visual Studio (with all Service Packs installed).

1. In Visual Studio select File ➤ New Project.

2. Enter a name for your add-in and a file location. Table 25 - 1 shows the result.

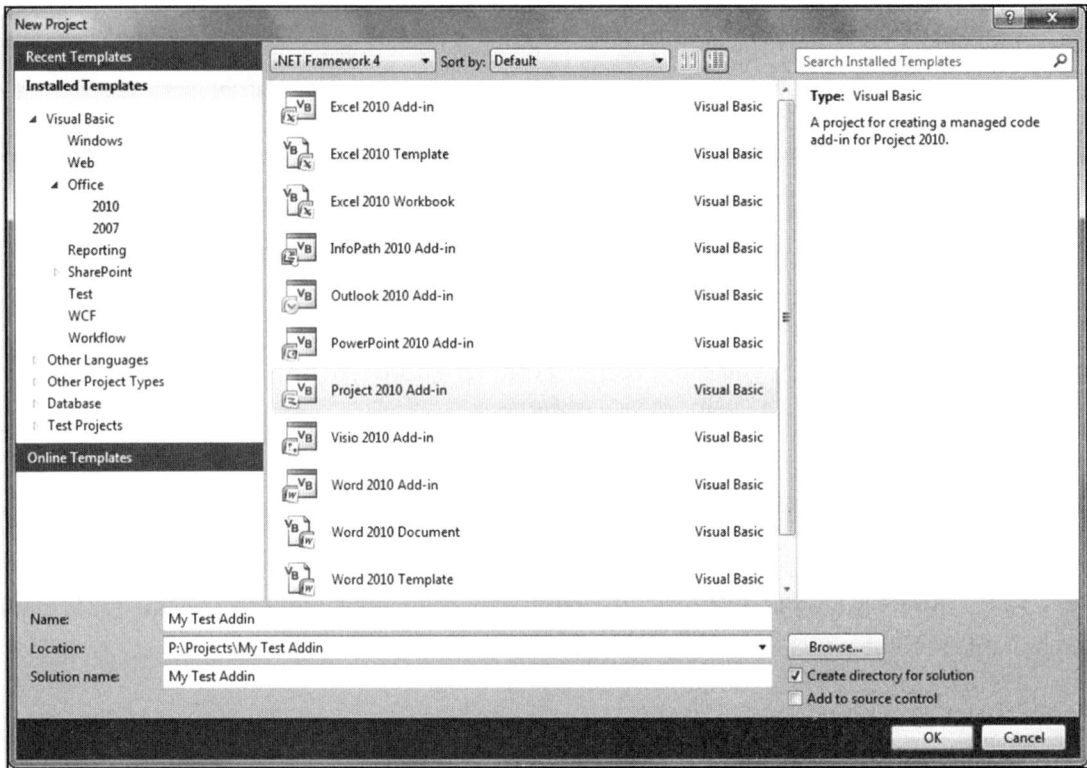

Figure 25 - 1: Your New Project for VB and Project 2010

3. Click the *OK* button to create the structure of your add-in. Depending on the speed of your PC, this may take a few seconds or more.

4. At the top of the page add the *Imports System.Windows.Forms* code for VB or for C# add the *using System.Windows.Forms;* code.

5. In the *Startup()* procedure, enter the code listed in Table 25 - 2:

Language	Code
C# 2008	`MessageBox.Show("All set to go!");`
C# 2010	`MessageBox.Show(prompt: "All set to go!");`
VB	`MessageBox.Show(text:="All set to go!")`

Table 25 - 2: Code for each Language

Note that the *MessageBox* code has many overlays and that one of them only has a prompt parameter. In this case, C# does not need the other parameters replaced by the missing object.

6. Now press **F5** to build your add-in and start debugging.

Visual Studio starts Microsoft Project with your add-in. Note that Project starts, and then appears to freeze for some seconds before the message appears. While Project appears to start and displays menus available for you to select; in reality, Project is still finishing its start up in the background. Microsoft Project only loads add-ins after it completes its start up. This is why there is a pause before you see the "All set to go!" message. You can do nothing about this pause, which is a small disadvantage of add-ins.

Security Options for Add-ins

If your add-in does not work, there may be a security setting preventing it from running. To check the settings in the Project client:

Action	Project 2010	Project 2007 and earlier
Set Add-in security settings to allow add-ins to run	1. Select File ➤ Options 2. Click the *Trust Center* tab 3. Click the *Trust Center Settings* button 4. Click the *Add-ins* tab 5. Make sure all check boxes are clear 6. Click the *OK* button	1. Select Tools ➤ Macro Security 2. Click the *Trusted Publishers* tab 3. Make sure the *Trust all installed Add-ins and templates* option is checked 4. Click the *OK* button

Table 25 - 3: Enabling Add-in security options

Figure 25 - 2 and Figure 25 – 3 show the end result.

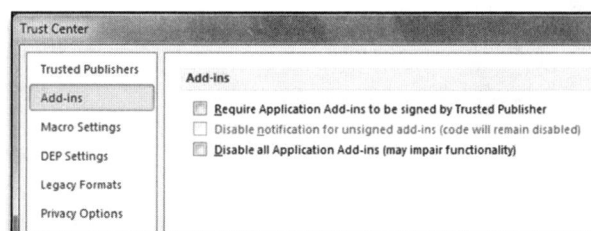

Figure 25 - 2: Final Add-in Security Settings for Project 2007 and earlier

Figure 25 - 3: Final Add-in Security Settings for Project 2010

Disabling and Removing Add-ins

Now, every time Project starts, the add-in runs on your PC. Table 25 - 4 details how to disable or remove an add-in.

Action	Project 2010	Project 2007 and earlier
Add *Add-ins* command to *Tools* menu	A *Com Add-ins* icon already exists under the *Developer* tab	1. Click Tools ➤ Customize ➤ Toolbars. 2. Click the *Commands* tab, and then click the *Tools* option in the *Categories* list. 3. Drag the *COM Add-ins* command from the *Commands* box to the *Tools* menu bar. When the *Tools* menu appears, point to where you want the *COM Add-ins* command to appear on the menu, and then release the mouse button. 4. In the *Customize* dialog, click the *Close* button.
Show *Add-ins* dialog	From the *Developer* tab, click the *Com Add-ins* icon.	Click Tools ➤ Com Add-ins.
Disable Add-in	Clear the checkmark against the add-in you want to disable.	Clear the checkmark against the add-in you want to disable.
Remove Add-in	Select the add-in then click the *Remove* button.	Select the add-in then click the *Remove* button.

Table 25 - 4: Displaying the Com Add-in command

Module 26

Your First Add-in

Learning Objectives

After completing this module, you will be able to:

- Create Add-ins for Project
- Convert VBA code to VB and C#
- Use the methodology for developing Add-ins

Inside Module 26

Converting a Sample Macro into an Add-in

As an example, I show a macro that allows the user to change all selected tasks to *not constrained*, change duration format, task type, estimated flag and, for Project 2010 only, the task mode (manually or automatically scheduled). With each of the following sections, I follow the methodology I suggested in Module 25. All C# code is for Visual Studio 2010 only.

The VBA Macro

To use the macro, first select all tasks to change then run the macro. A *UserForm* code controls what changes you need to make. To keep the *UserForm* code to a minimum I put most of it into a module and call it from the *UserForm* events. Files *Module 26 Project 2010 Sample Code – Your First Add-in.mpp* for Project 2010 and *Module 26 Sample Code – Your First Add-in.mpp* for Project 2007 and earlier, contain all of the code. Figure 26 - 1 shows the *UserForm* code in the VBA macro ready to accept change instructions.

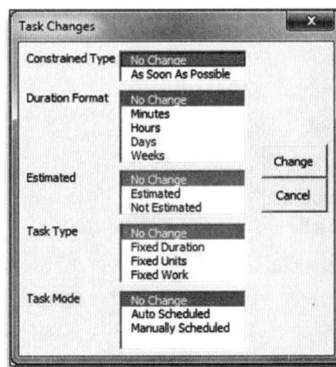

Figure 26 - 1: The VBA UserForm and options

The event code for the UserForm follows:

```
Private Sub Cancel_Click()
    frmChanges.Hide
    With frmChanges
        .lbConstrained.Value = "No Change"
        .lbDurationFormat.Value = "No Change"
        .lbEstimated.Value = "No Change"
        .lbTaskType.Value = "No Change"
        .lbTaskMode.Value = "No Change"
    End With
End Sub

Private Sub Change_Click()
    MakeChanges
End Sub

Private Sub UserForm_Initialize()
'Set up all Listboxes
    With frmChanges
        With .lbConstrained
            .AddItem "No Change"
```

```
            .AddItem "As Soon As Possible"
            .Value = "No Change"
      End With

      With .lbDurationFormat
         .Clear
         .AddItem "No Change"
         .AddItem "Minutes"
         .AddItem "Hours"
         .AddItem "Days"
         .AddItem "Weeks"
         .Value = "No Change"
      End With

      With .lbEstimated
         .Clear
         .AddItem "No Change"
         .AddItem "Estimated"
         .AddItem "Not Estimated"
         .Value = "No Change"
      End With

      With .lbTaskType
         .Clear
         .AddItem "No Change"
         .AddItem "Fixed Duration"
         .AddItem "Fixed Units"
         .AddItem "Fixed Work"
         .Value = "No Change"
      End With

      With .lbTaskMode
         .Clear
         .AddItem "No Change"
         .AddItem "Auto Scheduled"
         .AddItem "Manually Scheduled"
         .Value = "No Change"
      End With

'Controls don't line up easily, so I add this code to force even spacing
      .lbDurationFormat.Top = .lbConstrained.Top + .lbConstrained.Height + 5
      .lblDurationFormat.Top = .lbDurationFormat.Top
      .lbEstimated.Top = .lbDurationFormat.Top + .lbDurationFormat.Height + 5
      .lbTaskType.Top = .lbEstimated.Top + .lbEstimated.Height + 5
      .lbTaskMode.Top = .lbTaskType.Top + .lbTaskType.Height + 5
      .Height = .lbTaskMode.Top + .lbTaskMode.Height + 25

'Make Label tops same as their fields
      .lblDurationFormat.Top = .lbDurationFormat.Top
      .lblEstimated.Top = .lbEstimated.Top
      .lblTaskType.Top = .lbTaskType.Top
      .lblTaskMode.Top = .lbTaskMode.Top

'If not Version 2010, hide TaskMode Fields
      If Val(Application.Version) < 14 Then
         .lbTaskMode.Visible = False
```

```
            .lblTaskMode.Visible = False
            .Height = .lbTaskType.Top + .lbTaskType.Height + 25
        Else
            .lbTaskMode.Visible = True
            .lblTaskMode.Visible = True
            .Height = .lbTaskMode.Top + .lbTaskMode.Height + 25
        End If
    End With
End Sub
```

The *Cancel_Click* event resets all settings and hides the *UserForm* code which I call *frmChanges*. The *Change_Click* event runs when you click the *Change* button. The code calls the *MakeChanges* procedure in the VBA module which I name *ChangeCode*.

You saw most of the *UserForm_Initialize* code in Module 07. The last few lines are new however. The *UserForm* code does not allow easy alignment and spacing of controls, so I add lines to programmatically space the controls out and size the height of the form. Figure 26 - 1, shown previously, reveals how neat and evenly spaced the result is.

The *Application .Version* statement returns a text string with the version number. For Project 2010 the version returned is "14.0". I add the following code to automatically display a toolbar to run the macro. I explained all of this code in previous modules.

```
Private Sub Project_Open(ByVal pj As Project)
Dim MyBar As CommandBar
Dim MyButton As CommandBarButton
    On Error Resume Next
    Set MyBar = CommandBars("My Bar")
    If MyBar Is Nothing Then
        Set MyBar = CommandBars.Add(Name:="My Bar", Position:=msoBarFloating, _
                        Temporary:=True)
        MyBar.Visible = True
    End If

    Set MyButton = MyBar.Controls("MyButton")
    If MyButton Is Nothing Then
        Set MyButton = MyBar.Controls.Add(Type:=msoControlButton)
        With MyButton
            .Style = msoButtonCaption
            .Caption = "Change Task Settings"
            .OnAction = "Macro ""ShowMakeChangesForm"""
        End With
    End If
End Sub
```

This code lives in the *ThisProject* file.

For help on creating UserForms in Project VBA, see Module 07.

Converting VBA to VB

To convert the VBA code into an add-in, I first demonstrate using VB and then using C# for Project 2010. To start the conversion, first create a new VSTO project as follows:

1. Close any open project (solution or add-in) in Visual Studio.

2. Create a new VB project for your version of Project as we did for the environment check at the beginning of this module. Call this Project *ChangeTaskSettingsVB*.

3. The entire *ThisAddin* module is as follows and includes the *ThisProject* code converted to VB:

```vb
Imports System.Windows.Forms

Public Class ThisAddIn
    Private commandBar As Office.CommandBar
    Private WithEvents ChangeButton As Office.CommandBarButton

    Private Sub ThisAddIn_Startup() Handles Me.Startup
        'projApp declared in ChangeCode.vb

        projApp = Globals.ThisAddIn.Application

        If commandBar Is Nothing Then
            Dim barPosition As Integer = 1
            Dim isMenuBar As Boolean = False
            Dim isTemporary As Boolean = True
            commandBar = Application.CommandBars.Add("ChangeBar", barPosition, _
                        isMenuBar, isTemporary)
        End If
        Try
            ChangeButton = DirectCast(commandBar.Controls.Add( _
                    Office.MsoControlType.msoControlButton), Office.CommandBarButton)
            ChangeButton.Style = Office.MsoButtonStyle.msoButtonCaption
            ChangeButton.Caption = "Change Selected Tasks"
            ChangeButton.Tag = "Change Selected Tasks"
            ChangeButton.TooltipText = _
                                "Changes duration format, estimated and more"
            commandBar.Visible = True
        Catch ex As ArgumentException
            MessageBox.Show(ex.Message, "Error adding toolbar button", _
                    MessageBoxButtons.OK, MessageBoxIcon.[Error])
        End Try

    End Sub

    Private Sub ChangeButton_Click(ByVal Ctrl As _
            Microsoft.Office.Core.CommandBarButton, _
```

```
            ByRef CancelDefault As Boolean) Handles ChangeButton.Click
        ShowChangesForm
    End Sub
End Class
```

This code creates a command bar in all versions of Project. In Project 2010, however, the button appears in the *Add-in* tab as I discussed in Module 05. The *ThisAddin* code will not compile until you copy and convert the form and code from the *VBA_Code* module.

Note that the code is very similar to the *ThisProject* code. The main difference is the setting of the global *projApp* variable so that you can use it to access all project data in the other modules. You now use the *projApp* variable exactly as if you are controlling Project from Excel or controlling Excel using Project and the *xlApp* variable described in Module 12.

1. Click Project ➤ Add Module and name the module *ChangeCode.vb*.

2. In the module enter:

```
Imports System.Windows.Forms

Module ChangeCode

    Public projApp As MSProject.Application
    Friend formChanges As frmChanges

End Module
```

This code provides global variables for the project application and the *Changes* form in a way that allows you to use them in all modules.

3. Select Build ➤ Build ChangeTaskSettings. I regularly build my code frequently, as it is easier to fix problems as they occur rather than dealing with a long list of errors the first time I build. Remember, one step at a time!

4. Copy the code from the VBA *VBA_Code* module.

Note that just pasting the code into Visual Studio does some of the conversion. Pasting the code underneath the *Friend formChanges As frmChanges* row creates a whole heap of error messages, the *Error List* view (Click View ➤ Error List to see all errors) shows 8 errors and 0 warnings. I can either paste a little at a time or immediately start resolving the list. Here I choose the latter and resolve the 8 errors as follows.

1. The first error is *Option Explicit*. This is on by default in VB so I can either delete this line or click the *Error Correction Options* icon as shown in Figure 26 - 2.

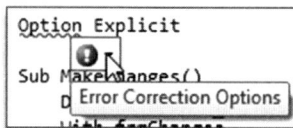

Figure 26 - 2: The Error Correction Options icon

Figure 26 - 3 shows the result of clicking on the *Error Correction Options* icon for *Option Explicit*.

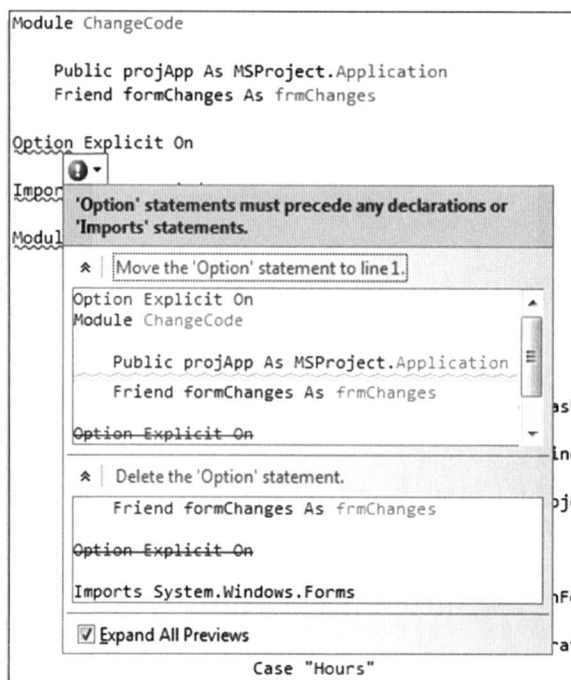

Figure 26 - 3: Error Options

No harm in stating the obvious and as a reminder for me when thinking in VBA mode, I select the first option *Move the 'Option' statement to line 1*.

2. I choose the same option for the *Imports* line and move it to the top.

3. The *Dim Tsk As* task causes error 2. As you learned in Module 13, to refer to *Microsoft Project* objects (such as *Task*) from Excel, I had to create a *Project* object, which I named *projApp*. I must do the same with Visual Studio. Creating a Project add-in automatically adds a reference to Microsoft Project, so the following code fixes this error.

```
Dim Tsk As MSProject.Task
```

4. Error 3 is the first of two errors referring to the UserForm. UserForms cannot be copied to Visual Studio (VB or C#) so shortly I show you how to create a replacement Windows form. I leave these 2 errors until later.

340

5. Error 4 is the *ActiveSelection* error, which I resolve with a qualifier, as are errors 6 and 7.

Fixing these errors (except for the UserForm) creates new errors, as the compiler gets further into your code. These new errors are all the same, they need qualifying so that your add-in knows from where to read the constants, methods and properties. For example *pjASAP* becomes *MSProject.PjConstraint.pjASAP* and *pjMinutes* becomes *MSProject.PjFormatUnit.pjMinutes*. After fixing all these errors, the final code becomes:

```
Option Explicit On

Imports System.Windows.Forms

Module ChangeCode

    Public projApp As MSProject.Application
    Friend formChanges As frmChanges

    Sub MakeChanges()
        Dim Tsk As MSProject.Task
        For Each Tsk In projApp.ActiveSelection.Tasks
            If Not Tsk Is Nothing Then
                Select Case formChanges.lbConstrained.Text
                    Case "As Soon As Possible"
                        Tsk.ConstraintType = MSProject.PjConstraint.pjASAP
                    Case Else
                End Select

                Select Case formChanges.lbDurationFormat.Text
                    Case "Minutes"
                        Tsk.Duration = projApp.DurationFormat(Tsk.Duration, _
                            MSProject.PjFormatUnit.pjMinutes)
                    Case "Hours"
                        Tsk.Duration = projApp.DurationFormat(Tsk.Duration, _
                            MSProject.PjFormatUnit.pjHours)
                    Case "Days"
                        Tsk.Duration = projApp.DurationFormat(Tsk.Duration, _
                            MSProject.PjFormatUnit.pjDays)
                    Case "Weeks"
                        Tsk.Duration = projApp.DurationFormat(Tsk.Duration, _
                            MSProject.PjFormatUnit.pjWeeks)
                    Case Else
                End Select

                Select Case formChanges.lbEstimated.Text
                    Case "Estimated"
                        Tsk.Estimated = True
                    Case "Not Estimated"
                        Tsk.Estimated = False
                    Case Else
                End Select

                Select Case formChanges.lbTaskType.Text
                    Case "Fixed Duration"
                        Tsk.Type = MSProject.PjTaskFixedType.pjFixedDuration
                    Case "Fixed Units"
                        Tsk.Type = MSProject.PjTaskFixedType.pjFixedUnits
```

```
                    Case "Fixed Work"
                        Tsk.Type = MSProject.PjTaskFixedType.pjFixedWork
                    Case Else
                End Select
            End If
        Next Tsk

    End Sub

    Public Sub ShowChangesForm()
        If formChanges Is Nothing Then
            formChanges = New frmChanges
        End If
        formChanges.Show()
    End Sub
End Module
```

This code now compiles except for the *frmChanges* code. Note the close similarity to VBA code. This conversion does not take long to do. All you have to do now is add the form, then test thoroughly.

Converting VBA to C# 2010

The process is the same; just creating an *Office* project (add-in) for C# creates a reference to the correct version of Project.

Warning: At the time of writing, C# had bugs such that the following code did not work as expected. Service Pack 1 should resolve these problems, but until then VB appears to be the more reliable tool. You may need to edit the following C# code to run it successfully, so please do not rely on it. The download for this book contains up-to-date information as it becomes available.

The entire *ThisAddIn_Startup* code is:

```
using System;
using System.Collections.Generic;
using System.Linq;
using System.Text;
using System.Xml.Linq;
using System.Windows.Forms;
using MSProject = Microsoft.Office.Interop.MSProject;
using Office = Microsoft.Office.Core;

namespace CSChangeTaskSettings {
    public partial class ThisAddIn {
        private Office.CommandBar commandBar;
        private Office.CommandBarButton ChangeButton;
        private MSProject.Application projApp;
```

```
        private void ThisAddIn_Startup(object sender, System.EventArgs e) {
            //projApp declared in ChangeCode.vb
            frmChanges frm = new frmChanges();

            projApp = Globals.ThisAddIn.Application;
            projApp.ActiveProject.Tasks.Add("Task 1");

            if (commandBar == null) {
                int barPosition = 1;
                bool isMenuBar = false;
                bool isTemporary = true;
                commandBar = Application.CommandBars.Add("ChangeBar",
                                        barPosition, isMenuBar, isTemporary);
            }
            try {
                ChangeButton = (Office.CommandBarButton)commandBar.Controls.Add
                                    (Office.MsoControlType.msoControlButton);
                ChangeButton.Style = Office.MsoButtonStyle.msoButtonCaption;
                ChangeButton.Caption = "Change Selected Tasks";
                ChangeButton.Tag = "Change Selected Tasks";
                ChangeButton.TooltipText =
                                    "Changes duration format, estimated and more";

                commandBar.Visible = true;
            }
            catch (ArgumentException ex) {
                MessageBox.Show(ex.Message, "Error adding toolbar button",
                        MessageBoxButtons.OK, MessageBoxIcon.Error);
            }
        }

        //VSTO generated code
    }
}
```

The contents of the *ChangeCode.cs* file are:

```
using System;
using System.Collections.Generic;
using System.Linq;
using System.Text;
using System.Windows.Forms;
using MSProject = Microsoft.Office.Interop.MSProject;

namespace CSChangeTaskSettings {
    class ChangeCode {
        public frmChanges formChanges = new frmChanges();

        private MSProject.Application projApp;

        void MakeChanges() {
            projApp = Globals.ThisAddIn.Application;
            foreach (MSProject.Task Tsk in projApp.ActiveSelection.Tasks) {
                if (Tsk != null) {
```

```
                switch (formChanges.lbConstrained.Text) {
                    case "As Soon As Possible":
                        Tsk.ConstraintType = MSProject.PjConstraint.pjASAP;
                        break;
                    default:
                        break;
                }

                switch (formChanges.lbDurationFormat.Text) {
                    case "Minutes":
                        Tsk.Duration = projApp.DurationFormat(Tsk.Duration,
                                        MSProject.PjFormatUnit.pjMinutes);
                        break;
                    case "Hours":
                        Tsk.Duration = projApp.DurationFormat(Tsk.Duration,
                                        MSProject.PjFormatUnit.pjHours);
                        break;
                    case "Days":
                        Tsk.Duration = projApp.DurationFormat(Tsk.Duration,
                                        MSProject.PjFormatUnit.pjDays);
                        break;
                    case "Weeks":
                        Tsk.Duration = projApp.DurationFormat(Tsk.Duration,
                                        MSProject.PjFormatUnit.pjWeeks);
                        break;
                    default:
                        break;
                }

                switch (formChanges.lbEstimated.Text) {
                    case "Estimated":
                        Tsk.Estimated = true;
                        break;
                    case "Not Estimated":
                        Tsk.Estimated = false;
                        break;
                    default:
                        break;
                }

                switch (formChanges.lbTaskType.Text) {
                    case "Fixed Duration":
                        Tsk.Type = MSProject.PjTaskFixedType.pjFixedDuration;
                        break;
                    case "Fixed Units":
                        Tsk.Type = MSProject.PjTaskFixedType.pjFixedUnits;
                        break;
                    case "Fixed Work":
                        Tsk.Type = MSProject.PjTaskFixedType.pjFixedWork;
                        break;
                    default:
                        break;
                }
            }
        }
    }
}
```

```
}
```

I leave it to the C# professionals to work out what does what!

Replacing the UserForm

Unfortunately, we cannot convert UserForms so you must completely re-create the UserForm in VBA with a Windows form in Visual Studio. The good news is that Windows forms in Visual Studio are much richer, have many more controls, can easily interface with databases and much, much more. I create the form, name it *frm-Changes* and the result is shown in Figure 26 - 4.

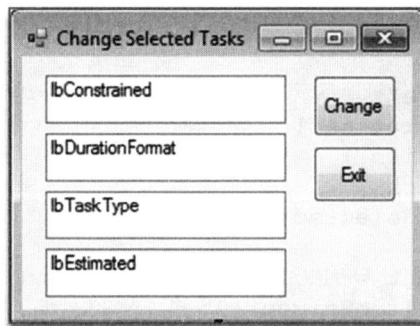

Figure 26 - 4: The Visual Studio Form

Notice that I set all fields to the same height as I rely on code to automatically set each field's height and then the height of the form as well. The ability to set the height of each ListBox with code is just one example of the extra power Visual Studio offers compared to VBA's UserForms. The VB code for the form's class follows:

```
Public Class frmChanges

    Public Sub New()

        ' This call is required by the designer.
        InitializeComponent()
        ' Add any initialization after the InitializeComponent() call.
        'Set up all Listboxes
        With Me.lbConstrained.Items
            .Add("No Change")
            .Add("As Soon As Possible")
            lbConstrained.SetSelected(0, True)
        End With
        Me.lbConstrained.Height = Me.lbConstrained.Items.Count * _
            Me.lbConstrained.ItemHeight + 5

        With Me.lbDurationFormat.Items
            .Clear()
            .Add("No Change")
            .Add("Minutes")
            .Add("Hours")
            .Add("Days")
            .Add("Weeks")
            lbDurationFormat.SetSelected(0, True)
```

```
            End With
            Me.lbDurationFormat.Height = Me.lbDurationFormat.Items.Count * _
                Me.lbDurationFormat.ItemHeight + 5

            With Me.lbEstimated.Items
                .Clear()
                .Add("No Change")
                .Add("Estimated")
                .Add("Not Estimated")
                lbEstimated.SetSelected(0, True)
            End With
            Me.lbEstimated.Height = Me.lbEstimated.Items.Count * _
                Me.lbEstimated.ItemHeight + 5

            With Me.lbTaskType.Items
                .Clear()
                .Add("No Change")
                .Add("Fixed Duration")
                .Add("Fixed Units")
                .Add("Fixed Work")
                lbTaskType.SetSelected(0, True)
            End With
            Me.lbTaskType.Height = Me.lbTaskType.Items.Count * _
                Me.lbTaskType.ItemHeight + 5

            'Controls don't line up easily, so I add this code to force even spacing
            lbDurationFormat.Top = lbConstrained.Top + lbConstrained.Height + 5
            lbEstimated.Top = lbDurationFormat.Top + lbDurationFormat.Height + 5
            lbTaskType.Top = lbEstimated.Top + lbEstimated.Height + 5
            Me.Height = lbTaskType.Top + lbTaskType.Height + 50
    End Sub

    Private Sub Cancel_Click(ByVal sender As Object, ByVal e _
                As System.EventArgs) Handles Cancel.Click
        Me.Close()
    End Sub

    Public Sub Change_Click(ByVal sender As Object, ByVal e As _
                System.EventArgs) Handles Change.Click
        MakeChanges()
    End Sub

End Class
```

All of the preceding sample code should be familiar to VB developers. I use ListBoxes for simplicity, but there is nothing stopping you from using any other controls. As a comparison, here is the same code in C# 2010:

```
using System;
using System.Collections.Generic;
using System.ComponentModel;
using System.Data;
```

```csharp
using System.Drawing;
using System.Linq;
using System.Text;

namespace ChangeTaskSettingsCS {
    public partial class frmChanges : Form {
        public frmChanges() {
            InitializeComponent();

            //Set up all Listboxes
            this.lbConstrained.Items.Add("No Change");
            this.lbConstrained.Items.Add("As Soon As Possible");
            this.lbConstrained.SetSelected(0, true);
            this.lbConstrained.Height = this.lbConstrained.Items.Count * _
                this.lbConstrained.ItemHeight + 5;

            this.lbDurationFormat.Items.Clear();
            this.lbDurationFormat.Items.Add("No Change");
            this.lbDurationFormat.Items.Add("Minutes");
            this.lbDurationFormat.Items.Add("Hours");
            this.lbDurationFormat.Items.Add("Days");
            this.lbDurationFormat.Items.Add("Weeks");
            this.lbDurationFormat.SetSelected(0, true);
            this.lbDurationFormat.Height = this.lbDurationFormat.Items.Count * _
                this.lbDurationFormat.ItemHeight + 5;

            this.lbEstimated.Items.Clear();
            this.lbEstimated.Items.Add("No Change");
            this.lbEstimated.Items.Add("Estimated");
            this.lbEstimated.Items.Add("Not Estimated");
            this.lbEstimated.SetSelected(0, true);
            this.lbEstimated.Height = this.lbEstimated.Items.Count * _
                this.lbEstimated.ItemHeight + 5;

            this.lbTaskType.Items.Clear();
            this.lbTaskType.Items.Add("No Change");
            this.lbTaskType.Items.Add("Fixed Duration");
            this.lbTaskType.Items.Add("Fixed Units");
            this.lbTaskType.Items.Add("Fixed Work");
            this.lbTaskType.SetSelected(0, true);
            this.lbTaskType.Height = this.lbTaskType.Items.Count * _
                this.lbTaskType.ItemHeight + 5;

        //Controls don't line up easily, so I add this code to force even spacing
            lbDurationFormat.Top = lbConstrained.Top + lbConstrained.Height + 5;
            lbEstimated.Top = lbDurationFormat.Top +
                            lbDurationFormat.Height + 5;
            lbTaskType.Top = lbEstimated.Top + lbEstimated.Height + 5;
            this.Height = lbTaskType.Top + lbTaskType.Height + 50;
        }
    }
}
```

Figure 26 - 5 shows the form when running.

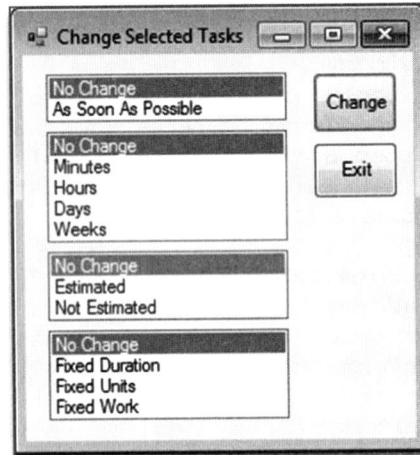

Figure 26 - 5: The Form When Running

Error Handling in Add-ins

You cannot create shrink wrap applications developed in VBA so most VBA macros are custom developed for in-house users or for a specific client. Distribution to large numbers of users, or shrink wrapping for sale are big reasons for developing an add-in. Add-ins, therefore, warrant more time spent automatically handling errors to help reduce support costs as much as possible.

VBA handles run time errors either with an *On Error Resume Next* or *On Error Goto* label. VB supports the same techniques, but the *Try Catch* structure available in VB and C# is much better. I recommend converting all VBA error handling to use the *Try Catch* structure. The code to insert a new task to the end of the project, then link it to its predecessor is:

```
Set Tsk = ActiveProject.Tasks.Add("New Task Name")
Tsk.TaskDependencies.Add From:=ActiveProject.Tasks( _
        ActiveProject.Tasks.Count - 1), Type:=pjFinishToStart, Lag:=0
```

In VB I use:

```
Try
    Tsk = projApp.ActiveProject.Tasks.Add("New Task Name")
    Tsk.TaskDependencies.Add From:=ActiveProject.Tasks( _
        ActiveProject.Tasks.Count - 1), Type:=pjFinishToStart, Lag:=0
```

```
Catch ex As Exception
   MessageBox.Show(ex.toString)
End Try
```

Or in C#:

```
Try {
   Tsk = projApp.ActiveProject.Tasks.Add("New Task Name")
   Tsk.TaskDependencies.Add From:= projApp.ActiveProject.Tasks(
         projApp.ActiveProject.Tasks.Count - 1),
         Type:=pjFinishToStart, Lag:=0 }
Catch (InvalidCastException e) {
   MessageBox.Show(e)
}
```

You can test either for one statement or for many statements in the *Try* block of code.

Hands On Exercise

Exercise 26-1

For any version of Project, write an add-in that reads data from the active project and writes to any database to which you have access, Microsoft Access, SQL Server, Oracle, etc.

1. Create a form to allow selection of what data the add-in will export.

2. Write the VB or C# code to export the required data to your database.

Exercise 26-2

If you have Project 2010, update the form to include task mode changes (between manually scheduled and auto scheduled). Note that for task mode values to change, you must save the file in Project 2010 format.

1. Add an extra ListBox called *lbTaskMode*.

2. Add code to *frmChanges.vb* to add suitable items for the ListBox (Tip: copy the code for one of the other ListBoxes and be sure to change all occurrences of the copied ListBox name to *lbTaskMode*.

3. Add an extra line at the end of *Sub New* in *frmChanges.vb* to align the top of the *lbTaskMode* ListBox and edit the *Me.lbTaskType.Height* row to use *lgTaskMode*, which is now the last control on the form.

VSTO and Project Events

In Microsoft Project, there are two types of events: Project level and Task/Resource/Assignment level. Project level events are the simplest to code and operate at the application level. Examples are *before save* and *after open*. The second type of events operate at the individual project level and are more complicated to handle as they require code in three different locations to enable. For more information on Microsoft Project events, see Module 09.

Using VSTO makes it is easier to code events as it treats all events the same way and they all live in the *ThisAdd-In.vb* file.

To add an event in VB:

1. Open the *ThisAddIn.vb* file.

2. Select Application from the *Object* pick list in the top left corner of the code window as shown in Figure 26 - 6.

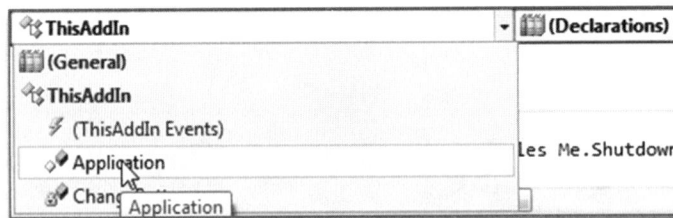

Figure 26 - 6: Selecting the Application Object

3. The *Declarations* pick list now shows all available events as partly shown in Figure 26 - 7.

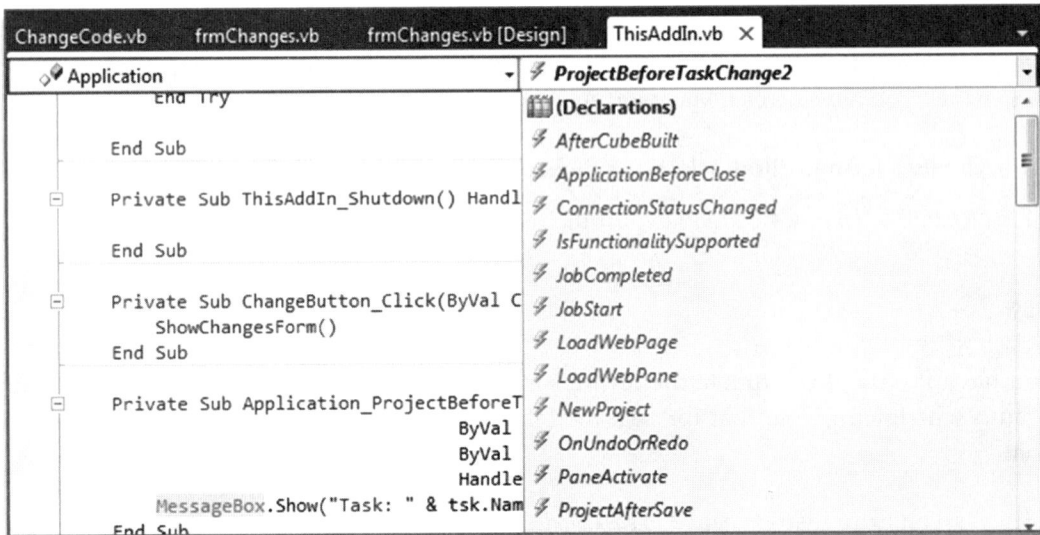

Figure 26 - 7: The Declarations pick list showing some of the available events

4. Enter the code you want for your selected event. Figure 26 - 8 shows two sample events that display relevant messages when I add either a new task or I change a task column.

```
Application                                          ▼  ⚡ ProjectBeforeTaskChange2                              ▼
                                                                                                               ⧧
☐   Private Sub Application_ProjectBeforeTaskChange2(ByVal tsk As Microsoft.Office.Interop.MSProject.Task, _
                           ByVal Field As Microsoft.Office.Interop.MSProject.PjField, _
                           ByVal NewVal As Object, ByVal Info As Microsoft.Office.Interop.MSProject.EventInfo) _
                           Handles Application.ProjectBeforeTaskChange2
          MessageBox.Show("Task: " & tsk.Name & "  Field: " & projApp.FieldConstantToFieldName(Field) & " changed")
    End Sub

☐   Private Sub Application_ProjectTaskNew(ByVal pj As Microsoft.Office.Interop.MSProject.Project, _
                           ByVal ID As Integer) Handles Application.ProjectTaskNew
          MessageBox.Show("Task: " & pj.Tasks(ID).Name & " added")
    End Sub
```

Figure 26 - 8: Code for two sample events

> ℹ️ At the time of writing, the release version of Project and VSTO for Visual Studio 2010 had a bug such that Tsk.Name does not return the name of the task it interrupts for Vb or C# when used in an event. Hopefully, this will be remedied in an early update, or at least the first Service Pack.

To add an event in C#:

1. In the *ThisAddIn.cs* file, at the end of the *ThisAddIn_Startup* code, type *this.Application*

2. Type a period and in the *IntelliSense* pick list that appears, press *p* to scroll to all supported project events. Select *ProjectBeforeSave2* and press the **Tab** key.

3. Type += *then* tab again and Visual Studio automatically creates the event code for you. I end up with the following code:

```csharp
    this.Application.ProjectBeforeSave2 +=
            new MSProject._EProjectApp2_ProjectBeforeSave2EventHandler
            (Application_ProjectBeforeSave2);
} //End of ThisAddIn_Startup code

void Application_ProjectBeforeSave2
        (MSProject.Project pj, bool SaveAsUi, MSProject.EventInfo Info)
{
    throw new NotImplementedException();
}
```

4. Replace the *throw new NotImplementedException();* code with your code.

For the event code to be properly inserted, be sure to follow the above instructions exactly. Each tab key press is important.

Creating a Button on the Project 2010 Ribbon

In Module 05, I showed you how to add a toolbar and button for Project 2007 and earlier. In Project 2010 that code still works but Project 2010 automatically adds the button to the *Add-ins* tab. The code for this is already in the *ThisAddin* file. In VSTO, there is a simpler and easier way to create the button and add an image to the button. To add a button to the *Add-ins* ribbon, do the following:

1. In the *ChangeTaskSettings* add-in, click Project ➤ Add New Item.

2. Click the *Office* template then the *Ribbon (Visual Designer)* item as shown in Figure 26 - 9.

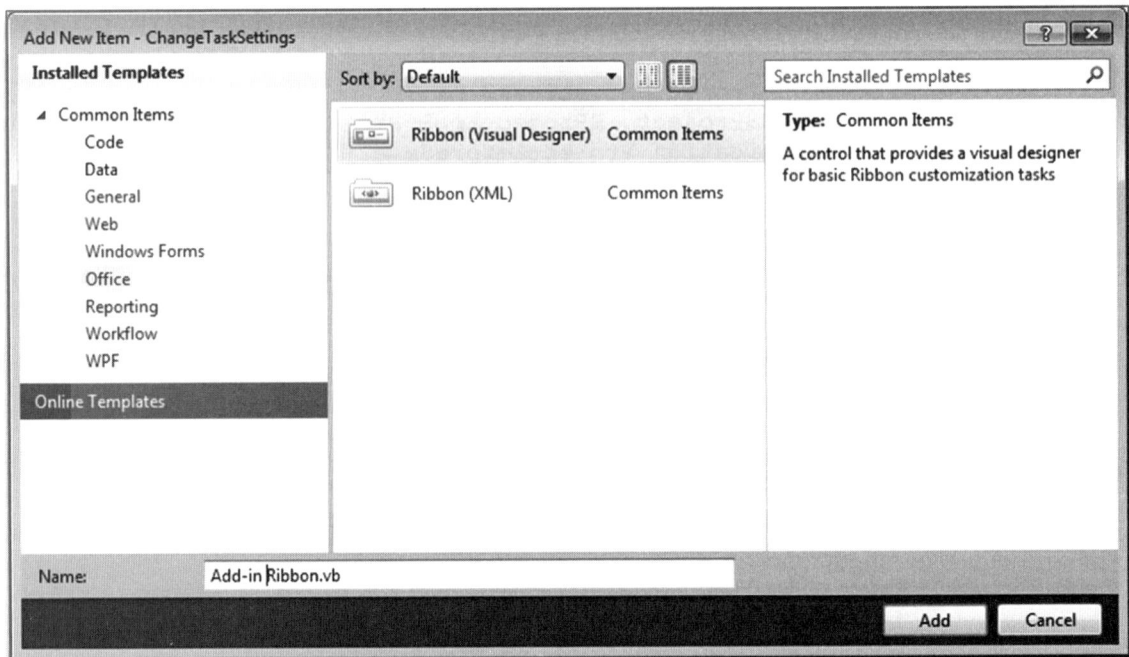

Figure 26 - 9: Adding a Button to the Add-in Ribbon

3. Click the *Add* button and the *Add-in* designer appears as shown in Figure 26 - 10.

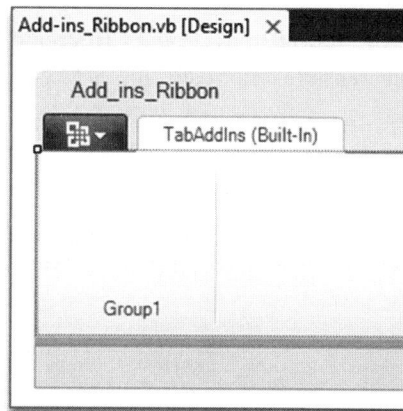

Figure 26 - 10: The Ribbon Designer

4. Expand the *Office Ribbon Controls* tab in the toolbox, and then drag a button control to *Group1* in the *Add-ins_Ribbon [Design]* tab.

5. This add-in only needs one button so the *Group* feature is unnecessary. Click on the *Group1* control then clear its label property to hide it.

6. Click the *button1* control, change the *Label* property to *Change Task Settings*, and change the *Name* property to *rbtnChangeTaskSettings*. Figure 26 - 11 shows the result.

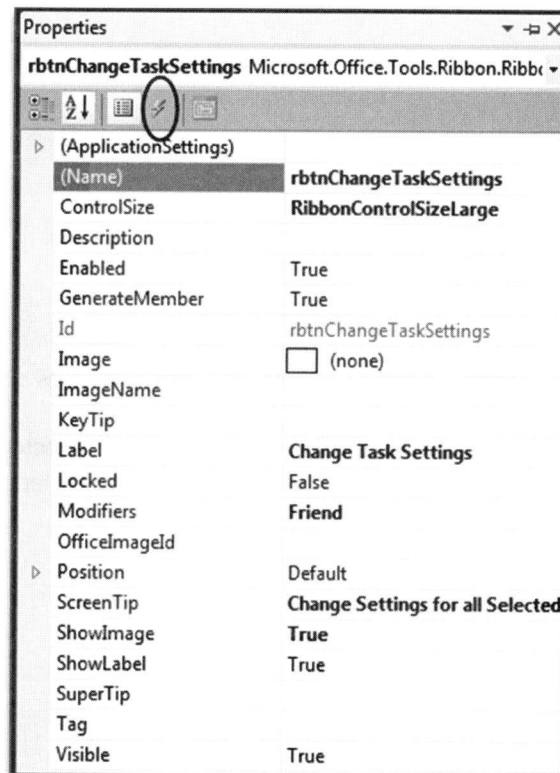

Figure 26 - 11: Button properties after editing

7. Now add the code. Click the *button* control to select it then click the *Events* icon in the *Properties* toolbar. The *Events* icon has a vertical ellipse drawn around it as shown previously in Figure 26 - 11.

8. Double-click the *Click* event in the dialog that appears to create the *Click* event handler. Here you just need to add the call to *ShowChangesForm()*. The result looks like Figure 26 - 12.

```vb
Imports Microsoft.Office.Tools.Ribbon

Public Class Add_ins_Ribbon
    Private Sub Add_ins_Ribbon_Load(ByVal sender As System.Object, _
                ByVal e As RibbonUIEventArgs) Handles MyBase.Load

    End Sub

    Private Sub rbtnChangeTaskSettings_Click(ByVal sender As System.Object, _
                ByVal e As Microsoft.Office.Tools.Ribbon.RibbonControlEventArgs) _
                Handles rbtnChangeTaskSettings.Click
        ShowChangesForm()
    End Sub
End Class
```

Figure 26 - 12: Final Event Handler Code

9. Now build and test the add-in. If the new button works, you can remove the original button by deleting the *Commandbar* code added to *ThisAddin* code earlier in this module.

Hands On Exercise

Exercise 26-3

Add code to update % complete for all milestones whose predecessors are 100% complete.

1. Write code in VBA to loop through all predecessors of all selected milestones (apply the *Milestones* filter then select all tasks). Make sure it works as expected.

2. In the *ChangeTaskSettings* add-in, add a *BeforeSave* event.

3. Copy and convert the VBA event code to your VSTO *BeforeSave2* event code.

4. Add an *Option* button to the *Change* form to let the user decide whether to update the % *complete* milestone.

> Note that some milestones may have a predecessor with lag. This may mean that even though all predecessors are 100% complete, the milestone itself may not be due yet. An order task followed by a receive order task is an example. Therefore, test that the milestone's date is less than today's date.

Developing 64 Bit Add-ins

Project 2010 comes in 32-bit and 64-bit formats. To run Project 64-bit requires Windows Vista SP1 64-bit (or later) or Windows 7 64-bit. You cannot mix Office 32-bit and 64-bit versions so Project 64-bit requires you to install Office 64-bit if you need it on the same PC.

32-bit add-ins cannot run in 64-bit applications and vice versa. To develop an add-in for Project 64-bit versions you need to build a 64-bit version of your add-in. To create a 64-bit version of your add-in you use the code and forms etc. you already have. By default they are in 32-bit. To compile the code and build a 64-bit solution do the following:

1. With your VSTO project open in Visual Studio click Project ➢ VSTOProjectName Properties

2. Click the *Compile* tab

3. Click the *Advanced Compile Options* button

4. Select *x64* in the *TargetCPU* drop down as shown in Figure 26 - 13

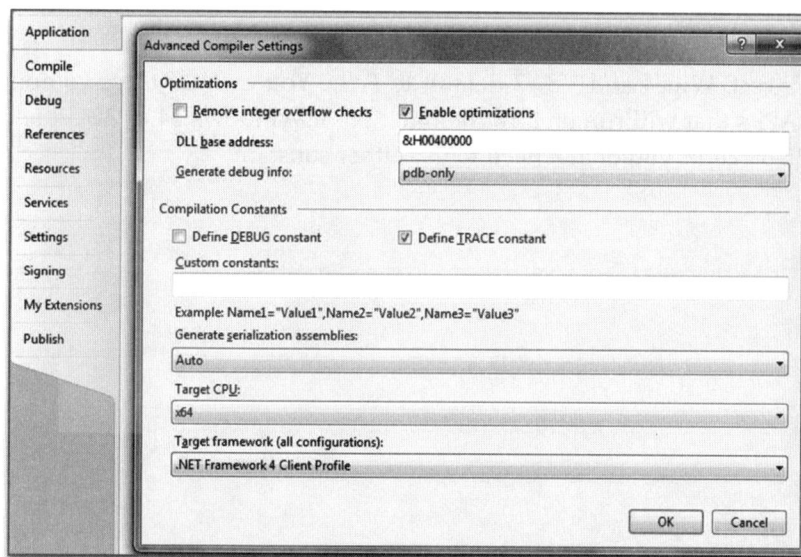

Figure 26 - 13: Selecting to build a 64-bit Add-in

Now build, test and deploy as normal. To build a new 32-bit version, reset the *Target CPU* option to *x32*. If you build a deployment project, it can be in 32-bit or 64-bit format.

Provided your code uses only built-in features of Visual Studio (including all calls to the Framework, Windows Forms etc.) your add-in works unchanged. However, any calls to a Windows API require recoding to 64-bit pointers instead of 32-bit pointers. Search the internet using the search string *Compatibility Between the 32-bit and 64-bit Versions of Office 2010* and look at the page with that string as its title to learn more and see some examples or look at http://msproj.com/1007.

Project 2010 uses VBA version 7. VBA 7 is the same as VBA 6 except for changes to accommodate 64-bit applications. In particular, there are two new conditional compilation constants: Win64 and VB7. Win64 returns *True* if you are running on a 64-bit version of Windows. VBA7 returns *True* if the code is running in VBA version 7 (Office 2010). The following code works in any version of Project:

```
#If Win64 Then
    Debug.Print "Windows 64"
#Else
    Debug.Print "Windows 32"
#End If
#If VBA7 Then
    Debug.Print "VBA 7"
#Else
    Debug.Print "VBA 6 or earlier"
#End If
```

The *Immediate* window in the Visual Basic Editor (VBE) shows the following when the system runs the above code on a 64-bit version of Windows and Project 2010:

```
Win 32
VBA 7
```

In earlier versions of Project, Win64 and VBA7 default to *False*. You can use these compilation constants to add code to call Windows API's that will run on any combination of Windows 64 or 32-bit and Office application 32 or 64-bit. If you write 32-bit code, you do not need to use either constant.

Module 27

Deploying your Add-in

Learning Objectives

After completing this module, you will be able to:

- Understand the different deployment options
- Create a Click Once deployment

Inside Module 27

Deployment Choices for Add-ins

You essentially have two choices regarding how to deploy your add-in, the *ClickOnce* setup or a *Standard* setup project. The attraction of the *ClickOnce* setup for an *Office* add-in is that the user simply clicks once on a link in their web browser or on a *setup.exe* file and the add-in installs automatically along with all required files such as the *.Net Framework*, etc. The installation automatically tests for updated versions, so the deployment is a set and forget experience. A *Standard* setup.exe method allows more flexible setup options; but you do not usually need it for *Office* add-ins. I provide instructions on creating a separate installation project for this second type; but otherwise I recommend you use the *ClickOnce* setup. Table 27 - 1 details the pros and cons of the ClickOnce approach.

Advantages	Disadvantages
• Little user interaction • Automated updates • Little effort for the developer • Automatically installs pre-requisites if user is logged on as an admin (can be pushed automatically using SMS) • Automatic update rollback	• Always deploys as a single solution, cannot be part of a greater whole • Cannot deploy additional files or registry keys • Cannot interact with the user to configure the installation • Cannot brand the installation

Table 27 - 1: ClickOnce pros and cons

ClickOnce Deployment

To create a *ClickOnce* setup:

1. Configure solution to use required *Framework* version – click Project ➢ ChangeTaskSettings Properties.

2. Edit the publish\ folder to be *ChangeTaskSettings_Publish*\ so it is a location you can search for and recognize.

3. Click the *Prerequisites* button.

4. Select the *Framework* version and use 3.5 SP1 unless your add-in contains version 4 specific features.

5. Click the *OK* button, then click the *Updates* button and select how often the add-in looks for updates.

6. Click the *OK* button, then click the *Options* button and change anything you need.

7. Click the *OK* button. You can click the *Publish Now* button but I show the normal *Publish* method.

8. Click Build ➢ Publish ChangeTaskSettings.

9. The *Publish* wizard starts as shown in Figure 27 - 1. Note that the system takes the *Publish* location from the edits in step 2 above.

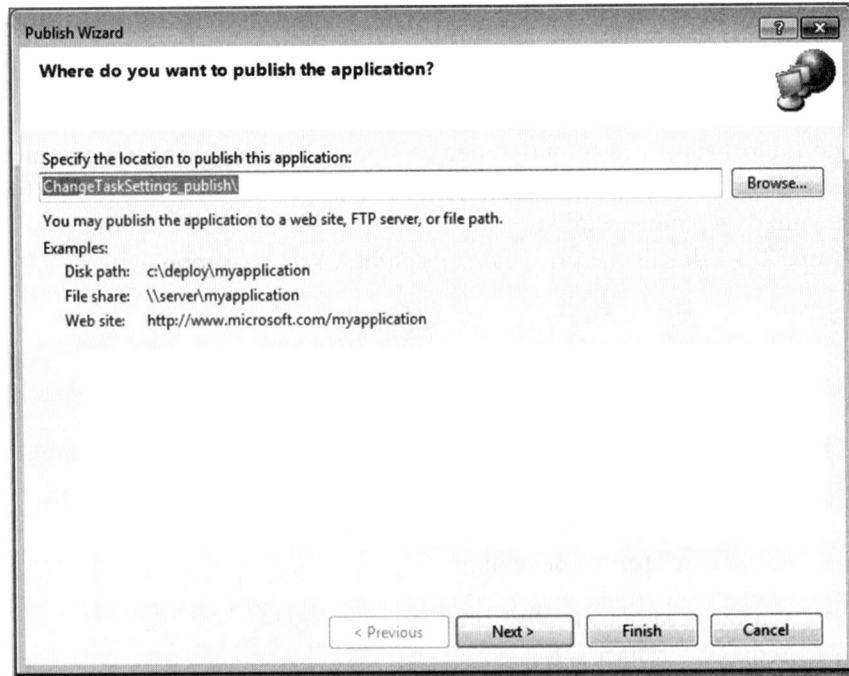

Figure 27 - 1: Step 1 of the Publish Wizard

10. Click the *OK* button and step 2 lets you choose the installation path as shown in Figure 27 - 2.

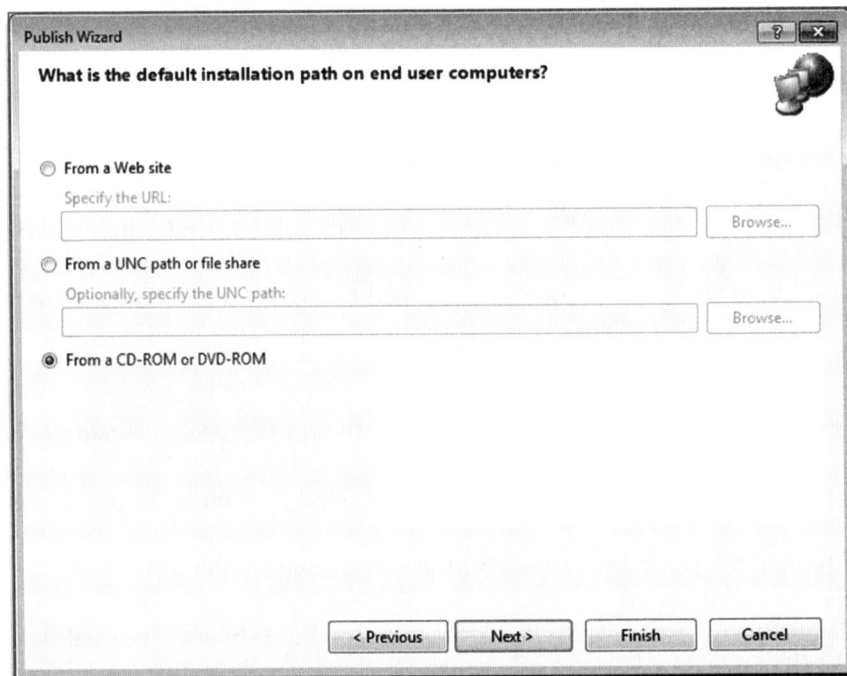

Figure 27 - 2: Step 2 of the Publish Wizard

11. A final *Summary* step follows step 2, so click the *Finish* button or click the *Next* button then the *Finish* button to start the publish process.

To deploy your add-in, find and copy the contents of the *ChangeTaskSettings_publish* folder to a CD, DVD, network folder or a USB memory stick. If you want your add-in to automatically look for updates, then you need to specify a location such as a network drive that is always available.

Run the *Setup.exe* file to install the add-in on any PC with Project installed.

If you specify a website or UNC path then the system publishes the program files there. Have your users run setup.exe from the location you provided and ensure they have the relevant permissions.

Windows Installer Deployment

Table 27 - 2 shows advantages and disadvantages of deploying with Windows Installer (MSI file).

Advantages	Disadvantages
• Can deploy additional components and registry settings	• Requires advanced configuration
• Can interact with the user to configure the installation.	• Higher developer effort required
• Custom branding of the installation	• No automated updates

Table 27 - 2: Windows Installer pros and cons

To deploy using *Windows* installer, you need to add a setup project to your add-in solution. To add a setup project:

1. In Visual Studio click File ➤ Add ➤ New Project.

2. Under *Other Project Types* in the *Installed Templates* list select the *Setup Project* option if you want to do things manually, otherwise I use the Setup Wizard.

3. Name the project; I name my project *InstallChangeSettings* as shown in Figure 27 - 3: Adding a Setup Project.

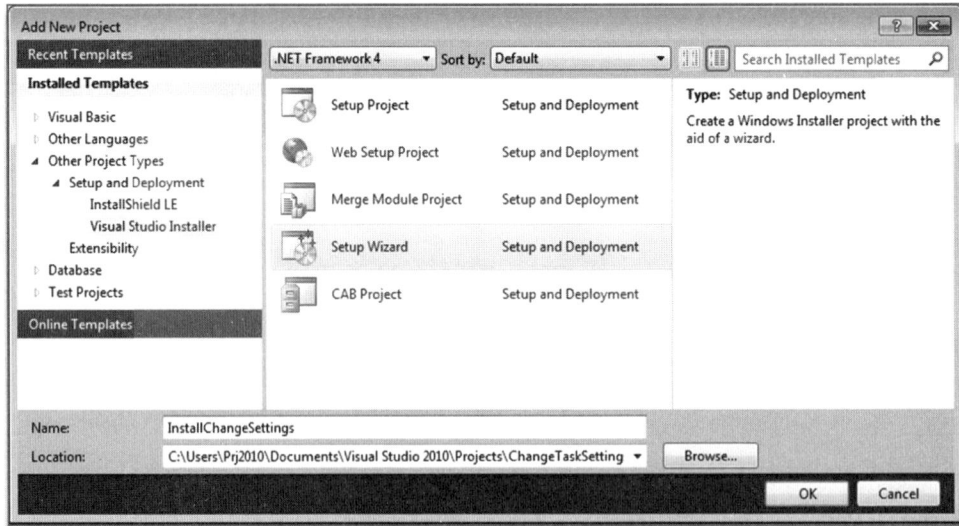

Figure 27 - 3: Adding a Setup Project

4. Click the *OK* button then the *Next* button to go past the welcome page of the Setup Wizard.

5. On step 2 of 5 I choose the *Create a setup* option for a Windows application.

6. On step 3 of 5 I choose the *Primary Output* option from the *ChangeTaskSettings* add-in. This option copies the *DLL* or *EXE* file built by Visual Studio.

7. Step 4 of 5 allows you to include any additional files you want.

8. Step 5 of 5 is a summary, so click the *Finish* button. Now the system displays a view of the folders that it will create for the target machine. By right-mouse clicking on them you can add more files.

9. The Solution Explorer for the *ChangeTaskSettings* add-in now looks as shown in Figure 27 - 4.

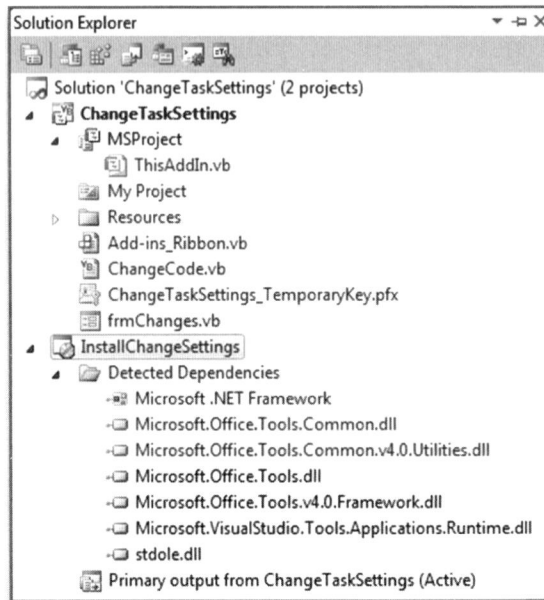

Figure 27 - 4: The final Solution Explorer

Index

You may also need these books!

Buy direct from our website or your favorite bookseller

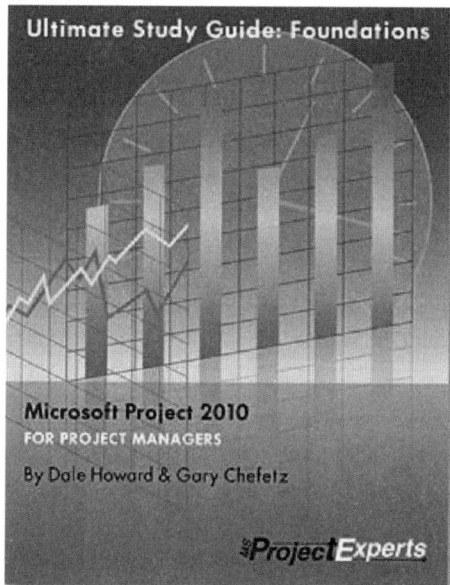

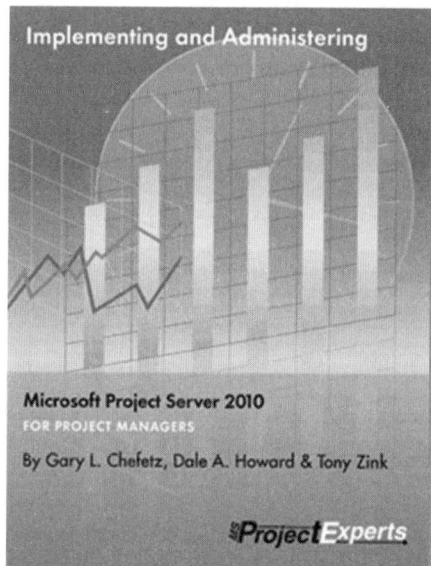

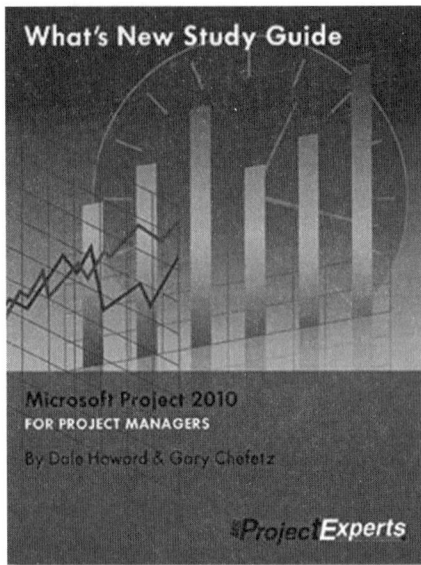

What's New Study Guide Microsoft Project 2010

ISBN 978-1-934240-16-8

A learning guide to get you up to speed with the revolutionary new features in Microsoft Office Project 2010. Learn how to use manually scheduled tasks, the team planner, and the new user interface. The content of this book derives from the Ultimate Study Guide: Foundations, Microsoft Project 2010.

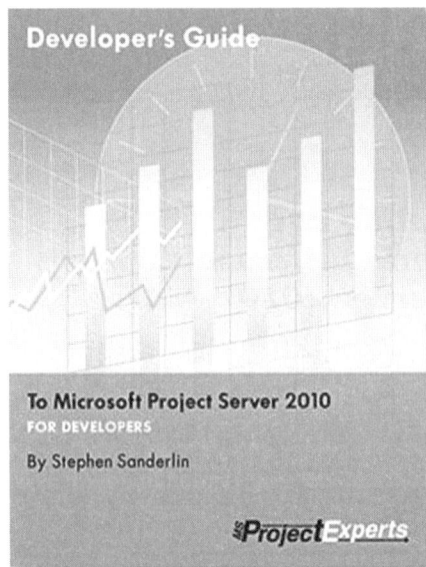

Developer's Guide To Microsoft Project Server 2010

ISBN 978-1-934240-08-3

The first book covering development for Project Server. A complete guide to the PSI, including sample code that you can use to build your own solutions.

MSProjectExperts provides a complete line of Microsoft Project and Project Server courseware covering every role in the enterprise. Each book has its own Instructor documentation and file downloads to support classroom training or self-study. Contact us at (646) 736-1688 for more information or visit our website at:

http://www.msprojectexperts.com

MSProjectExperts

CONSULTING

TRAINING

BOOKS AND COURSEWARE

SUPPORT

You deserve the best, do not settle for less! MSProjectExperts is a Microsoft Gold Certified Partner specializing in Microsoft Office Project Server since its first release. This is not something we "also do," it's all we do. Microsoft recognizes our consultants as being among the world's top experts with three Microsoft Project MVPs on staff.

MSProjectExperts

90 John Street, Suite 404

New York, NY 10038

(646) 736-1688

To learn more about MSProjectExperts:

http://www.msprojectexperts.com

For the best Project and Project Server training available:

http://www.projectservertraining.com

To learn more about our books:

http://www.projectserverbooks.com

For FAQs and other free support:

http://www.projectserverexperts.com